The Deep Learning Revolution

The Deep Learning Revolution

Terrence J. Sejnowski

The MIT Press
Cambridge, Massachusetts
London, England

This book was set in ITC Stone Sans Std and ITC Stone Serif Std by Toppan Best-set Premedia Limited. Printed and bound in the United States of America.

Library of Congress Cataloging-in-Publication Data

Names: Sejnowski, Terrence J. (Terrence Joseph), author.
Title: The deep learning revolution / Terrence J. Sejnowski.
Description: Cambridge, MA : The MIT Press, 2018. | Includes bibliographical
    references and index.
Identifiers: LCCN 2017044863 | ISBN 9780262038034 (hardcover : alk. paper)
Subjects: LCSH: Machine learning. | Big data. | Artificial intelligence--Social aspects.
Classification: LCC Q325.5 .S45 2018 | DDC 006.3/1--dc23 LC record available at
    https://lccn.loc.gov/2017044863

10 9 8 7 6 5 4 3 2 1

For Bo and Sol, Theresa, and Joseph
In memory of Solomon Golomb

Contents

Preface

If you use voice recognition on an Android phone or Google Translate on the Internet, you have communicated with neural networks[1] trained by deep learning. In the last few years, deep learning has generated enough profit for Google to cover the costs of all its futuristic projects at Google X, including self-driving cars, Google Glass, and Google Brain.[2] Google was one of the first Internet companies to embrace deep learning; in 2013, it hired Geoffrey Hinton, the father of deep learning, and other companies are racing to catch up.

The recent progress in artificial intelligence (AI) was made by reverse engineering brains. Learning algorithms for layered neural network models are inspired by the way that neurons communicate with one another and are modified by experience. Inside the network, the complexity of the world is transformed into a kaleidoscope of internal patterns of activity that are the ingredients of intelligence. The network models that I worked on in the 1980s were tiny compared with today's models, which now have millions of artificial neurons and which are dozens of layers deep. What made it possible for deep learning to make big breakthroughs on some of the most difficult problems in artificial intelligence was persistence, big data, and a lot more computer power.

We're not good at imagining the impact of a new technology on the future. Who could have predicted in 1990, when the Internet went commercial, what impact it would have on the music business? On the taxi business? On political campaigns? On almost all aspects of our daily lives? There was a similar failure to imagine how computers would change our lives. Thomas J. Watson, the president of IBM, is widely quoted as saying in 1943: "I think there is a world market for maybe five computers."[3] What's hard to imagine are the uses to which a new invention will be put, and inventors are no better than anyone else at predicting what those uses will be. There is a lot of room between the utopian and doomsday scenarios that are being predicted for deep learning and AI, but even the most imaginative science fiction writers are unlikely to guess what their ultimate impact will be.

The first draft of *The Deep Learning Revolution* was written in a few focused weeks after hiking in the Pacific Northwest and meditating on the remarkable recent shift in the world of artificial intelligence, which had its origin many decades earlier. It is a story about a small group of researchers challenging an AI establishment that was much better funded and at the time the "only game in town." They vastly underestimated the difficulty of the problems and relied on intuitions about intelligence that proved to be misleading.

Life on earth is filled with many mysteries, but perhaps the most challenging of these is the nature of intelligence. Nature abounds with intelligence in many forms, from humble bacterial to complex human intelligence, each adapted to its niche in nature. Artificial intelligence will also come in many forms that will take their particular places on this spectrum. As machine intelligence based on deep neural networks matures, it could provide a new conceptual framework for biological intelligence.

The Deep Learning Revolution is a guide to the past, present, and future of deep learning. Not meant to be a comprehensive history of the field, it is rather a personal view of key conceptual advances and the community of researchers who made them. Human memory is fallible and shifts with every retelling of a story, a process called "reconsolidation." The stories in this book stretch over forty years, and even though some are as vivid to me as if they occurred yesterday, I am well aware that the details have been edited by my memory's retellings over time.

Part I provides the motivation for deep learning and the background needed to understand its origins; part II explains learning algorithms in several different types of neural network architectures; and part III explores the impact that deep learning is having on our lives and what impact it may have in years to come. But, as the New York Yankees' philosopher Yogi Berra once said: "It's tough to make predictions, especially about the future." Text boxes in eight of the chapters to follow provide technical background to the story; timelines at the beginning of the three parts keep track of events that bear on that story and extend over sixty years.

I Intelligence Reimagined

Timeline

1956—The Dartmouth Artificial Intelligence Summer Research Project gave birth to the field of AI and motivated a generation of scientists to explore the potential for information technology to match the capabilities of humans.

1962—Frank Rosenblatt published *Principles of Neurodynamics: Perceptrons and the Theory of Brain Mechanisms,* which introduced a learning algorithm for neural network models with a single layer of variable weights—the precursor of today's learning algorithms for deep neural network models.

1962—David Hubel and Torsten Wiesel published "Receptive Fields, Binocular Interaction and Functional Architecture in the Cat's Visual Cortex," which reported for the first time the response properties of single neurons recorded with a microelectrode. Deep learning networks have an architecture similar to the hierarchy of areas in the visual cortex.

1969—Marvin Minsky and Seymour Papert published *Perceptrons*, which pointed out the computational limitations of a single artificial neuron and marked the beginning of a neural network winter.

1979—Geoffrey Hinton and James Anderson organized the Parallel Models of Associative Memory workshop in La Jolla, California, which brought together a new generation of neural network pioneers and led to publication of Hinton and Anderson's collected volume by the same title in 1981.

1987—The First Neural Information Processing Systems (NIPS) Conference and Workshop was held at the Denver Tech Center, bringing together researchers from many fields.

1 The Rise of Machine Learning

Not too long ago it was often said that computer vision could not compete with the visual abilities of a one-year-old. That is no longer true: computers can now recognize objects in images about as well as most adults can, and there are computerized cars on the road that drive themselves more safely than an average sixteen-year-old could. And rather than being told how to see or drive, computers have learned from experience, following a path that nature took millions of years ago. What is fueling these advances is gushers of data. Data are the new oil. Learning algorithms are refineries that extract information from raw data; information can be used to create knowledge; knowledge leads to understanding; and understanding leads to wisdom. Welcome to the brave new world of deep learning.[1]

Deep learning is a branch of machine learning that has its roots in mathematics, computer science, and neuroscience. Deep networks learn from data the way that babies learn from the world around them, starting with fresh eyes and gradually acquiring the skills needed to navigate novel environments. The origin of deep learning goes back to the birth of artificial intelligence in the 1950s, when there were two competing visions for how to create an AI: one vision was based on logic and computer programs, which dominated AI for decades; the other was based on learning directly from data, which took much longer to mature.

In the twentieth century, when computers were puny and data storage was expensive by today's standards, logic was an efficient way to solve problems. Skilled programmers wrote a different program for each problem, and the bigger the problem, the bigger the program. Today computer power and big data are abundant and solving problems using learning algorithms is faster, more accurate, and more efficient. The same learning algorithm can be used to solve many difficult problems; its solutions are much less labor intensive than writing a different program for every problem.

Learning How to Drive

The $2 million cash prize for the Defense Advanced Research Projects Agency (DARPA) Grand Challenge in 2005 was won by Stanley, a self-driving car instrumented by Sebastian Thrun's group at Stanford, who taught it how to navigate across the desert in California using machine learning. The 132-mile course had narrow tunnels and sharp turns, including Beer Bottle Pass, a winding mountain road with a sheer drop-off on one side and a rock face on the other (figure 1.1). Rather than follow the traditional AI approach by writing a computer program to anticipate every contingency, Thrun drove Stanley around the desert (figure 1.2), and it learned for itself to predict how to steer based on sensory inputs from its vision and distance sensors.

Thrun later founded Google X, a skunk works for high-tech projects, where the technology for self-driving cars was developed further. Google's self-driving cars have since logged 3.5 million miles driving around the San Francisco Bay Area. Uber has deployed a fleet of self-driving cars in Pittsburgh. Apple is moving into self-driving cars to extend the range of

Figure 1.1
Sebastian Thrun with Stanley, the self-driving automobile that won the 2005 DAR-PA Grand Challenge. This breakthrough jump-started a technological revolution in transportation. Courtesy of Sebastian Thrun.

Figure 1.2
Beer Bottle Pass. This challenging terrain was near the end of the 2005 DARPA Grand Challenge for a vehicle to drive unassisted by a human through a 132-mile off-road desert course. A truck in the distance is just beginning the climb. Courtesy of DARPA.

products that its operating systems control, hoping to repeat its successful foray into the cell phone market. Seeing a business that had not changed for 100 years transformed before their eyes, automobile manufacturers are following in their tracks. General Motors paid $1 billion for Cruise Automation, a Silicon Valley start-up that is developing driverless technology, and invested an additional $600 million in 2017 in research and development.[2] In 2017, Intel purchased Mobileye, a company that specializes in sensors and computer vision for self-driving cars, for $15.3 billion dollars. The stakes are high in the multitrillion-dollar transportation sector of the economy.

Self-driving cars will soon disrupt the livelihoods of millions of truck and taxi drivers. Eventually, there will be no need to own a car in a city when a self-driving car can show up in a minute and take you safely to your destination, without your having to park it. The average car today is only used 4 percent of the time, which means it needs to be parked somewhere 96 percent of the time. But because self-driving cars can be serviced and parked outside cities, vast stretches of city land now covered with parking lots can be repurposed for more productive uses. Urban planners are already thinking ahead to the day when parking lots become parkland.[3] Parking lanes along streets can become real bike lanes. Many other car-related businesses will be affected, including auto insurance agencies and body shops. No more speeding or parking tickets. There will be fewer deaths from drunk drivers and from drivers falling asleep at the wheel. Time wasted commuting to work will be freed for other purposes. According to the U.S. Census Bureau, in 2014, 139 million Americans spent an average of 52 minutes commuting to and from work each workday. That amounts to 29.6 billion hours per year, or an astounding 3.4 million years of human lives that could have been put to better use.[4] Highway capacity will be increased by a factor of four by caravaning.[5] And, once developed and widely used, self-driving cars that can drive themselves home without a steering wheel will put an end to grand theft auto. Although there are many regulatory and legal obstacles in the way, when self-driving cars finally become ubiquitous, we will indeed be living in a brave new world. Trucks will be the first to become autonomous, probably in 10 years; taxis in 15 years and passenger cars in 15 to 25 years from start to finish.

The iconic position that cars have in our society will change in ways that we cannot imagine and a new car ecology will emerge. Just as the introduction of the automobile more than 100 years ago created many new industries and jobs, there is already a fast-growing ecosystem being created around self-driving cars. Waymo, the self-driving spin-off from Google, has invested $1 billion over 8 years and has constructed a secretive testing facility in California's central valley with a 91-acre fake town, including fake bicycle riders and fake auto breakdowns.[6] The goal is to broaden the training data to include special and unusual circumstances, called edge cases. Rare driving events that occur on highways often lead to accidents. The difference with self-driving cars is that when one car experiences a rare event, the learning experience will propagate to all other self-driving cars, a form of collective intelligence. Many similar test facilities are being constructed by other self-driving car companies. These create new jobs that did not exist before, and new supply chains for the sensors and lasers that are needed to guide the cars.[7]

Self-driving cars are just the most visible manifestation of a major shift in an economy being driven by information technology (IT). Information flows through the Internet like water through city pipes. Information accumulates in massive data centers run by Google, Amazon, Microsoft, and other IT companies that require so much electrical power that they need to be located near hydroelectric plants, and streaming information generates so much heat that it needs rivers to supply the coolant. In 2013, data centers in the United States consumed 10 million megawatts, equivalent to the power generated by thirty-four large power plants.[8] But what is now making an even bigger impact on the economy is how this information is used. Extracted from raw data, the information is being turned into knowledge about people and things: what we do, what we want, and who we are. And, more and more, computer-driven devices are using this knowledge to communicate with us through the spoken word. Unlike the passive knowledge in books that is externalized outside brains, knowledge in the cloud is an external intelligence that is becoming an active part of everyone's lives.[9]

Learning How to Translate

Deep learning is used at Google today in more than 100 services, from Street View to Inbox Smart Reply and voice search. Several years ago, engineers at Google realized that they had to scale up these compute-intensive applications to cloud levels. Setting out to design a special-purpose chip for deep learning, they cleverly designed the board to fit into a hard disk drive slot in their data center racks. Google's tensor processing unit (TPU) is now deployed on servers around the world, delivering an order-of-magnitude improvement in performance for deep learning applications.

An example of how quickly deep learning can change the landscape is the impact it has had on language translation—a holy grail for artificial intelligence since it depends on the ability to understand a sentence. The recently unveiled new version of Google Translate based on deep learning represents a quantum leap improvement in the quality of translation between natural languages. Almost overnight, language translation went from a fragmented hit-and-miss jumble of phrases to seamless sentences (figure 1.3). Previous computer methods searched for combinations of words that could be translated together, but deep learning looks for dependencies across whole sentences.

Alerted about the sudden improvement of Google Translate, on November 18, 2016, Jun Rekimoto at the University of Tokyo tested the new system by having it translate the opening of Ernest Hemingway's "The Snows of Kilimanjaro" into Japanese and then back into English—with the following result (guess which one is the original Hemingway):

> 1: Kilimanjaro is a snow-covered mountain 19,710 feet high, and is said to be the highest mountain in Africa. Its western summit is called the Masai "Ngaje Ngai," the House of God. Close to the western summit there is the dried and frozen carcass of a leopard. No one has explained what the leopard was seeking at that altitude.

Figure 1.3
Japanese signs and menus instantly translated into English by Google Translate, which is now an app on your smart phone. This is especially useful if you need to find the right train in Japan.

> 2: Kilimanjaro is a mountain of 19,710 feet covered with snow and is said to be the highest mountain in Africa. The summit of the west is called "Ngaje Ngai" in Masai, the house of God. Near the top of the west there is a dry and frozen dead body of leopard. No one has ever explained what leopard wanted at that altitude.[10]

(Hemingway is #1.)

The next step will be to train larger deep learning networks on paragraphs to improve continuity across sentences. Words have long cultural histories. Vladimir Nabokov, the Russian writer and English-language novelist who wrote *Lolita*, came to the conclusion that it was impossible to translate poetry between languages. His literal translation of Aleksandr Pushkin's *Eugene Onegin* into English, annotated with explanatory footnotes on the cultural background of the verses, made his point.[11] Perhaps Google Translate will be able to translate Shakespeare someday by integrating across all of his poetry.[12]

Learning How to Listen

Another holy grail of artificial intelligence is speech recognition. Until recently, speaker-independent speech recognition by computers was limited to narrow domains, such as airline reservations. Today, it is unlimited. A summer research project at Microsoft Research by an intern from the University of Toronto in 2012 dramatically improved the performance of Microsoft's speech recognition system (figure 1.4).[13] In 2016, a team at Microsoft announced that its deep learning network with 120 layers had achieved human-level performance on a benchmark test for multi-speaker speech recognition.[14]

The consequences of this breakthrough will ripple through society over the next few years, as computer keyboards are replaced by natural language interfaces. This is already happening with digital assistants as Amazon's Alexa, Apple's Siri, and Microsoft's Cortana leapfrog one another into homes everywhere. Just as typewriters became obsolete with the widespread use of

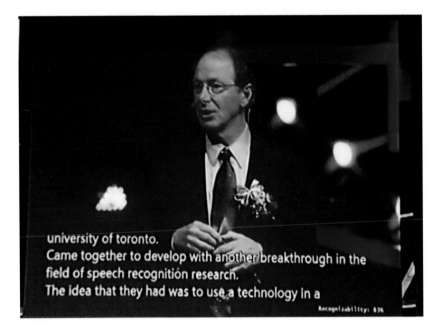

Figure 1.4
Microsoft Chief Research Officer Rick Rashid in a live demonstration of automated speech recognition using deep learning on October 25, 2012, at an event in Tianjin, China. Before an audience of 2,000 Chinese, Rashid's words, spoken in English, were recognized by the automated system, which first showed them in subtitles below Rashid's screen image and then translated them into spoken Chinese. This high-wire act made newsfeeds worldwide. Courtesy of Microsoft Research.

personal computers, so computer keyboards will someday become museum pieces.

When speech recognition is combined with language translation, it will become possible to communicate across cultures in real time. *Star Trek*'s Universal Translator is within our reach (figure 1.4). Why did it take so long for speech recognition and language translation by computers to reach human levels of performance? Is it just a coincidence that these and other cognitive capabilities of computers are reaching threshold at the same time? All these breakthroughs are being driven by big data.

Learning How to Diagnose

Skin Deep

Service industries and professions will also be transformed as machine learning matures and is applied to many other problems where big data is available. Medical diagnosis based on the records of millions of patients will become more accurate. A recent study applied deep learning to 130,000 dermatological images for more than 2,000 different diseases—a medical database ten times larger than used previously (figure 1.5).[15] The study's network was trained to diagnose each disease from a "test set" of new images it had not seen before. Its diagnostic performance on the new images was comparable to and in some cases better than that of twenty-one expert dermatologists. It will soon be possible for anyone with a smartphone to take a photo of a suspicious skin lesion and have it diagnosed instantly, a process that now requires a visit to a doctor's office, a long wait for the lesion to be screened by an expert—and payment of a substantial bill. This will greatly expand the scope and quality of dermatological care. If individuals can quickly get an expert assessment, they will see their doctors office at an early stage of a skin disease, when it is easier to treat. All doctors will become better at diagnosing rare skin diseases with the help of deep learning.[16]

Deep Cancer

The detection of metastatic breast cancer in images of lymph node biopsies on slides is done by experts who make mistakes, mistakes that have deadly consequences. This is a pattern recognition problem for which deep learning should excel. And indeed, a deep learning network trained on a large dataset of slides for which ground truth was known reached an accuracy of 0.925, good but not as good as experts who achieved 0.966 on the same test set.[17] However, when the predictions of deep learning were combined

Figure 1.5
Artist's impression of a deep learning network diagnosing a skin lesion with high accuracy, cover of February 2, 2017, issue of *Nature*.

with the human expert, the result was an almost perfect 0.995. They do better together than either alone because deep learning networks and human experts have different ways of looking at the same data. Many more lives can be saved. This points toward a future in which man and machine work together as partners rather than competitors.

Deep Sleep

If you have a serious sleep problem, which 70 percent of us will have sometime during our lifetimes, after waiting months to see your doctor (unless your problem is urgent), you will be directed to a sleep clinic, where you will be observed overnight attached to dozens of electrodes to record your electroencephalogram (EEG) and muscle activity while you sleep. In the course of each night, you will enter into slow-wave sleep and, periodically, into rapid-eye-movement (REM) sleep, during which you will dream, but insomnia, sleep apnea, restless leg syndrome, and many other sleep disorders can disrupt this pattern. If you had trouble sleeping at home, sleeping in a strange bed connected by wires to ominous medical equipment can be a real challenge. A sleep expert will look over your EEG recordings and mark the sleep stages in blocks of 30 seconds, which takes several hours to score each eight hours of sleep. You will eventually get back a report on abnormalities in your sleep pattern and a bill for $2,000.

The sleep expert will have been trained to look for telltale features that characterize the different sleep stages, based on a system devised in 1968 by Anthony Rechtshaffen and Alan Kales.[18] But, because the features are often ambiguous and inconsistent, experts agree only 75 percent of the time on how to interpret them. In contrast, Philip Low, a former graduate student in my lab, used unsupervised machine learning to automatically detect sleep stages with a time resolution of 3 seconds and a concordance with human experts of 87 percent, in less than a minute of computer time. Moreover, this required recording from only a single location on the head rather than many contacts and a bundle of wires that take a long time to put on and take off. In 2007, we launched a start-up company, Neurovigil, to bring this technology to sleep clinics, but they showed little interest in disrupting their cash flow from human scoring. Indeed, with an insurance code to bill patients, they had no incentive to adopt a cheaper procedure. Neurovigil found another market in large drug companies that run clinical trials and need to test the effects of their drugs on sleep patterns, and it is now entering the market for long-term care facilities, where elderly often have progressive sleep problems.

The sleep clinic model is flawed because health problems can't be reliably diagnosed based on such restricted circumstances: Everyone has a different baseline, and departures from that baseline are the most informative. Neurovigil already has a compact device, the iBrain, which can record your EEG at home, transmit the data to the Internet and analyze the data longitudinally for trends and anomalies. This will allow doctors to detect health problems early when it is easier to treat them and to stop the development of chronic illnesses. There are other diseases whose treatment would benefit from continuous monitoring, such as type 1 diabetes, for which the level of sugar in the blood could be monitored and regulated by delivery of insulin.

Access to cheap sensors that can record data continuously is having a major impact on diagnosis and treatment of other chronic diseases.

There are several lessons to be learned from the Neurovigil experience. Although having better and cheaper technology does not translate easily into a marketable new product or service, even a far superior one, when an incumbent is entrenched in the market, there are secondary markets where the new technology can have a more immediate impact and buy time to improve and better compete. This is how the technologies of solar energy and of many other new industries entered the market. In the long run, sleep monitoring and new technologies with demonstrated advantages will reach patients at home and eventually be integrated into medical practice.

Learning How to Make Money

More than 75 percent of trading on the New York Stock Exchange is automated (figure 1.6), fueled by high-frequency trades that move into and out of positions in fractions of a second. (When you don't have to pay for each transaction, even small advantages can be parlayed into big profits.) Algorithmic trading on a longer time scale takes into account longer-term trends based on big data. Deep learning is getting better and better at making both more money and higher profits.[19] The problem with predicting the financial markets is that the data are noisy and conditions are not stationary—psychology can change overnight after an election or international conflict. This means that an algorithm that predicts stock values today may not work tomorrow. In practice, hundreds of algorithms are used and the best ones are continually combined to optimize returns.

Back in the 1980s, when I was consulting for Morgan Stanley on neural network models of stock trading, I met David Shaw, a computer scientist who specialized in designing parallel computers. On leave of absence from Columbia University, Shaw was working as a quantitative analyst, or "quant," in the early days of automated trading. He would go on to start his own investment management firm on Wall Street, the D. E. Shaw Group, and he is now a multibillionaire. The D. E. Shaw Group has been highly successful, but not as successful as another hedge fund, Renaissance Technologies, which was founded by James Simons, a distinguished mathematician and former chair of the Mathematics Department at Stony Brook University. Simons made $1.6 billion in 2016 alone, and this wasn't even his best year.[20] Called "the best physics and mathematics department in the world,"[21] Renaissance "avoids hiring anyone with even the slightest whiff of Wall Street bona fides."[22]

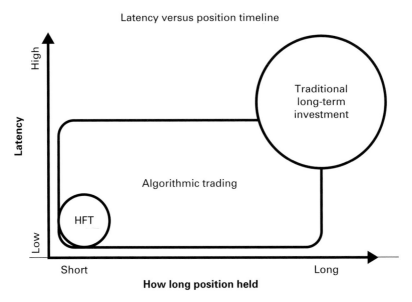

Latency versus position timeline

Figure 1.6
Machine learning is driving algorithmic trading, which is faster than traditional long-term investment strategies and more deliberate than high-frequency trading (HFT) in stock markets. Many different kinds of machine learning algorithms are combined to achieve best returns.

No longer involved in the daily operation of D. E. Shaw, David Shaw is now engrossed in D. E. Shaw Research, which has built a special-purpose parallel computer, called "Anton," that performs protein folding much faster than any other computer on the planet.[23] Simons has retired from overseeing Renaissance and has started a foundation that funds research on autism and other programs in the physical and biological sciences. Through the Simons Institute for the Theory of Computing at UC Berkeley, the Simons Center for the Social Brain at MIT, and the Flatiron Institute in New York, Shaw's philanthropy has had a major impact on advancing computational methods for data analysis, modeling, and simulation.[24]

Financial services more broadly are undergoing a transformation under the banner of financial technology, or "fintech," as it has come to be called. Information technology such as block chain, which is a secure Internet ledger that replaces financial middlemen in transactions, is being tested on a small scale but could soon disrupt multitrillion-dollar financial markets. Machine learning is being used to improve credit evaluation on loans, to accurately deliver business and financial information, to pick up signals on social media that predict market trends, and to provide biometric security for financial transactions. Whoever has the most data wins, and the world is awash with financial data.

Learning the Law

Deep learning is just beginning to affect the legal profession. Much of the routine work of associates in law firms who charge hundreds of dollar an hour will be automated, especially in large, high-value commercial offices. In particular, technology-assisted review, or discovery, will be taken over by artificial intelligence, which can sort through thousands of documents for legal evidence without getting tired. Automated deep learning systems will also help law firms comply with the increasing complexity of governmental regulations. They will make legal advice available for the average person who cannot now afford a lawyer. Not only will legal work be cheaper; it will be much faster, a factor that is often more important than its expense. The world of law is well on its way to becoming "Legally Deep."[25]

Learning How to Play Poker

Heads-up no-limit Texas hold 'em is one of the most popular versions of poker, commonly played in casinos, and the no-limit betting form is played at the main event of the World Series of Poker (figure 1.7). Poker is challenging because, unlike chess, where both players have access to the same information, poker players have imperfect information, and, at the highest levels of play, skills in bluffing and deception are as important as the cards that are dealt.

The mathematician John von Neumann, who founded mathematical game theory and pioneered digital computers, was particularly fascinated with poker. As he put it: "Real life consists of bluffing, of little tactics of deception, of asking yourself what is the other man going to think I mean to do. And that is what games are about in my theory."[26] Poker is a game that reflects parts of human intelligence that were refined by evolution. A deep learning network called "DeepStack" played 44,852 games against thirty-three professional poker players. To the shock of poker experts, it beat the best of the poker players by a sizable margin, one standard deviation, but it beat the thirty-three players overall by four standard deviations—an immense margin.[27] If this achievement is replicated in other areas where human judgment based on imperfect information is paramount, such as politics and international relations, the consequences could be far reaching.[28]

Figure 1.7
Heads-up no-limit Texas hold 'em. Aces in the hole. Bluffing in high stakes poker has been mastered by DeepStack, which has beaten professional poker players at their own game by a wide margin.

Learning How to Play Go

In March 2016, Lee Sedol, the Korean Go 18-time world champion, played and lost a five-game match against DeepMind's AlphaGo (figure 1.8), a Go-playing program that used deep learning networks to evaluate board positions and possible moves.[29] Go is to Chess in difficulty as chess is to checkers. If chess is a battle, Go is a war. A 19×19 Go board is much larger than an 8×8 chessboard, which makes it possible to have several battles raging in different parts of the board. There are long-range interactions between battles that are difficult to judge, even by experts. The total number of legal board positions for Go is 10^{170}, far more than the number of atoms in the universe.

In addition to several deep learning networks to evaluate the board and choose the best move, AlphaGo had a completely different learning system, one used to solve the temporal credit assignment problem: which of the many moves were responsible for a win, and which were responsible for a loss? The basal ganglia of the brain, which receive projections from the entire cerebral cortex and project back to it, solve this problem with a temporal difference algorithm and reinforcement learning. AlphaGo used the same learning algorithm that the basal ganglia evolved to evaluate sequences of

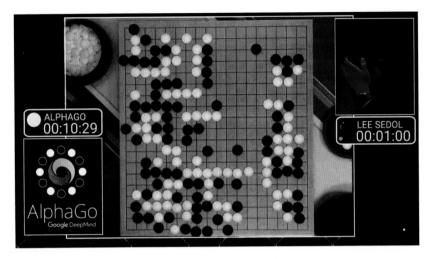

Figure 1.8
Go board during play in the five-game match that pitted Korean Go champion Lee
Sedol against AlphaGo, a deep learning neural network that had learned how to play
Go by playing itself.

actions to maximize future rewards (a process that will be explained in chapter 10). AlphaGo learned by playing itself—many, many times

The Go match that pitted AlphaGo against Lee Sedol had a large following in Asia, where Go champions are national figures and treated like rock
stars. AlphaGo had earlier defeated a European Go champion, but the level
of play was considerably below the highest levels of play in Asia, and Lee
Sedol was not expecting a strong match. Even DeepMind, the company
that had developed AlphaGo, did not know how strong their deep learning
program was. Since its last match, AlphaGo had played millions of games
with several versions of itself and there was no way to benchmark how
good it was.

It came as a shock to many when AlphaGo won the first three of five
games, exhibiting an unexpectedly high level of play. This was riveting
viewing in South Korea, where all the major television stations had a running commentary on the games. Some of the moves made by AlphaGo
were revolutionary. On the thirty-eighth move in the match's second game,
AlphaGo made a brilliantly creative play that surprised Lee Sedol, who took
nearly ten minutes to respond. AlphaGo lost the fourth game, a face-saving
win for humans, and ended the match by winning four games to one (figure 1.9).[30] I stayed up into the wee hours of those March nights in San
Diego and was mesmerized by the games. They reminded me of the time

I sat glued to the TV in Cleveland on June 2, 1966, at 1:00 a.m., as the Surveyor robotic spacecraft landed on the moon and beamed back the first photo of a moonscape.[31] I witnessed these historic moments in real time. AlphaGo far exceeded what I and many others thought was possible.

On January 4, 2017, a Go player on an Internet Go server called "Master" was unmasked as AlphaGo 2.0 after winning sixty out of sixty games against some of the world's best players, including the world's reigning Go champion, the nineteen-year-old prodigy Ke Jie of China. It revealed a new style of play that went against the strategic wisdom of the ages. On May 27, 2017, Ke Jie lost three games to AlphaGo at the Future of Go Summit in Wuzhen, China (figure 1.10). These were some of the best Go games ever played, and hundreds of millions of Chinese followed the match. "Last year, I think the way AlphaGo played was pretty close to human beings, but today I think he plays like the God of Go," Ke Jie concluded.[32]

After the first game, which he lost by a razor-thin margin of one-half point, Ke Jie said that he "was very close to winning the match in the middle of the game" and that he was so excited "I could feel my heart thumping! Maybe because I was too excited I made some stupid moves. Maybe that's the weakest part of human beings."[33] What Ke Jie experienced was an emotional overload, but a less elevated level of emotions is needed to reach peak performance. Indeed, stage actors know that if they don't have butterflies in their stomachs before their performances, they won't be

Figure 1.9
Lee Sedol after losing the Go Challenge Match in March 2016.

Figure 1.10
Demis Hassabis (left) and Ke Jie meet after the historic Go match in China in 2017, holding a board with Ke Jie's signature. Courtesy of Demis Hassabis.

in good form. Their performances follow an inverted U-shaped curve, with their best ones in an optimal state between low and high levels of arousal. Athletes call this being "in the zone."

AlphaGo also defeated a team of five top players on May 26, 2017. These players have analyzed the moves made by AlphaGo and are already changing their strategies. In a new version of "ping-pong diplomacy," the match was hosted by the Chinese government. China is making a large investment in machine learning, and a major goal of their brain initiative is to mine the brain for new algorithms.[34]

The next chapter in this Go saga is even more remarkable, if that is possible. AlphaGo was jump-started by supervised learning from 160,000 human Go games before playing itself. Some thought this was cheating—an autonomous AI program should be able to learn how to play Go without human knowledge. In October, 2017, a new version, called AlphaGo Zero, was revealed that learned to play Go starting with only the rules of the game, and trounced AlphaGo Master, the version that beat Kie Jie, winning 100 games to none.[35] Moreover, AlphaGo Zero learned 100 times faster and with 10 times less compute power than AlphaGo Master. By completely ignoring human knowledge, AlphaGo Zero became super-superhuman.

There is no known limit to how much better AlphaGo might become as machine learning algorithms continue to improve.

AlphaGo Zero had dispensed with human play, but there was still a lot of Go knowledge handcrafted into the features that the program used to represent the board. Maybe AlphaGo Zero could improve still further without any Go knowledge. Just as Coca-Cola Zero stripped all the calories from Coca-Cola, all domain knowledge of Go was stripped from AlphaZero. As a result, AlphaZero was able to learn even faster and decisively beat AlphaGo Zero.[36] To make the point that less is more even more dramatically, AlphaZero, without changing a single learning parameter, learned how to play chess at superhuman levels, making alien moves that no human had ever made before. AlphaZero did not lose a game to Stockfish, the top chess program already playing at superhuman levels. In one game, AlphaZero made a bold bishop sacrifice, sometimes used to gain positional advantage, followed by a queen sacrifice, which seemed like a colossal blunder until it led to a checkmate many moves later that neither Stockfish nor humans saw coming. The aliens have landed and the earth will never be the same again.

AlphaGo's developer, DeepMind, was cofounded in 2010 by neuroscientist Demis Hassabis (figure 1.10, left), who had been a postdoctoral fellow at University College London's Gatsby Computational Neuroscience Unit (directed by Peter Dayan, a former postdoctoral fellow in my lab and winner of the prestigious Brain Prize in 2017 along with Raymond Dolan and Wolfram Schultz for their research on reward learning). DeepMind was acquired by Google for $600 million in 2014. The company employs more than 400 engineers and neuroscientists in a culture that is a blend between academia and start-ups. The synergies between neuroscience and AI run deep and are quickening.

Learning How to Become More Intelligent

Is AlphaGo intelligent? There has been more written about intelligence than any other topic in psychology except consciousness, both of which are difficult to define. Psychologists since the 1930s distinguish between fluid intelligence, which uses reasoning and pattern recognition in new situations to solve new problems, without depending on previous knowledge, and crystallized intelligence, which depends on previous knowledge and is what the standard IQ tests measure. Fluid intelligence follows a developmental trajectory, reaching a peak in early adulthood and decreasing with age, whereas crystallized intelligence increases slowly and asymptotically as you age until fairly late in life. AlphaGo displays both crystallized and fluid intelligence in a rather narrow domain, but within this domain, it has demonstrated surprising creativity. Professional expertise is also based on learning in narrow domains. We are all professionals in the domain of language and practice it every day.

The reinforcement learning algorithm used by AlphaGo can be applied to many problems. This form of learning depends only on the reward given to the winner at the end of a sequence of moves, which paradoxically can improve decisions made much earlier. When coupled with many powerful deep learning networks, this leads to many domain-dependent bits of intelligence. And, indeed, cases have been made for different domain-dependent kinds of intelligence: social, emotional, mechanical, and constructive, for example.[37] The "*g* factor" that intelligence tests claim to measure is correlated with these different kinds. There are reasons to be cautious about interpreting IQ tests. The average IQ has been going up all over the world by three points per decade since it was first studied in the 1930s, a trend called the "Flynn effect." There are many possible explanations for the Flynn effect, such as better nutrition, better health care, and other environmental factors.[38] This is quite plausible because the environment affects gene regulation, which in turn affects brain connectivity, leading to changes in behavior.[39] As humans increasingly are living in artificially created environments, brains are being molded in ways that nature never intended. Could it be that humans have been getting smarter over a much longer period of time? For how long will the increase in IQ continue? The incidence of people playing computers in chess, backgammon, and now Go has been steadily increasing since the advent of computer programs that play at championship levels, and so has the machine augmented intelligence of the human players.[40] Deep learning will boost the intelligence not just of scientific investigators but of workers in all professions.

Scientific instruments are generating data at prodigious rate. Elementary particle collisions at the Large Hadron Collider (LHC) in Geneva generate 25 petabyes of data each year. The Large Synoptic Sky Telescope (LSST) will generate 6 petabytes of data each year. Machine learning is being used to analyze the huge physics and astronomy datasets that are too big for humans to search by traditional methods.[41] For example, DeepLensing is a neural network that recognizes images of distant galaxies that have been distorted by light bending by "gravitational lenses" around another galaxy along the line of sight. This allows many new distant galaxies to be automatically discovered. There are many other "needle-in-a-haystack" problems in physics and astronomy for which deep learning vastly amplifies traditional approaches to data analysis.

The Shifting Job Market

Introduced by banks in the late 1960s to dispense cash to account holders 24/7, a much-welcomed convenience for those in need of cash before or after normal banking hours, automated teller machines (ATMs) have since acquired the ability to read handwritten checks. And though they reduced routine work for bank tellers, there are more bank tellers than before providing customers with personalized services such as mortgage and investment advice, and new ATM repair jobs[42]—just as the steam engine displaced manual laborers, on the one hand, but gave rise to new jobs for skilled workers who could build and maintain steam engines and drive steam locomotives, on the other. So, too, Amazon's online marketing has displaced many workers from local brick-and-mortar retail stores but has also created 380,000 new jobs for workers in the distribution and delivery of the goods sold by it and by the many businesses under its umbrella.[43] And as jobs that now require human cognitive skills are taken over by automated AI systems, there will be new jobs for those who can create and maintain these systems.

Job turnover is nothing new. Farmworkers in the nineteenth century were displaced by machines, and new jobs were created at city factories made possible by machines, all of which required an educational system to train workers in new skills. The difference is that, today, the new jobs being opened up by artificial intelligence will require new, different, and ever-changing skills in addition to traditional cognitive skills.[44] So we will need to learn throughout our lifetimes. For this to happen, we will need a new educational system that is based at the home rather than the school.

Fortunately, just as the need for finding new jobs has become acute, the Internet has made available free massive open online courses (MOOCs) to acquire new knowledge and skills. Though still in their infancy, MOOCs are evolving rapidly in the education ecosystem and hold great promise for delivering quality instruction to a wider range of people than ever before. When coupled with the next generation of digital assistants, MOOCs could be transformational. Barbara Oakley and I developed a popular MOOC called "Learning How to Learn" that teaches you how to become a better learner (figure 1.11) and a follow-up MOOC called "Mindshift" that teaches you how to reinvent yourself and change your lifestyle (both MOOCs will be described in chapter 12).

As you interact with the Internet, you are generating big data about yourself that is machine readable. You are being targeted by ads generated

Learning How to Learn

Figure 1.11
"Learning How to Learn," a massive open online course (MOOC) that teaches you how to become a better learner is the most popular MOOC on the Internet, with over 3 million learners. Courtesy of Terrence Sejnowski and Barbara Oakley.

from the digital bread crumbs you have left behind on the Internet. The information you reveal on Facebook and other social media sites can be used to create a digital assistant that knows you better than almost anyone else in the world and will not forget anything, becoming, in effect, your virtual doppelganger. By pressing both Internet tracking and deep learning into service, the educational opportunities for the children of today's children will be better than the best available today to wealthy families. These grandchildren will have their own digital tutors, who will accompany them throughout the trajectory of their education. Not only will education become more individualized; it will become more precise. There are already a wide range of educational experiments under way throughout the world at programs like the Kahn Academy and funded by the Gates, Chan-Zuckerberg, and other philanthropic foundations that are testing software to make it possible for all children to progress at their own pace throughout their formal education and to adapt to the specific needs of each child.[45] The widespread availability of digital tutors will free teachers from the repetitive parts of teaching, like grading, and allow them to do what humans do best—emotional support for struggling students and intellectual inspiration for gifted students. Educational technology—edtech—is moving rapidly ahead, and the transition to precision education could be quite fast compared to self-driving cars because the obstacles it must overcome are much less daunting, the demand is much greater, and education in the U.S. is a trillion-dollar market.[46] One major concern will be who has access to the internal files of the digital assistants and digital tutors.

Is Artificial Intelligence an Existential Threat?

When AlphaGo convincingly beat Lee Sedol at Go in 2016, it fueled a reaction that had been building over the last several years concerning the

dangers that artificial intelligence might present to humans. Computer scientists signed pledges not to use AI for military purposes. Stephen Hawking
and Bill Gates made public statements warning of the existential threat
posed by AI. Elon Musk and other Silicon Valley entrepreneurs set up a
new company, OpenAI, with a one-billion-dollar nest egg and hired Ilya
Sutskever, one of Geoffrey Hinton's former students, to be its first director. Although OpenAI's stated goal was to ensure that future AI discoveries would be publicly available for all to use, it had another, implicit and
more important goal—to prevent private companies from doing evil. For,
with AlphaGo's victory over world Go champion Sedol, a tipping point had
been reached. Almost overnight, artificial intelligence had gone from being
judged a failure to being perceived as an existential threat.

This is not the first time an emergent technology has seemed to pose an
existential threat. The invention, development, and stockpiling of nuclear
weapons threatened to blow up the world, but somehow we have managed
to keep that from happening, at least until now. When recombinant DNA
technology first appeared, there was fear that deadly engineered organisms
would be set loose to cause untold suffering and death across the globe.
Genetic engineering is now a mature technology, and so far we have managed to survive its creations. The recent advances in machine learning pose
a relatively modest threat compared to nuclear weapons and killer organisms. We will also adapt to artificial intelligence, and, indeed, this is already
happening.

One of the implications of DeepStack's success is that a deep learning
network can learn how to become a world-class liar. What deep networks
can be trained to do is limited only by the trainer's imagination and data. If
a network can be trained to safely drive a car, it can also be trained to race
Formula 1 cars, and someone probably is willing to pay for it. Today it still
requires skilled and highly trained practitioners to build products and services using deep learning, but as the cost of computing power continues to
plummet and as software becomes automated, it will soon become possible
for high school students to build AI applications. Otto, the highest-earning
online e-commerce company in Germany for clothing, furnishings, and
sport, is using deep learning to predict ahead of time what its customers are likely to order based on their past history of ordering and then to
preorder it for them.[47] With 90 percent accuracy, customers receive mer-
chandise almost before they order it. Done automatically without human
intervention, preordering not only saves the company millions of euros a
year in reduced surplus stock and product returns but also results in greater

customer satisfaction and retention. Rather than displacing Otto's workers, deep learning has boosted their productivity. AI can make you more productive at your job.

Although the major high-tech companies have pioneered deep learning applications, machine learning tools are already widely available and many other companies are beginning to benefit. Alexa, a wildly popular digital assistant operating in tandem with the Amazon Echo smart speaker, responds to natural language requests based on deep learning. Amazon Web Services (AWS) has introduced toolboxes called "Lex," "Poly" and "Comprehend" that make it easy to develop the same natural language interfaces based on automated test-to-speech, speech recognition and natural language understanding, respectively. Applications with conversational interactions are now within the reach of smaller businesses that can't afford to hire machine learning experts. AI can enhance customer satisfaction.

When chess-playing computer programs eclipsed the best human chess players, did that stop people from playing chess? On the contrary, it raised their level of play. It also democratized chess. The best chess players once came from big cities like Moscow and New York that had a concentration of grandmasters who could teach younger players and raise their level of play. Chess-playing computer programs made it possible for Magnus Carlson, who grew up in a small town in Norway, to become a chess grandmaster at thirteen, and today he is the world chess champion. The benefits of artificial intelligence will affect not just the playing of games, however, but every aspect of human endeavor, from art to science. AI can make you smarter.[48]

Back to the Future

The Deep Learning Revolution has two intertwined themes: how human intelligence evolved and how artificial intelligence is evolving. The big difference between the two kinds of intelligence is that it took human intelligence many millions of years to evolve, but artificial intelligence is evolving on a trajectory measured in decades. Although this is warp speed even for cultural evolution, fastening our seat belts may not be the right response.

The recent breakthroughs in deep learning were not the overnight successes that you might have gathered from press reports. The story behind the shift from artificial intelligence based on symbols, logic, and rules to deep learning networks based on big data and learning algorithms is not generally known. *The Deep Learning Revolution* tells that story and explores the origins and consequences of deep learning from my perspective both as a pioneer in developing learning algorithms for neural networks in the 1980s and as the president of the Neural Information Processing Systems (NIPS) Foundation, which has overseen discoveries in machine learning and deep learning over the last thirty years. My colleagues and I in the neural network community were for many years the underdogs, but our persistence and patience eventually prevailed.

2   The Rebirth of Artificial Intelligence

Marvin Minsky was a brilliant mathematician and a founder of the MIT Artificial Intelligence Laboratory (MIT AI Lab).[1] Founders set the direction and the culture of a field, and, thanks in no small part to Minsky, artificial intelligence at MIT in the 1960s was a bastion of cleverness. Bubbling over with more ideas per minute than anyone else I knew, he could convince you that his take on a problem was right, even when common sense told you otherwise. I admired his boldness and his cleverness—but not the direction that he took AI.

Child's Play?

Blocks World is a good example of a project that came out of the MIT AI Lab in the 1960s. To simplify the problem of vision, Blocks World consisted of rectangular building blocks that could be stacked to create structures (figure 2.1). The goal was to write a program that could interpret a command, such as "Find a large yellow block and put it on top of the red block," and plan the steps needed for a robot arm to carry out the command. This seems like child's play, but a large, complex program had to be written, one that became so cumbersome that it could not be readily debugged and was effectively abandoned when the student who wrote the program, Terry Winograd, left MIT. This seemingly simple problem was much harder than anyone thought it would be, and, even if it had succeeded, there was no direct path from Blocks World to the real world, where objects come in many shapes, sizes, and weights, and not all angles are right angles. Compared to a controlled laboratory setting where the direction and level of lighting can be fixed, in the real world, lighting can vary dramatically from place to place and time to time, which greatly complicates the task of object recognition for computers.

Figure 2.1
Marvin Minsky watching a robot stacking blocks around 1968. Blocks World was a simplified version of how we interact with the world, but it was far more complex than anyone imagined, and was not solved until 2016 by deep learning.

In the 1960s, the MIT AI Lab received a large grant from a military research agency to build a robot that could play Ping-Pong. I once heard a story that the principal investigator forgot to ask for money in the grant proposal to build a vision system for the robot, so he assigned the problem to a graduate student as a summer project. I once asked Marvin Minsky whether the story was true. He snapped back that I had it wrong: "We assigned the problem to undergraduate students." A document from the archives at MIT confirms his version of the story.[2] What looked like it would be an easy problem to solve proved to be quicksand that swallowed a generation of researchers in computer vision.

Why Vision Is a Hard Problem

We rarely have difficulty identifying what an object is despite differences in the location, size, orientation, and lighting of the object. One of the earliest ideas in computer vision was to match a template of the object with the pixels in the image, but that approach failed because the pixels of the two images of the same object in different orientations don't match. For example, consider the two birds in figure 2.2. If you shift the image of one bird over the other, you can get a part to match, but the rest is out of register; but you can get a fairly good match to an image of another bird species in the same pose.

Figure 2.2
Zebra finches consulting with each other. We have no difficulty seeing that they are the same species. But because they have different orientations to the viewer it is difficult to compare them with templates even though they have almost identical features.

Progress in computer vision was made by focusing not on pixels but on features. For example, birders have to become experts in distinguishing between different species that may differ in only a few subtle markings. A practical and popular book on identifying birds has only one photograph of a bird, but many schematic drawings pointing out the subtle differences between them (figure 2.3).[3] A good feature is one that is unique to one bird species, but because the same features are found on many species, what makes it possible to identify a bird is the unique combination of several field marks such as wing bars, eye stripes, and wing patches. And when these field marks are shared by closely related species, there are calls and songs that distinguish one from another. Drawings or paintings of birds are much better at directing our attention to the relevant distinguishing features than are photographs, which are filled with hundreds of less relevant features (figure 2.3).

The problem with this features-based approach is not just that it is very labor intensive to develop feature detectors for the hundreds of thousands of different objects in the world, but that, even with the best feature detectors, ambiguities arise from images of objects that are partially occluded, which makes recognizing objects in cluttered scenes a daunting task for computers.

Figure 2.3
Distinctive feature that can be used to discriminate between similar birds. The arrows point toward the location of where to find wing bars that are especially important for telling apart families of warblers: Some are conspicuous, some obscure, some double, some long, some short. From Peterson, Mountfort, and Hollom, *Field Guide to the Birds of Britain and Europe*, 5th ed., p.16.

Little did anyone suspect in the 1960s that it would take fifty years and a millionfold increase in computer power before computer vision would reach human levels of performance. The misleading intuition that it would be easy to write a computer vision program is based on activities that we find easy to do, such as seeing, hearing, and moving around—but that took evolution millions of years to get right. Much to their chagrin, early AI pioneers found the computer vision problem to be extremely hard to solve. In contrast, they found it much easier to program computers to prove mathematical theorems—a process thought to require the highest levels of intelligence—because computers turn out to be much better at logic than we are. Being able to think logically is a late development in evolution and, even in humans, requires training to follow a long line of logical propositions to a rigorous conclusion, whereas, for most problems we need to solve to survive, generalizations from previous experiences work well for us most of the time.

Expert Systems

Popular in the 1970s and 1980s, AI expert systems were developed to solve problems like medical diagnosis using a set of rules. Thus an early expert system, MYCIN, was developed to identify the bacteria responsible for infectious diseases such as meningitis.[4] Following the expert system approach, MYCIN's developers had first to collect facts and rules from infectious disease experts, as well as symptoms and medical histories from the patients, then to enter these into the system's computer, and finally to program the computer to make inferences using logic. The developers ran into difficulties in collecting the facts and rules from the experts, however, especially in the more complex domains, where the best diagnosticians rely not on rules but on pattern recognition based on experience, which is difficult to codify,[5] and where their system had to be continually updated as new facts were discovered and old rules became obsolete. And they encountered further difficulties in collecting and entering the patients' symptoms and medical histories into the system's computer, a process that could take a half hour or longer per patient, more time than a busy physician could afford. Not surprisingly, MYCIN was never used clinically. Although many expert systems were written for other applications such as toxic spill management, mission planning for autonomous vehicles, and speech recognition, few are in use today.

Researchers tried many different approaches in the early decades of AI, but their approaches were more clever than they were practical. Not only did they underestimate the complexity of real-world problems, but the solutions they proposed scaled badly. In complex domains, the number of rules can be enormous, and as new facts are added by hand, keeping track of exceptions to and interactions with other rules becomes impractical. Douglas Lenat, for example, started a project called "Cyc" in 1984 to codify common sense, which seemed like a good idea at the time but turned out to be a nightmare in practice.[6] We take for granted a boundless number of facts about the way the world works, most of which are based on experience. For example, a cat falling from 40 feet will probably avoid harm,[7] but a human falling from the same height probably won't.

Another reason why progress in early AI was so slow was that digital computers were incredibly primitive and memory forbiddingly expensive by today's standards. But because digital computers are highly efficient at logical operations, symbol manipulation, and the application of rules, it is not too surprising that these computational primitives would be favored in the twentieth century. Thus Allen Newell and Herbert Simon, two computer scientists from Carnegie Mellon University, were able to write a computer program called "Logic Theorist" in 1955 that could prove the logical theorems in *Principia Mathematica*, Alfred North Whitehead and Bertrand Russell's attempt to systematize all of mathematics. There were great expectations in these early days that intelligent computers were just around the corner.

AI pioneers who sought to write computer programs with the functionality of human intelligence did not care how the brain actually achieved intelligent behavior. When I asked Allen Newell why, he told me that he personally had been open to insights from brain research, but that there simply hadn't been enough known at the time to be of much use. Basic principles of brain function were just emerging in the 1950s, led by the work of Alan Hodgkin and Andrew Huxley, who explained how signals from the brain are carried over a long distance by all-or-none electrical spikes in nerves, and of Bernard Katz, who discovered clues to how these electrical signals are converted into chemical signals at synapses, which communicate between neurons.[8]

Although, by the 1980s, more was both known about the brain and more widely accessible outside the field of biology, the brain itself had become irrelevant for the new generation of AI researchers, whose goal was to write a program that was functionally equivalent to how the brain worked. In philosophy this stance was called functionalism, which for many was a good excuse to ignore the messy details in biology. But a small group of AI researchers who were not part of the mainstream believed that an approach to artificial intelligence inspired by the actual biology of the brain and variously called "neural networks," "connectionism," and "parallel distributed processing" could eventually solve difficult problems that had eluded logic-based AI.

I was one of that group.

Into the Lion's Den

In 1989, Michael Dertouzos, head of MIT's Computer Science Laboratory, invited me to give a distinguished lecture at MIT on my pioneering approach to AI based on neural networks (figure 2.4). On arriving there, I was warmly greeted by Dertouzos, who, as we rode together in the elevator, told me that it was an MIT tradition for the distinguished lecturer to take five minutes to open a discussion with faculty and students on his or her topic over lunch. "And," he added as the doors of the elevator opened, "they hate what you do."

The room was packed with perhaps as many as a hundred people, which surprised even Dertouzos. Scientists were standing in circles three rows deep: the first row for senior faculty, junior faculty in the second row, and students in the rows beyond them. And I was in the center, stationed in front of the buffet, the main dish. What could I possibly say in five minutes that could make any difference to an audience that hated what I was doing?

I improvised: "That fly on the food has a brain with only 100,000 neurons; it weighs a milligram and consumes a milliwatt of power," I said,

Figure 2.4
Terry Sejnowski talking about scaling laws for the cortex shortly after he moved to the Salk Institute in 1989. Courtesy of Ciencia Explicada.

winging it. "The fly can see, it can fly, it can navigate, and it can find food. But what is truly remarkable is that it can reproduce itself. MIT owns a supercomputer that costs $100 million: it consumes a megawatt of power and is cooled by a huge air-conditioner. But the biggest cost of the super-computer is human sacrifice in the form of programmers to feed its voracious appetite for programs. That supercomputer can't see, it can't fly, and although it communicates with other computers, it can't mate or reproduce itself. What is wrong with this picture?"

After a long pause, a senior faculty member spoke, "Because we haven't written the vision program yet." (The Department of Defense had recently poured $600 million into its Strategic Computing Initiative, a program that ran from 1983 to 1993 but came up short on building a vision system to guide a self-driving tank.)[9] "Good luck with that," was my reply.

Gerald Sussman, who made several important applications of AI to real-world problems, including a system for high-precision integration for orbital mechanics, defended the honor of MIT's approach to AI with an appeal to the classic work of Alan Turing, who had proven that the Turing machine, a thought experiment, could compute any computable function. "And how long would that take?" I asked. "You had better compute quickly or you will be eaten," I added, then walked across the room to pour myself a cup of coffee. And that was the end of the dialogue with the faculty.

"What is wrong with this picture?" is a question that every student in my lab can answer. But the first two rows of my lunchtime audience were stumped. Finally, a student in the third row offered this reply: "The digital computer is a general-purpose device, which can be programmed to compute anything, though inefficiently, but the fly is a special-purpose computer that can see and fly but can't balance my checkbook." This was the right answer. The vision networks in the fly eye evolved over hundreds of millions of years, and its vision algorithms are embedded in the networks themselves. This is why you can reverse engineer vision by working out the wiring diagram and information flow through the neural circuits of the fly eye, and why you can't do that for a digital computer, where the hardware by itself needs software to specify what problem is being solved.

I recognized Rodney Brooks smiling in the back of the crowd, someone I had once invited to a workshop on computational neuroscience in Woods Hole on Cape Cod, Massachusetts. Brooks is from Australia, and, in the 1980s, he was a junior faculty member in the MIT AI Lab, where he built walking robotic insects using an architecture that did not depend on digital logic. He would eventually become the lab's director and go on to found iRobot, the company that makes Roombas.

The room where I gave my lecture that afternoon was huge and filled with a large contingent of undergraduate students, the next generation looking to the future rather than the past. I talked about a neural network that learned how to play backgammon, a project I collaborated on with Gerald Tesauro, a physicist at the Center for Complex Systems Research at the University of Illinois in Urbana-Champaign. Backgammon is a race to the finish between two players, with pieces that move forward based on each roll of the dice, passing over one another on the way. Unlike chess, which is deterministic, backgammon is governed by chance: the uncertainty with every roll of the dice makes it more difficult to predict the outcome of a particular move. It is a highly popular game in the Middle East, where some make a living playing high-stakes backgammon.

Rather than write a program based on logic and heuristics to handle all possible board positions, an impossible task given that there are 10^{20} possible backgammon board positions, we had the network learn to play through pattern recognition by watching a teacher play.[10] Gerry went on to create the first backgammon program that played at world-championship levels by having the backgammon network play itself (a story that will be told in chapter 10).

After my lecture, I learned that there was a front page article in the *New York Times* that morning about how government agencies were slashing funding for artificial intelligence. Although this was the beginning of an AI winter for mainstream researchers, it didn't affect me or the rest of my group, for whom the neural network spring had just begun.

But our new approach to AI would take twenty-five years to deliver real-world applications in vision, speech, and language. Even in 1989, I should have known it would take this long. In 1978, when I was a graduate student at Princeton, I extrapolated Moore's law for the exponential increase in computing power, doubling every 18 months, to see how long it would take to reach brain levels of computing power and concluded it would happen in 2015. Fortunately, that did not deter me from charging ahead. My belief in neural networks was based on my intuition that if nature had solved these problems, we should be able to learn from nature how to solve them, too. The twenty-five years I had to wait was not even a blink of the eye compared to the hundreds of millions of years it took nature.

Inside the visual cortex, neurons are arranged in a hierarchy of layers. As sensory information is transformed cortical layer by cortical layer, the representation of the world becomes more and more abstract. Over the decades, as the number of layers in neural network models increased, their performance continued to improve until finally a critical threshold was reached that allowed us to solve problems we could only dream about solving in the 1980s. Deep learning automates the process of finding good features that distinguish different objects in an image, and that is why computer vision is so much better today than it was five years ago.

By 2016, computers had become a million times faster and computer memory had increased by a billion times from megabytes to terabytes. It became possible to simulate neural networks with millions of units and billions of connections, compared with networks in the 1980s that had only hundreds of units and thousands of connections. Though still tiny by the standards of a human brain, which has a hundred billion neurons and a million billion synaptic connections, today's networks are now large enough to demonstrate proof of principle in narrow domains.

Deep learning in deep neural networks has arrived. But before there were deep networks, we had to learn how to train shallow networks.

3 The Dawn of Neural Networks

The only existence proof that any of the hard problems in artificial intelligence can be solved is the fact that, through evolution, nature has already solved them. But there were clues in the 1950s for how computers might actually achieve intelligent behavior, if AI researchers would take an approach that was fundamentally different from symbol processing.

The first clue was that our brains are powerful pattern recognizers. Our visual systems can recognize an object in a cluttered scene in one-tenth of a second, even though we may have never seen that particular object before and even when the object is in any location, of any size, and in any orientation to us. In short, our visual system behaves like a computer that has "recognize object" as a single instruction.

The second clue was that our brains can learn how to perform many difficult tasks through practice, from playing the piano to mastering physics. Nature uses general-purpose learning to solve specialized problems, and humans are champion learners. This is our special power. The organization of our cerebral cortex is similar throughout, and deep learning networks are found in all our sensory and motor systems.[1]

The third clue was that our brains aren't filled with logic or rules. Yes, we can learn how to think logically or follow rules, but only after a lot of training, and most of us aren't very good at it. This is illustrated by typical performances on a logical puzzle called the "Wason selection task" (figure 3.1).

The correct selections are the card with "8" and the brown card. In the original study, only 10 percent of subjects got the right answer.[2] But most subjects had no trouble getting the right answer when the logic test was grounded in a familiar context (figure 3.2).

Reasoning seems to be domain specific, and the more familiar we are with a domain, the easier it is for us to solve problems in that domain. Experience makes it easier to reason within a domain because we can use examples we have encountered to intuit solutions. In physics, for example,

Figure 3.1
Each of these four cards has a number on one side and a field of color covering the entire other side. Which card(s) must you turn over in order to test the truth of the proposition that if a card shows an even number on one face, then its opposite face is red? (From "Wason selection task," Wikipedia.)

Figure 3.2
Each card has an age on one side, and a drink on the other. Which card(s) must be turned over to test the law that, if you are drinking alcohol, then you must be over 18? (From "Wason selection task," Wikipedia.)

we learn a domain like electricity and magnetism by solving many problems, not by memorizing formulas. If human intelligence were based purely on logic, it should be domain general, which it isn't.

The fourth clue is that our brains are filled with billions and billions of tiny neurons that are constantly communicating with one another. This suggests that, for solutions to the hard problems in artificial intelligence, we should be looking into computers with massively parallel architectures rather than those with von Neumann digital architectures through which data and instructions are fetched and executed one at a time. Yes, it is true that a Turing machine can compute any computable function given enough memory and enough time, but nature had to solve problems in real time. To do this, it made use of the brain's neural networks that, like the most powerful computers on the planet, have massively parallel processors. Algorithms that run efficiently on them will eventually win out.

Early Pioneers

In the 1950s and 1960s, shortly after Norbert Wiener introduced cybernetics, based on communications and control systems in both machines and living creatures,[3] there was an explosion of interest in self-organizing systems. As a small sample of the ingenious creations that explosion gave rise to, Oliver Selfridge created Pandemonium,[4] a pattern recognition device in which feature-detecting "demons" vied with one another for the right to represent objects in images (a metaphor for deep learning; figure 3.3); and Bernard Widrow and his student Ted Hoff at Stanford invented the LMS (least mean squares) learning algorithm,[5] which, along with its successors, is used extensively for adaptive signal processing in numerous applications from noise cancellation to financial forecasting. Here I will focus on just one of the pioneers of those early decades, Frank Rosenblatt (figure 3.4), whose perceptron is the direct antecedent of deep learning.[6]

Learning from Examples

Undeterred by our lack of understanding about brain function, neural network AI pioneers plunged ahead with cartoon versions of neurons and how they are connected with one another. Frank Rosenblatt at Cornell University (figure 3.4) was one of the earliest to mimic the architecture of our visual system for automatic pattern recognition.[7] He invented a deceptively simple network called a "perceptron," a learning algorithm that could learn how to classify patterns into categories, such as letters of the alphabet. Algorithms are step-by-step procedures that you follow to achieve particular goals, much as you would a recipe to bake a cake (chapter 13 will explain algorithms in general).

If you understand the basic principles for how a perceptron learns to solve a pattern recognition problem, you are halfway to understanding how deep learning works. The goal of a perceptron is to determine whether an input pattern is a member of a category, such as cats, in an image. Box 3.1 explains how the inputs to a perceptron are transformed by a set of weights from the input units to the output unit. The weights are a measure of the influence that each input has on the final decision made by the output unit. But how can we find a set of weights that can correctly classify inputs?

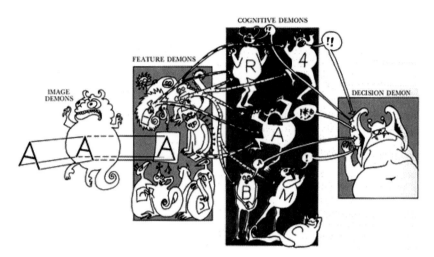

Figure 3.3

Pandemonium. Oliver Selfridge imagined that there were demons in the brain that were responsible for extracting successively more complex features and abstractions from sensory inputs, resulting in decisions. Each demon at each level is excited if it is a match to input from an earlier level. The decision demon weighs the degree of excitement and importance of its informants. This form of evidence evaluation is a metaphor for current deep learning networks, which have many more levels. From Peter H. Lindsay and Donald A. Norman, *Human Information Processing: An Introduction to Psychology*, 2nd ed. (New York: Academic Press, 1977), figure 3-1. Wikipedia Commons: https://commons.wikimedia.org/wiki/File:Pande.jpg.

The traditional way that an engineer solves this problem is to handcraft the weights based on analysis or an ad hoc procedure. This is labor intensive and often depends on intuition as much as on engineering. An alternative is to use an automatic procedure that learns from examples, the same way that we learn about objects in the world. Many examples are needed including those not in the category, especially if they are similar, such as dogs if the goal is to recognize cats. The examples are passed to the perceptron one at a time and corrections are automatically made to the weights if there is a classification error.

The beauty of the perceptron learning algorithm is that it is guaranteed to find a set of weights automatically if such a set of weights exists and if enough examples are available. The learning takes place incrementally after each of the examples in the training set is presented and the output compared with the correct answer. If the answer is correct, no changes are made to the weights, but if it isn't correct (1 when it should be 0, or 0 when

NEW NAVY DEVICE LEARNS BY DOING

Psychologist Shows Embryo of Computer Designed to Read and Grow Wiser

WASHINGTON, July 7 (UPI) —The Navy revealed the embryo of an electronic computer today that it expects will be able to walk, talk, see, write, reproduce itself and be conscious of its existence.

The embryo—the Weather Bureau's $2,000,000 "704" computer—learned to differentiate between right and left after fifty attempts in the Navy's demonstration for newsmen.

The service said it would use this principle to build the first of its Perceptron thinking machines that will be able to read and write. It is expected to be finished in about a year at a cost of $100,000.

Dr. Frank Rosenblatt, designer of the Perceptron, conducted the demonstration. He said the machine would be the first device to think as the human brain. As do human beings, Perceptron will make mistakes at first, but will grow wiser as it gains experience, he said.

Dr. Rosenblatt, a research psychologist at the Cornell Aeronautical Laboratory, Buffalo, said Perceptrons might be fired to the planets as mechanical space explorers.

Figure 3.4

Frank Rosenblatt at Cornell deep in thought. He invented the perceptron, an early precursor of deep learning networks, which had a simple learning algorithm for classifying images into categories. Article in the *New York Times*, July 8, 1958, from a UPI wire report. The perceptron machine was expected to cost $100,000 on completion in 1959, or around $1 million in today's dollars; the IBM 704 computer that cost $2 million in 1958, or $20 million in today's dollars, could perform 12,000 multiplies per second, which was blazingly fast at the time. But the much less expensive Samsung Galaxy S6 phone, which can perform 34 billion operations per second, is more than a million times faster. Photo courtesy of George Nagy.

Box 3.1

The Perceptron

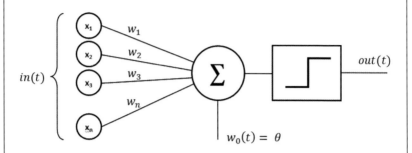

A perceptron is a neural network with one artificial neuron that has an input layer and a set of connections linking the input units to the output unit. The goal of a perceptron is to classify patterns presented to input units. The basic operation performed by the output unit is to sum up the values of each input (x_n) multiplied by its connection strength, or weight (w_n), to the output unit. In the diagram above, a weighted sum of the inputs ($\Sigma_{i=1, ..., n}\ w_i\ x_{i,}$) is compared to the threshold θ and passed through a step function that gives an output of "1" if the sum is greater than the threshold and an output of "0" otherwise. For example, the input could be the intensities of pixels in an image, or more generally, features that are extracted from the raw image, such as the outline of objects in the image. Images are presented one at a time, and the perceptron decides whether or not the image is a member of a category, such as the category of cats. The output can only be in one of two states, "on" if the image is in the category or "off" if it isn't. "On" and "off" correspond to the binary values 1 and 0, respectively. The perceptron learning algorithm is

$\delta\,w_i = \alpha\,\delta\,x_i$

δ = output—teacher,

where both the output and teacher are binary, so that $\delta = 0$ if the output is correct , and $\delta = +1$ or -1 If the output is not correct, depending on the difference.

it should be 1), then the weights are changed slightly so that the next time the same input is given, it is closer to getting the correct answer (box 3.1). It is important that the changes occur gradually so that the weights can feel the tugs from all the training examples, and not just from the last one.

If this explanation of perceptron learning isn't clear, there is a much neater geometric way to understand how a perceptron learns to classify inputs. For the special case of two inputs, it is possible to plot the inputs on a two-dimensional graph. Each input is a point in the graph and the two weights in the network determine a straight line. The goal of learning is to move the line around so that it cleanly separates the positive and negative examples (figure 3.5). For three inputs, the space of inputs is three-dimensional, and the perceptron specifies a plane that separates the positive and negative training examples. The same principle holds even in the general case, when the dimensionality of the space of inputs can be quite high and impossible to visualize.

Eventually, if a solution is possible, the weights will stop changing, which means the perceptron has correctly classified all of the examples in the training set. But, in what is called "overfitting," it is also possible that there are not enough examples in the set, and the network has simply memorized the specific examples without being able to generalize to new ones. To avoid overfitting, it is important to have another set of examples,

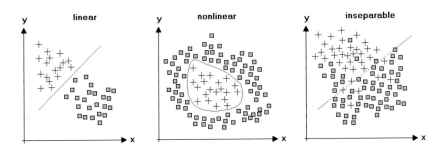

Figure 3.5
Geometric explanation for how two object categories are discriminated by a perceptron. The objects have two features, such as size and brightness, which have values (x,y) and are plotted on each graph. The two types of objects (pluses and squares) in the panel on the left can be separated by a straight line that passes between them; this discrimination can be learned by a perceptron. The two types of objects in the other two panels cannot be separated by a straight line, but those in the center panel can be separated by a curved line. The objects in the panel on the right would have to be gerrymandered to separate the two types. The discriminations in all three panels could be learned by a deep learning network if enough training data were available.

called a "test set," that wasn't used to train the network. At the end of training, the classification performance on the test set is a true measure of how well the perceptron can generalize to new examples whose respective categories are unknown. Generalization is the key concept here. In real life, we never see the same object the same way or encounter the same situation, but if we can generalize from previous experience to new views or situations, we can handle a broad range of real-world problems.

SEXNET

As an example of how a perceptron can be used to solve a real-world problem, consider how you would tell a male from a female face, taking away hair, jewelry, and secondary sexual characteristics such as Adam's apples, which tend to be larger in males. Beatrice Golomb, a postdoctoral fellow in my lab in 1990, used faces of college students from a database she obtained as inputs to a perceptron that was trained to classify the sex of a face with an 81 percent accuracy (figure 3.6).[8] The faces that the perceptron had difficulty classifying were also difficult for humans to classify, and members of my lab achieved an average performance of 88 percent on the same set of faces. Beatrice also trained a multilayer perceptron (which will be introduced in chapter 8) that achieved a 92 percent accuracy,[9] better than people from my lab. At a talk she gave at the 1991 Neural Information Processing Systems (NIPS) Conference, she concluded: "Since experience improves performance, this should suggest that people in the lab need to spend more time engaged in discriminating sex." She called her multilayer perceptron the "SEXNET." In the question-and-answer period, someone asked whether SEXNET could be used to detect transvestite faces. "Yes," said Beatrice, to which Ed Posner, the founder of the NIPS conferences, retorted, "That would be the DRAGNET."[10]

---▶

Figure 3.6
What is the sex of this face—male or female? A perceptron was trained to discriminate male from female faces. The pixels from the image of a face (top) are multiplied by the corresponding weights (bottom), and the sum is compared to a threshold. The size of each weight is depicted as the area of the pixel. Positive weights (white) are evidence for maleness and negative weights (black) favor femaleness. The nose width, the size of the region between the nose and mouth, and image intensity around the eye region are important for discriminating males, whereas image intensity around the mouth and cheekbone is important for discriminating females. From M. S. Gray, D. T. Lawrence, B. A. Golomb, and T. J. Sejnowski, "A Perceptron Reveals the Face of Sex," Neural Computation 7 (1995): 1160–1164, figure 1.

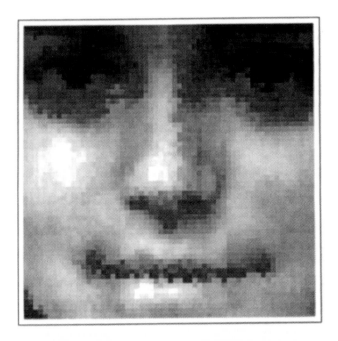

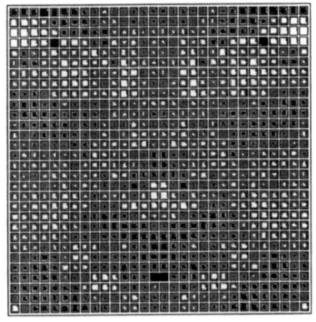

What makes discriminating male from female faces an interesting task is that, although we are quite good at it, we can't articulate exactly what the differences between male and female faces are. Since no single feature is definitive, this pattern recognition problem depends on combining evidence from a large number of low-level features. The advantage of the perceptron is that the weights provide clues to which parts of the face are the most informative about sex (figure 3.6). Surprisingly, the philtrum (the space between the nose and lips) was the most distinctive feature, which is noticeably larger in most males. Regions around the eyes (larger in males) and upper cheeks (larger in females) also had high informational value for classifying sex. The perceptron weighs evidence from all these locations to make a decision, and so do we although we might not be able to describe how we do it.

Rosenblatt's proof of the "perceptron convergence theorem" in 1957 was a breakthrough, and his demonstrations were impressive. Backed by the Office of Naval Research, he built a custom-hardware analog computer with 400 photocells as input, with weights that were variable resistance potentiometers adjusted by motors. Analog signals vary continuously with time, just like the signals from vinyl phonograph records. Given a collection of pictures with and without tanks in them, Rosenblatt's perceptron learned how to recognize tanks even in new images. This was written up in the *New York Times* and caused a sensation (figure 3.4).[11]

The perceptron inspired a beautiful mathematical analysis of pattern separation in high-dimensional spaces. When points live in a space that has thousands of dimensions. we cannot rely on our intuition about distances between points in the three-dimensional space we live in. The Russian mathematician Vladimir Vapnik introduced a classifier based on this analysis, called the "Support Vector Machine,"[12] which generalized the perceptron and is widely used in machine learning. He found a way to automatically find a flat surface that maximally separates points from the two categories (figure 3.5, linear). This makes generalization more robust to measurement error of the points in the space, and, when coupled with the "kernel trick," which is a nonlinear extension, the Support Vector Machine algorithm has become a mainstay in machine learning.[13]

Perceptrons Eclipsed

But there was a limitation that made the perceptron line of research problematic. The caveat above, "if such a set of weights exists," raised the question of what problems can and cannot be solved by perceptrons.

Embarrassingly simple distributions of points in two dimensions cannot be separated by a perceptron (figure 3.5, nonlinear). It turned out that the tank perceptron was not a tank classifier, but a time of day classifier. It is much more difficult to classify tanks in images; indeed, it cannot be done with a perceptron. This also shows that, even when a perceptron has learned something, it may not be what you think it has learned. The final blow to the perceptron was a 1969 tour de force mathematical treatise, *Perceptrons* by Marvin Minsky and Seymour Papert.[14] Their definitive geometric analysis showed that the capabilities of perceptrons are limited: they can only separate categories that are linearly separable (figure 3.5). The cover of their book illustrates a geometric problem that Minsky and Papert proved the perceptron could not solve (figure 3.7). Although, at the end of their book, Minsky and Papert considered the prospect of generalizing single- to multiple-layer perceptrons, one layer feeding into the next, they doubted there would ever be a way to train even these more powerful perceptrons. Unfortunately, many took this doubt to be definitive, and the field was abandoned until a new generation of neural network researchers took a fresh look at the problem in the 1980s.

In a perceptron, each input contributes independent evidence to the output unit. But what if several inputs need to be combined in ways that make decisions dependent on the combination and not on each input separately? This is why a perceptron cannot distinguish whether a spiral is connected or not: a single pixel carries no information on whether it is on the inside or the outside. Although in multilayer feedforward networks, combinations of several inputs can be formed in intermediate layers between the input and output units, no one in the 1960s knew how to train a network with even a single layer of such "hidden units" between the input and output layers.

Frank Rosenblatt and Marvin Minsky had been classmates at the Bronx High School of Science in New York City. They debated their radically different approaches to artificial intelligence at scientific meetings, where participants tilted toward Minsky's approach. But despite their differences, each man made important contributions to our understanding of perceptrons, which is the starting point for deep learning.

When Rosenblatt died in a boating accident in 1971 at age 43, the backlash against perceptrons was in full swing, and there were rumors that he might have committed suicide, or was it an outing gone tragically wrong?[15] What became clear was that a heroic period of discovering a new way of computing with neural networks was closing; a generation would pass before the promise of Rosenblatt's pioneering efforts was realized.

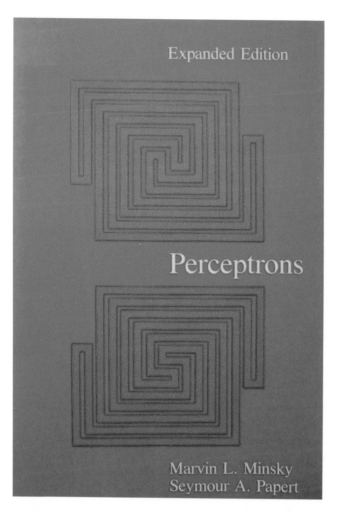

Figure 3.7
The book cover of an expanded edition of *Perceptrons*. The two red spirals look the same but they aren't. The top one is two disconnected spirals, but the bottom one is a single connected spiral, which you can verify by tracing the insides of the loops with a pencil. Minsky and Papert proved that a perceptron cannot distinguish between these two objects. Can you see the difference without tracing? Why not?

4 Brain-style Computing

"If I Only Had a Brain" was a song sung by the Scarecrow in the classic 1939 musical film *The Wizard of Oz*. What the Scarecrow did not know was that he already had a brain and could hardly have talked or sung without one, but the brain was only two days old, and his real problem was a lack of experience. With time, he learned about the world and was eventually recognized as the wisest man in all of Oz, wise enough to know his own limitations. In contrast, the Tin Woodman sang "If I Only Had a Heart." He and the Scarecrow debated which was more important, having a brain or having a heart. In Oz, as well as in the real world, cognition and emotion, both products of the brain, work together in a delicate balancing act with learning to create human intelligence. Drawing on this classic musical, the theme of this chapter is "If AI Only Had a Brain and a Heart."

How the Brain Works

Geoffrey Hinton (figure 4.1) and I had similar beliefs about the promise of neural network models when we met at a workshop that Geoffrey organized in 1979. We became fast friends and later collaborated on the discovery of a new type of neural network model called the "Boltzmann machine" (discussed in chapter 7), which would break a logjam that had been holding back learning in multilayer network models for a generation.

Every few years, I get a call from Geoffrey that begins with "I figured out how the brain works." Each time, he tells me about a clever new scheme for improving neural network models. It has taken many such schemes and refinements for deep learning in multilayered neural networks to achieve a level of performance comparable to humans in recognizing speech on cell phones and objects in photos. The public became aware of these capabilities just a few years ago; they are now well known, but they were a long time in coming.

A

B

Figure 4.1

(A) Geoffrey Everest Hinton early in his career. His middle name comes from a relative, George Everest, who surveyed India and figured out how to measure the height of the world's tallest mountain, which now bears his name. (B) Hinton in 1994. These two photos were taken fifteen years apart. Courtesy of Geoffrey Hinton.

Geoffrey received an undergraduate degree in psychology at the University of Cambridge and a doctorate in artificial intelligence from the University of Edinburgh. His thesis advisor was Christopher Longuet-Higgins, a distinguished chemist who invented an early network model of an associative memory. At that time, the dominant paradigm in artificial intelligence was based on writing programs that used symbols, logic, and rules to codify intelligent behavior; cognitive psychologists had adopted this approach to understanding human cognition, and especially language. Geoffrey was swimming against the tide. No one could have predicted that he would someday figure out how the brain—or at least something like the brain—works. His lectures are compelling, and he can explain abstract mathematical concepts with a clarity that requires little math to grasp. His wit and self-effacing humor are charming. Geoffrey is also by nature highly competitive, especially when it comes to the brain.

When we first met, Geoffrey was a postdoctoral fellow at the University of California, San Diego (UCSD), in the Parallel Distributed Processing (PDP) Group led by David Rumelhart and James McClelland. Geoffrey believed that networks of simple processing units, working together in parallel and learning from examples, were a better way to understand cognition. He was a central figure in the PDP Group, which was exploring how words and language could be understood as the spread of activity distributed over a large number of nodes in a network.

The traditional approach to language in cognitive science is based on symbolic representations. The word "cup," for example, is a symbol that stands for the concept of a cup, and not just any cup, but all cups. The beauty of symbols is that they allow us to compress complex ideas and manipulate them; the problem with symbols is that they are so compressed that it is difficult to ground them in the real world, where cups come in an infinite variety of forms, shapes, and sizes. There is no logical program that can specify what is and what is not a cup or that can recognize cups in images, even though most of us humans are quite good at knowing a cup when we see it. Abstract concepts like justice and peace are even more difficult for a logical program to pin down. An alternative is to represent cups by activity patterns over a very large population of neurons, which can capture both the similarities and differences between concepts. This endows a symbol with a rich internal structure that reflects its meaning. The problem was that no one in 1980 knew how to create these internal representations.

Geoffrey and I were not the only ones who believed in the potential of network models to mimic intelligent behavior in the 1980s. A number of researchers around the world, most of them toiling in isolation, shared our belief and went on to develop specialized network models. Christoph von der Malsburg, for one, developed a model of pattern recognition based on linking together artificial neurons that fired spikes[1] and later demonstrated that this approach could recognize faces in images.[2] Kunihiko Fukushima at Osaka University, for another, invented the Neocognitron,[3] a multilayered network model based on the architecture of the visual system that used convolutional filters and a simple form of Hebbian plasticity and was a direct precursor of deep learning networks. And, for a third, Teuvo Kohonen, an electrical engineer at Helsinki University, developed a self-organizing network that could learn to cluster similar inputs into a two-dimensional map, representing different speech sounds, for example, by different processing units in the map, with similar inputs activating neighboring regions of the output space.[4] A major advantage of the Kohonen network model was that it did not require a category label for each input (generating labels to train supervised networks is expensive). Kohonen had only one arrow in his quiver, but it was a very fine arrow.

In a promising early attempt to systematize probabilistic networks, Judea Pearl at the University of California, Los Angeles (UCLA), introduced belief networks that linked the items in the network with probabilities, such as the probabilities that the grass is wet because the sprinkler came on or because it rained.[5] Although Pearl's network model was a powerful framework for keeping track of cause and effect in the world, manually assigning all of the required probabilities proved impracticable. A breakthrough was needed for automatically finding the probabilities with learning algorithms (as will be discussed in part II).

These and other network-based models all had one fatal flaw in common: none of them worked well enough to solve problems in the real world. Moreover, the pioneers who developed them rarely collaborated with one another, making it even more difficult to make progress. As a consequence, very few in the leading AI research centers at MIT, Stanford, and Carnegie Mellon took neural networks seriously. Rule-based symbol processing received most of the funding—and generated most of the jobs.

Early Pioneers

In 1979, Geoffrey Hinton and James Anderson, a psychologist at Brown University, organized the Parallel Models of Associative Memory workshop in La Jolla, California.[6] Most participants were meeting one another for the first time. As a postdoctoral fellow of neurobiology at Harvard Medical School who had written only a few highly technical papers on neural networks published in obscure journals, I was surprised to be invited to the workshop. Geoffrey later told me that he had vetted me with David Marr (figure 4.2, middle), a towering figure in neural network modeling and a leading visionary at the MIT AI Lab. I first met Marr in a small workshop at Jackson Hole, Wyoming, in 1976. We had similar interests and he invited me to visit him and give a talk at MIT.

Marr received a bachelor's degree in mathematics and his doctorate in physiology from Cambridge University. His doctoral advisor was Giles Brindley, a physiologist who specialized on the retina and color vision but also was known for his work on musicology and the treatment of erectile

Figure 4.2
(Left to right) Tomaso Poggio, David Marr, and Francis Crick hiking in California in 1974. Francis enjoyed long discussions with visitors on many scientific issues. Courtesy of The Salk Institute for Biological Studies.

dysfunction. He famously dropped his pants during a lecture at a meeting of the American Urological Association in Las Vegas, Nevada, to demonstrate the effectiveness of a chemically-induced erection. Marr's doctoral dissertation described a neural network model of learning in the cerebellum, a part of the brain that is involved with fast motor control. He also developed neural network models of the hippocampus and the cerebral cortex, described in dense papers that have proven to be prescient.[7]

When I first met Marr at Jackson Hole, he had already moved to MIT, where he was working on vision and where, as a charismatic figure, he had attracted talented students to work with him. Pursuing a bottom-up strategy, he started at the retina, where light is converted to electrical signals, and asked how signals in the retina encoded the features of objects and how the visual cortex represented the surfaces and boundaries of objects. He and Tomaso Poggio (figure 4.2, left) developed an ingenious recurrent neural network model for stereo vision with feedback connections to detect the depth of an object from the slight lateral displacements of the images of dots in the two eyes in random-dot stereograms.[8] Binocular depth perception is the basis for how Magic Eye images pop out at you.[9]

Two years after Marr died of leukemia in 1980 at the age of 35, the book he was working on at the time, *Vision*, was published posthumously.[10] Ironically, despite the bottom-up approach Marr took to his research on vision, starting with the retina and modeling each succeeding stage of visual processing, his book is best known for advocating a top-down strategy, starting with a computational analysis of the problem to be solved, followed by building an algorithm to solve the problem, and finally by implementing the algorithm in hardware. But, even though this may be a good way to explain things after you have figured them out, it isn't such a good way to discover what's going on in the brain. The difficulty is in the first step, in deciding on what problem the brain is solving. Our intuition is often misleading, particularly when it comes to vision; we are exceptionally good at seeing, but the brain hides all the details from us. As a consequence, a pure top-down strategy is flawed, but so is a pure bottom up strategy. (Later chapters will explore how progress was made in understanding vision working from the inside out with learning algorithms.)

Also attending Hinton and Anderson's workshop in La Jolla was Francis Crick (figure 4.2, right), who with James Watson at Cambridge University had discovered the structure of DNA in 1953. Decades after his discovery, in 1977, Crick had moved to the Salk Institute for Biological Studies in La Jolla and shifted his research focus to neuroscience. He would invite researchers to visit him and have a long discussion on many topics in neuroscience, especially on vision, and David Marr was one of those visitors. At the end of Marr's book, there is a revealing discussion in the form of a Socratic dialogue, a dialogue I later learned had arisen from Marr's discussions with Crick. On moving to the Salk Institute in 1989, I, too, came to appreciate the value of having a dialogue with Crick.

George Boole and Machine Learning

In 1854, a self-taught British schoolteacher who had five daughters, some of whom were mathematically inclined, wrote a book entitled *An Investigation of the Laws of Thought*, which was the mathematical foundation for what is now called "Boolean logic." George Boole's insights into how to manipulate logical expressions are at the heart of digital computing and were a natural starting point for fledgling efforts in artificial intelligence in the 1950s. Geoffrey Hinton, who happens to be Boole's great-great-grandson, is proud to have a pen once used by Boole and handed down in his family.

In preparing a talk, I discovered that the full title of Boole's famous book is *An Investigation of the Laws of Thought, on Which Are Founded the Mathematical Theories of Logic and Probabilities* (figure 4.3). Although best remembered for its insights into logic, *Investigation* also has much to say about probability theory, which is at the heart of modern machine learning and can describe the uncertainties in the real world far better than logic. So Boole is also one of the fathers of machine learning. What an irony that a forgotten side of his thinking should flower 250 years later through his great-great-grandson. Boole would have been proud of him.

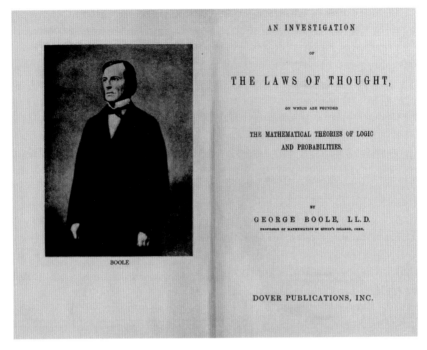

AN INVESTIGATION

OF

THE LAWS OF THOUGHT,

ON WHICH ARE FOUNDED

THE MATHEMATICAL THEORIES OF LOGIC
AND PROBABILITIES.

BY

GEORGE BOOLE, LL.D.
PROFESSOR OF MATHEMATICS IN QUEEN'S COLLEGE, CORK.

DOVER PUBLICATIONS, INC.

BOOLE

Figure 4.3
Although *The Laws of Thought* by George Boole is famous for investigating logic as a basis for thinking, note that it is also about probabilities. These two areas of mathematics inspired symbol processing and machine learning approaches to artificial intelligence, respectively.

The Humpty Dumpty Project

As a graduate student in the Physics Department at Princeton, I approached the problem of understanding the brain by writing down equations for networks of nonlinearly interacting neurons and by analyzing them,[11] much as physicists have over the centuries used mathematics to understand the nature of gravity, light, electricity, magnetism, and nuclear forces. Every night before bed, I would pray: "Dear Lord, let the equations be linear, the noise be Gaussian, and the variables be separable." These are the conditions that lead to analytic solutions, but because neural network equations turn out to be nonlinear, the noise associated with them non-Gaussian, and the variables nonseparable, they do not have explicit solutions. Moreover, simulating the equations on computers at that time was impossibly slow for large networks; even more discouraging, I had no idea whether I had the right equations.

Taking courses at Princeton, I discovered that exciting progress was being made by neuroscientists, whose relatively young science was founded forty-five years ago. Before that, research on the brain was carried out in many disciplines: biology, psychology, anatomy, physiology, pharmacology, neurology, psychiatry, bioengineering, and many others. At the first meeting of the Society for Neuroscience in 1971, Vernon Mountcastle personally greeted everyone at the door.[12] Today there are over 40,000 members of the society, and 30,000 show up at the annual meeting. I met this legendary neurophysiologist, who had discovered the cortical column and who had a formidable personality, at the Johns Hopkins University when I moved to the Department of Biophysics there for my first job in 1982.[13] I would work closely with Mountcastle in planning the Mind/Brain Institute at Johns Hopkins, the first institute of its kind in the world, established in 1994.

There are many different levels of investigation in the brain (figure 4.4), and important discoveries have been made at each of them; integrating all that knowledge is a formidable problem. This is reminiscent of the Humpty Dumpty nursery rhyme:

Humpty Dumpty sat on a wall,
Humpty Dumpty had a great fall.
All the king's horses and all the king's men
Couldn't put Humpty together again.

Although neuroscientists are very good at taking the brain apart, putting the pieces together poses a more difficult problem, one that requires synthesis rather than reduction, which is what I wanted to do. But first I had to know what the parts are, and the brain has lots of parts.

In a graduate seminar taught by Charles Gross, a psychologist who studied the monkey visual system at Princeton, I was impressed with the progress that had been made by David Hubel and Torsten Wiesel at Harvard Medical School in recording from single neurons in the visual cortex. If physics wasn't the royal road to understanding how the brain works, maybe neuroscience would be. For their pioneering work in the primary visual cortex, Hubel and Wiesel would receive a Nobel Prize in Physiology or Medicine in 1981. (Their discoveries, discussed in chapter 5, are the basis for deep learning, the subject of chapter 9.)

What I learned at Woods Hole

After finishing my doctorate in physics at Princeton in 1978, I attended a ten-week, in-depth summer course on experimental neurobiology at the

Levels of Investigation

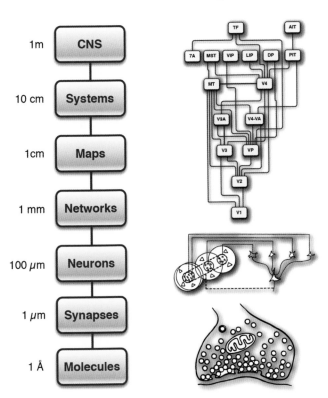

Figure 4.4

Levels of investigation in the brain. (Left) The spatial scale ranges from the molecular level at the bottom to the entire central nervous systems (CNS) at the top. Much is known about each of these levels, but the least understood is the network level with its small groups of highly interconnected neurons—the level modeled by artificial neural networks. (Right) Icons for synapse (bottom), simple cell in visual cortex (middle), and hierarchy of cortical areas in the visual cortex (top). Adapted from P. S. Churchland, and T. J. Sejnowski, "Perspectives on Cognitive Neuroscience," *Science*, 242 (1988): 741–745, figure 1.

Marine Biological Laboratory at Woods Hole. I arrived on the first day of the course in a casual blue sports coat and neatly pressed khaki pants, only to be taken aside by Story Landis, one of the course instructors, who bought me my first pair of jeans. Story was on the faculty in the Harvard Department of Neurobiology at the time and went on to become the director of the National Institute for Neurological Disorders and Stroke at the National Institutes of Health. She still reminds me of this incident.

After the summer course, I stayed on for a few weeks in September to wrap up a project I had started. Sharks and rays (which include skates) are able to sense very weak electrical fields; indeed, they can detect the signal from a 1.5-volt battery clear across the Atlantic Ocean. With this sixth sense, skates can navigate by the weak electrical signals from their motion through the earth's magnetic field, which generates microvolt signals in their electroreceptors. My project yielded spectacular electron microscope images of the skate electroreceptor.[14]

I was taking photos in the basement of Loeb Hall at Woods Hole when I received an unexpected call from Stephen Kuffler, who founded the Neurobiology Department at Harvard Medical School. Kuffler is a legend in neuroscience, and getting an offer to work with him as a postdoctoral fellow in his lab was life changing. I moved to Boston after finishing a brief postdoctoral fellowship with Alan Gelperin on mapping metabolic activity in the pedal ganglion of the garden slug *Limax maximus*.[15] I will never be able to eat a snail again without thinking about its brain. Alan descended intellectually from a line of neuroethologists, who study the neural basis of animal behavior. What I learned was that the so-called simpler nervous systems in invertebrates were actually more complex than those in organisms higher up the evolutionary ladder since invertebrates had to survive with many fewer neurons, each of which was highly specialized. I also came to understand that nothing in neuroscience makes any sense except in the light of behavior.[16]

In Kuffler's lab, I studied a late slow excitatory response at a synapse in the bullfrog sympathetic ganglion (figure 4.5) that was 60,000 times slower than the fast millisecond excitatory response at another synapse on the same neuron.[17] These ganglia contain the neurons that form the output of the bullfrog's autonomic nervous system, which regulates glands and internal organs. After stimulating the nerve to the synapse, I could walk to the coffeepot and back before the synaptic input to the neuron had reached a peak, which it would in around 1 minute, taking 10 minutes to recover. Synapses are the fundamental computational elements in the brain, and the diversity of synapse types is telling. This experience taught me that

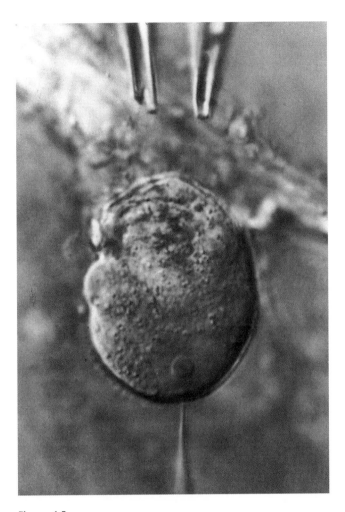

Figure 4.5
Bullfrog sympathetic ganglion cell. As neurons, these cells receive inputs from the spinal cord and innervate glands in the skin of bullfrogs. They are large and their electrical signals are easy to record with a microelectrode (bottom). They have no dendrites and can be electrically stimulated by a nerve (top, background) or with chemicals (top, pair of micropipettes). Stimulating the nerve elicits three different synaptic signals: a fast millisecond excitatory response, similar to that at the neuromuscular junction; a slower excitatory response that peaks in 10 seconds and lasts 1 minute; and a late slow excitatory response that peaks in 1 minute and last 10 minutes. This illustrates the broad range of times scales that are present in even the simplest neurons. From S. W. Kuffler, and T. J. Sejnowski, "Peptidergic and Muscarinic Excitation at Amphibian Sympathetic Synapses," *Journal of Physiology* 341 (1983): 257–278, plate I.

complexity might not be the royal road to understanding brain function. To understand the brain, I had to understand how, through evolution, nature had solved a large collection of problems long ago and passed those solutions on from species to species up the evolutionary ladder. We have ion channels in our brains that first evolved in bacteria billions of years ago.

The Missing Link

But if physics was too simple and biology too complex, where should I look for guidance? Unlike forces in physics, brain circuits have a purpose, which is to solve computational problems, like seeing and moving around, in order to survive in the world. Even a perfect physical model of how a neuron worked wouldn't tell us what its purpose was. Neurons are in the business of processing signals that carry information, and computation was

Figure 4.6
Terry Sejnowski and Geoffrey Hinton discussing network models of vision in Boston in 1980. This was one year after Geoffrey and I met at the Parallel Models of Associative Memory workshop in La Jolla and one year before I started my lab at Johns Hopkins in Baltimore and Geoffrey started his research group at Carnegie Mellon in Pittsburgh. Courtesy of Geoffrey Hinton.

the missing link in trying to understand nature. I have over the last forty years been pursuing this goal, pioneering a new field called "computational neuroscience."

After his stint as a postdoctoral fellow at UCSD, Geoffrey Hinton returned to England, where he had a research position with the Applied Psychology Unit of the Medical Research Council (MRC) at Cambridge. One day in 1981, he received a call at 2:00 a.m. from someone who introduced himself as Charles Smith, president of the System Development Foundation in Palo Alto, California.[18] Smith said that his foundation wanted to fund potentially promising but risky research that was unlikely to succeed and Geoffrey had been highly recommended to him. Geoffrey wasn't sure that this was for real. Good friend that he is, Geoffrey mentioned my research to Smith, telling him it was even more unlikely to succeed than his.

The foundation was indeed real and provided us with our first grants, which greatly speeded up our research. We could now afford to buy faster computers and to pay the students working with us. Geoffrey replaced his Apple II with a fancy Lisp machine[19] when he moved to Carnegie Mellon in Pittsburgh; I briefly had more computer power than the entire Computer Science Department when I moved to Johns Hopkins in Baltimore.[20] I was also able to buy the first modem that linked Hopkins to the ARPANET, a precursor to the Internet, so that Geoffrey and I could e-mail each other. We could not have asked for a better start to our careers as we set off in new directions (figure 4.6). I was fortunate to be funded over the years by the Office of Naval Research, which also supported Frank Rosenblatt and many other neural network researchers.

5 Insights from the Visual System

One of my earliest memories, before going to kindergarten, was peering over pieces of a jigsaw puzzle and matching them using shape, color, and context as cues. My parents would amaze their friends at parties by how quickly their toddler son could put jigsaw puzzles together. I did not know it then, but my brain was doing what brains do best—solving problems with pattern recognition. Science is filled with problems that are like puzzles with missing pieces and vague hints to the underlying picture. How brains solve problems is the ultimate puzzle.

The Helmholtz Club was a small cadre of vision scientists in Southern California from the San Diego, Los Angeles, and Irvine campuses of the University of California, Caltech, and the University of Southern California, who would meet each month in the afternoon on the Irvine campus.[1] Hermann von Helmholtz was a nineteenth-century physicist and physician who developed a mathematical theory and an experimental approach to vision that forms the basis for our current understanding of visual perception. As the club's secretary, it fell to me to recruit an outside speaker to give a talk to some fifteen to twenty members and their guests. This would be followed by a second talk by a club member. The talks were interactive, with ample time for in-depth discussion. One of the outside speakers expressed his surprise at those asking questions: "They actually wanted to know the answers." Intellectual high points for all who attended them, these monthly meetings were master classes in vision.[2]

Vision is our most acute and also our most studied sense. With two frontal eyes, we have exquisite binocular depth perception, and half of our cortex is visual. The special status of vision is captured by the saying "Seeing is believing." Ironically, that we can see so well has blinded us to the enormous computational complexity of the vision problem, solved by nature over hundreds of millions of year of evolution (as noted in chapter 2). The organization of the visual cortex has served as the inspiration for the most successful deep learning networks.

In one-tenth of a second, ten billion neurons in our visual cortex working together in parallel can identify a cup in a cluttered scene, even though we may never have seen that particular cup before and even when it might be in any location, of any size, and in any orientation to us. As a graduate student at Princeton, I was fascinated by vision and worked for a summer in the laboratory of Charles Gross, who studied the inferotemporal cortex of monkeys (figure 5.1), where he had discovered neurons that respond to complex objects like faces and, famously, toilet brushes.[3]

While at the Department of Neurobiology of the Harvard Medical School, I worked with Stephen Kuffler, who had earlier discovered how the ganglion cells in the retina encode visual scenes, and who probably would

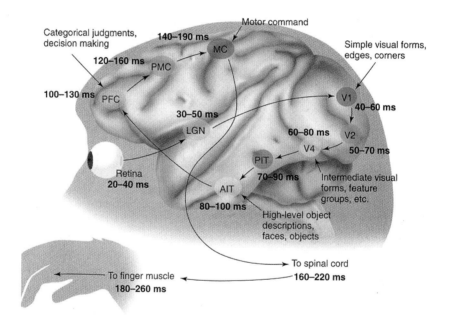

Figure 5.1

Schematic of the flow of information through the visual system of a macaque monkey. The arrows indicate projections between visual areas starting at the retina, with delays in milliseconds in the arrival of visual information occurring at each stage of visual processing. Visual perception in the macaque is similar to ours and we have the same stages of visual processing. LGN: lateral geniculate nucleus; V1: primary visual cortex; V2: secondary visual cortex; V4: visual area 4; AIT and PIT: anterior and posterior inferotemporal cortex; PFC: prefrontal cortex; PMC: premotor cortex; MC: motor cortex. From S. J. Thorpe and M. Fabre-Thorpe, "Seeking Categories in the Brain," *Science* 291, no. 5502 (2001): 261.

have received the Nobel Prize in Physiology or Medicine with David Hubel and Torsten Wiesel in 1981 for his discoveries in the retina, had he not died the year before. After moving to the Salk Institute in 1989, I would work with Francis Crick, who had shifted his research focus from molecular genetics to neuroscience in 1977 and was intent on finding the neural correlates of visual awareness. It was thus my privilege to be in the company of some of the greatest vision scientists of that time.

Vision from the Bottom Up

If we follow the signals generated by an image into the brain, we can see how it is transformed over and over again as it passes from one stage of processing to the next (figure 5.1). Vision starts in the retina, where photoreceptors convert light into electrical signals. There are two layers of neurons within the retina that process the visual signals in space and time, ending with the ganglion cells that project out into the optic nerves.

In a classic 1953 experiment whose results hold for all mammals, Stephen Kuffler (figure 5.2, left) recorded from the output neurons of the retina of a living cat while stimulating them to fire spikes in response to spots of light. He reported that some output neurons responded to a spot of light in their center when it went on, and others responded to a spot of light in their center when it went off. But, just outside the centers, the surrounding annulus had the opposite polarity: on-centers with off-surrounds and off-centers with on-surrounds (figure 5.3). The responses of ganglion cells to patterns of light are called "receptive field" properties.

I once asked Kuffler, whose main scientific interest was in the properties of synapses between neurons, what motivated him to study the retina. He said that since his lab at Johns Hopkins was in the Wilmer Eye Institute at the time, he felt guilty he was not working on eyes. Having pioneered the study of single ganglion cells in the retina, he handed off the project to two postdoctoral fellows in his lab, David Hubel and Torsten Wiesel (figure 5.2, right and center), and advised them to follow the signals into the brain. In 1966, Kuffler and his postdoctoral fellows moved to Harvard Medical School to start a new Department of Neurobiology.

Vision in the Cerebral Cortex

Hubel and Wiesel discovered that cortical neurons responded much better to oriented bars of light and contrast edges than to spots of light. The circuits in the cortex had transformed the input signals. They described

Figure 5.2

(Left to right) Stephen Kuffler, Torsten Wiesel, and David Hubel. The Department of Neurobiology at Harvard Medical School was founded in 1966, and this photo is from the early years. I never saw any of them wearing a tie in the lab on a workday so this must have been a special occasion. Courtesy of Harvard Medical School.

two principal types of cells: the oriented simple cell, which had on- and off- regions like the ganglion cells (figure 5.4), and the oriented complex cell that responded uniformly to oriented stimuli anywhere in the receptive field of the neuron (figure 5.5).

Each cortical neuron in the visual cortex can be thought of as a visual feature detector, which only becomes active when it receives inputs above a certain threshold for its preferred feature in a particular patch of the visual field. The feature each neuron prefers is determined by its connectivity with other neurons. The neocortex of mammals has six specialized layers. Hubel and Wiesel also discovered that the inputs from the two eyes are organized in alternating left, right columns in the middle layer (4) of the cortex, to which inputs originating from a relay station in the thalamus project. Monocular neurons in layer 4 project to neurons in the upper layers (2 and 3) that receive binocular inputs, which in turn project upstream to other cortical areas and downstream to the bottom layers (5 and 6) that

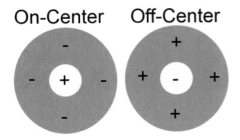

Figure 5.3
Response properties of ganglion cells in the retina. These two donuts represent the responses of two types ganglion cells in the retina that send coded messages to the brain so you can see. For the on-center type, a spot of light in the center coming on (+) and a spot of light in the annulus around the center going off (–) produce a burst of spikes. The opposite holds for the off-center type, in which a spot of light in the center going off (–) and a spot of light in the annulus around the center coming on (+) produce a burst of spikes. The changes in illumination carry important information about moving stimuli and contrast boundaries around an object. These properties were discovered by Stephen Kuffler in 1953.

project subcortically. The preferred orientation and ocular preference of every cell in a column is the same and varies smoothly across the cortex (figure 5.6).

Synapse Plasticity

If one eye of a cat is closed during the first few months of its life, cortical neurons that normally would be driven by both eyes become monocular, exclusively driven by the open eye.[4] Monocular deprivation drives changes in the strengths of synapses in the primary cortex, where inputs to neurons receive converging inputs from the two eyes for the first time. After the critical period of cortical plasticity in the primary visual cortex is over, the closed eye can no longer influence cortical neurons, resulting in a condition called "amblyopia." Although, uncorrected, misalignment or "strabismus," which is common in babies, will greatly reduce the number of cortical neurons that are binocular and preclude binocular depth perception,[5] a timely operation to align the eyes within the critical period can rescue binocular neurons.

Monocular deprivation is an example of the high degree of plasticity that is present during the early stages of development as the environment molds synaptic connections between neurons in the cortex and other parts of the brain. These activity-dependent changes ride on top of the continual

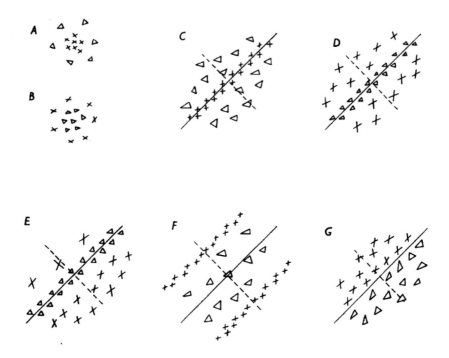

Figure 5.4

Receptive field for a simple cell in the cat primary visual cortex. This figure is from the 1962 paper by Hubel and Wiesel that discovered simple cells. Triangles are locations in the visual field where the onset a spot of light produces an on-response, and crosses are where the offset of a spot of light produces an off-response. (A) On-center cell in the retina (compare with figure 5.3, left). (B) Off-center cell in the retina (compare with figure 5.3, right). (C–G). Variety of simple cell receptive fields in the primary visual cortex, all of which are elongated compared to receptive fields in the retina, and with more complex arrangements of on-regions and off-regions. From D. H. Hubel and T. N. Wiesel, "Receptive Fields, Binocular Interaction and Functional Architecture in the Cat's Visual Cortex," *Journal of Physiology* 160, no. 1 (1962): 106–154.2, figure 2.

renewal that occurs in all cells. Even though most of the neurons in our brains are the same ones we had at birth,[6] nearly every component of those neurons and the synapses that connect them turns over every day. Proteins are replaced as they wear out, and lipids in the membrane are renewed. With so much dynamic turnover, it is a mystery how our memories are maintained over our lifetimes.

There is another possible explanation for the apparent longevity of memories: they may be like scars on our bodies that have survived as

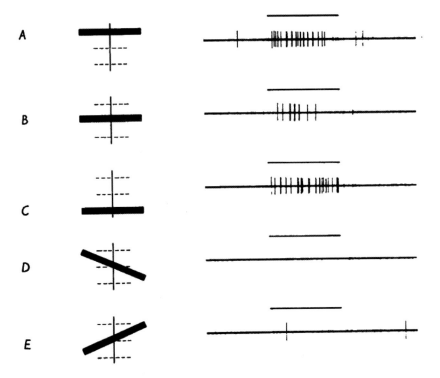

Figure 5.5
Responses from a complex cell in the cat primary visual cortex. This figure is from the 1962 paper by Hubel and Wiesel that discovered complex cells. A long, narrow black bar evokes a volley of spikes (vertical ticks) wherever it is placed anywhere within the receptive field (dashed lines) of a complex cell, provided the orientation is correct (upper three records). A non-optimal orientation gives a weaker response or none at all (lower two record). From D. H. Hubel and T. N. Wiesel, "Receptive Fields, Binocular Interaction and Functional Architecture in the Cat's Visual Cortex," Journal of Physiology 160, no. 1 (1962): 106–154.2, figure 7.

markers of past events in our lives. The place to look for these markers is not inside neurons, where there is constant turnover, but outside, in the space between neurons, where the extracellular matrix, made from proteoglycans that are like the collagen in scar tissue, is tough material that lasts many years.[7] If this conjecture is ever proven to be true, it means that our long-term memories are embedded in the brain's "exoskeleton," and we have been looking for them in the wrong places.[8]

Synapses contain many hundreds of unique proteins that control the release of neurotransmitters and the activation of receptors on the receiving

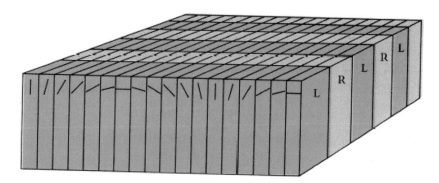

Figure 5.6

Ice cube model of a column of neurons in primary visual cortex. In a vertical penetration all neurons have the same orientation preference and ocular dominance. Under each square millimeter of cortex there is a complete set of orientations that change slowly across the surface of the cortex (front side of cube) and inputs from both eyes (right side of cube). From D. Hubel, *Eye, Brain and Vision* (New York: W. H. Freeman and Company, 1988), 131.

neuron. In most cases, synaptic strengths can be selectively increased or decreased over a wide range, which, in the cortex, is a factor of 100. (Examples of synaptic learning algorithms that have been discovered in the brain will be discussed in later chapters.) Even more remarkable, new synapses are constantly being formed in the cortex and old ones removed, making them among the most dynamic organelles in the body. There are around 100 different types of synapses in the brain, with glutamic acid the most common excitatory neurotransmitter in the cortex and another amino acid, gamma-aminobutyric acid (GABA), the most common inhibitory transmitter. There is also a wide range of time courses for the electrochemical influences that these neurotransmitter molecules have on other neurons. For example, the bullfrog sympathetic ganglion cell discussed in chapter 4 has synapses with time scales ranging from milliseconds to minutes.

Shape from Shading

Steven Zucker (figure 5.7), whose research focus is on a blend of computer vision and biological vision, has been working on a book to explain how vision works for as long as I have known him, which is more than thirty years. The problem is that Steve keeps discovering new things about vision and, as it did for Tristram Shandy, the protagonist of Laurence Sterne's novel, the end of his book keeps receding into the future the more that he

Figure 5.7
Steven Zucker at Yale University lit from the top right side of the picture. From the variation in the shading on his sweater you can perceive the shapes of the folds. The equations on the blackboard behind him, inspired by the visual cortex of monkeys, explain how. We see the same perceived shapes independently of the light source. Courtesy of Steven Zucker.

discovers. His approach to vision is based on the exquisitely regular structure of the primary visual cortex (figure 5.6), a structure unlike any found elsewhere in the cortex, where neurons are organized in an almost mosaic-like arrangement, begging for a geometrical interpretation. Most researchers in computer vision want to recognize objects by segmenting them from the background and identifying a few diagnostic features.

Steve was more ambitious and wanted to understand how we extract the shape of objects from surface shading and telltale signs of creases and folds. In an interview at the annual meeting of the Society for Neuroscience in 2006, Frank Gehry, the architect who designs buildings that look like ship's sails (figure 5.8), was asked how he got ideas for his buildings.[9] He replied that his inspiration came from looking at shapes of crumpled paper. But how does our visual system piece together the complex shape of the crumpled paper from the complex pattern of folds and shaded surfaces?

How do we perceive the shifting shapes of the surfaces on the Guggenheim Museum in Bilbao (figure 5.8)?

Steve Zucker recently was able to explain how we see folds in shaded images, based on the close relationship between the three-dimensional contours of the surface as seen on contour maps of mountains and the constant-intensity contours on images (figure 5.9).[10] The link is provided by the geometry of surfaces.[11] This explains the mystery of why our perception of shape is so insensitive to differences in the lighting and the surface properties of objects. It may also explain why we are so good at reading contour maps, where the contours are made explicit, and why we need only a few special internal lines to see the shapes of objects in cartoons.

In 1988, Sidney Lehky and I asked whether we could train a neural network with one layer of hidden units to compute the curvature of shaded surfaces.[12] We succeeded, and, to our surprise, the hidden units behaved like simple cells. But, on closer inspection, we discovered that not all of these "simple cells" were created equal. By looking at their projections to the output layer, which was trained to compute the curvature using a learning algorithm (discussed in chapter 8), we found that some of the hidden units were being used to decide between positive curvature (bulge) and negative curvature (bowl; figure 5.10). Like some simple cells, these units

Figure 5.8
Guggenheim Museum in Bilbao, Spain, designed by Frank Gehry. Shading and reflections from curved surfaces give a strong impression of form and motion. Tiny people on the walkway calibrate the scale of the edifice.

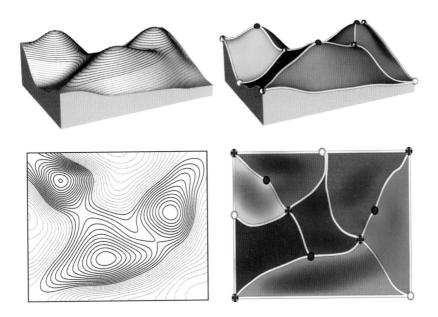

Figure 5.9
Altitude contours of a surface (top left) compared with isophotes (contours of constant intensity) of an image of the same surface (bottom left). Both give rise to the same parcellation between critical points as shown to the right of the contours. From Kunsberg and Zucker, "Critical Contours: An Invariant Linking Image Flow with Salient Surface Organization," figure 5. Courtesy of Dr. A. G. Gyulassy.

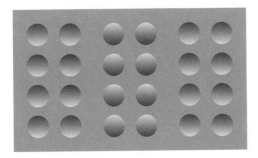

Figure 5.10
Curvature from shading. Our visual system can extract the shape of an object from the slowly varying changes in the brightness across an image within the bounding contour. You see eggs or egg cartons depending on direction of shading and your assumption about the direction of lighting (usually assumed to be overhead). Turn this book upside down to see them reverse. From V. S. Ramachandran, "Perception of Shape from Shading," *Nature* 331, no. 6152 (1988), figure 2.

were detectors; they tended to have either low activity or high activity, a bimodal distribution. By contrast, the other units in the hidden layer had graded responses and were functioning as filters that signaled to the output units the direction and magnitude of curvature.

The conclusion was a surprise: the function of a neuron is determined not simply by how it responds to inputs, but also by the neurons it activates downstream—by its "projective field." Until recently, the output of a neuron was much more difficult to determine than its inputs, but new genetic and anatomical techniques make it possible to track the axonal projections downstream with great precision, and new optogenetic techniques make it possible to selective stimulate specific neurons to probe their impact on perception and behavior.[13] Even so, our small network could only identify the curvature of hills or bowls, and we still don't know how globally organized perceptions, called "gestalts" in the psychology literature, are organized in the cortex.

Steve Zucker and I were once stranded at the old Stapleton International Denver Airport in 1984, our flights delayed by a snowstorm. Excited about computational neuroscience, which was still in its infancy, we dreamed up a workshop that would bring together computational and experimental researchers and decided to organize it at Woods Hole, where I had taken a summer course in neurobiology and had returned for several summers to work with Stephen Kuffler on physiological experiments at the Marine Biological Laboratory. Woods Hole is a beautiful Cape Cod village on the sea, not too far from Boston. Over the years, many of the leading researchers who study vision have come to this annual workshop, which has been another scientific high point for me. What emerged from these workshops was the beginning of a computational theory for the visual cortex, although confirmation of that theory would take another thirty years. (In chapter 9, we will see that the architecture of the most successful deep learning network is remarkably similar to that of the visual cortex.)

Visual Maps in the Cortex Are Hierarchically Organized

Jon Kaas and John Allman, while at the Neurophysiology Department of the University of Wisconsin in the early 1970s, explored the cortical areas that received inputs from the primary visual cortex and discovered that different areas had different properties. For example, they discovered a map of the visual field in an area they called the "middle temporal cortex" or "MT," whose neurons responded to oriented visual stimuli moving in a preferred direction. Allman mentioned to me that they had a difficult time getting the chairman of his department, Clinton Woolsey, to accept their discovery. In an earlier experiment, Woolsey's coarser recording techniques had missed the areas of extrastriate visual cortex that Kaas and Allman had later discovered with better recording techniques.[14] More recent studies were to find some two dozen visual areas in the monkey visual cortex.

In 1991 while at Caltech, David Van Essen made a careful study of the inputs and outputs of each visual area of the cortex and arranged them in a hierarchical diagram (figure 5.11). Sometimes used simply to illustrate the complexity of the cortex, his diagram resembles the subway map of a great city, with boxes representing the stops and the lines joining them the high-speed train routes. The visual input from the retinal ganglion cells (RGC) projects to the primary visual cortex (V1) at the bottom of the diagram. From there, the signals are transported up the hierarchy, each area specialized for a different aspect of vision, such as form perception. Near the top of the hierarchy on the right side of the diagram, the receptive fields of neurons in the anterior, central, and posterior areas of the inferotemporal cortex (AIT, CIT, and PIT) cover the entire visual field and respond preferentially to complex visual stimuli such as faces and other objects. Although we don't know how the neurons do this, we do know that the strengths of the connections can be altered by experience, so that neurons can learn how to respond to new objects. Van Essen has since moved to Washington University in St. Louis, where he is a co-director of the Human Connectome Project funded by the National Institutes of Health (NIH).[15] The goal of his research team there is to use imaging techniques based on magnetic resonance imaging (MRI)[16] to work out a long-range map of connections in the human cortex (figure 5.12).

The Birth of Cognitive Neuroscience

In 1988, I served on a committee for the McDonnell and Pew Foundations that interviewed prominent cognitive scientists and neuroscientists to get their recommendations on how to jumpstart a new field called "cognitive neuroscience."[17] The committee traveled around the world to meet with experts to get their advice on which scientific topics were the most promising and where to place new centers for cognitive neuroscience. We met at the Harvard Faculty Club on a hot August afternoon to interview Jerry Fodor, who is an expert on the language of thought and a champion of the modular mind. He started by throwing down the gauntlet, "Cognitive neuroscience is not a science and it never will be." He gave the impression that he had read all the neuroscience papers on vision and memory, and they did not come up to his standards. But when he remarked that "the

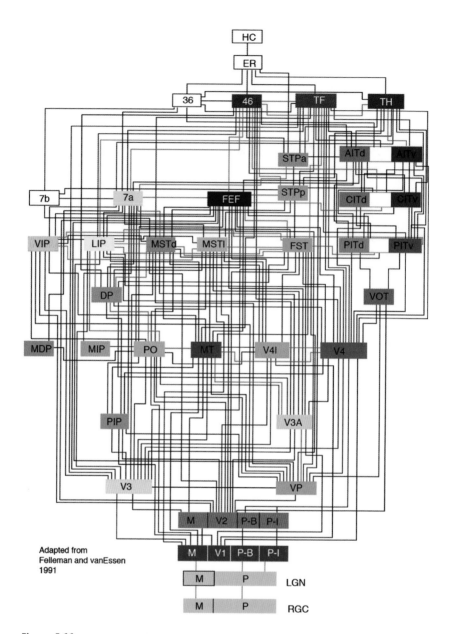

Figure 5.11

Hierarchy of visual areas in the monkey brain. Visual information from retinal ganglion cells (RGC) in the retina project to the lateral geniculate nucleus (LGN) of the thalamus, whose relay cells project to the primary visual cortex (V1). The hierarchy of cortical areas terminates in the hippocampus (HC). Nearly all of the 187 links in the diagram are bidirectional, with feedforward connection from a lower area and feedback connection from the higher area. From D. J. Felleman and D. C. Van Essen, "Distributed Hierarchical Processing in Primate Visual Cortex," *Cerebral Cortex* 1, no. 1 (1991): 30, figure 4.

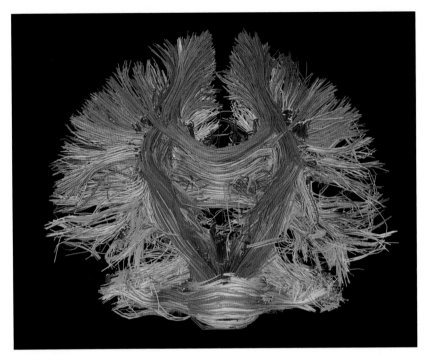

Figure 5.12
Human connectome. Long-range fiber tracts in the white matter of the cerebral cortex can be traced noninvasively with magnetic resonance imaging (MRI) based on the uneven diffusion of water molecules. The false colors label the directions of different pathways. From The Human Connectome Project.

McDonald Foundation is throwing away its money," John Bruer, the president of the McDonnell Foundation, was quick to point out that Fodor was confusing his foundation with the hamburger place down the road.

Unfazed, Fodor explained why the mind had to be thought of as a modular symbol-processing system running an intelligent computer program. Patricia Churchland, a philosopher at the University of California, San Diego, asked him whether his theory also applied to cats. "Yes," said Fodor, "cats are running the cat program." But when Mortimer Mishkin, an NIH neuroscientist studying vision and memory, asked him to tell us about discoveries made in his own lab, Fodor mumbled something I couldn't follow about using event-related potentials in a language experiment. Mercifully, at that moment, a fire drill was called and we all filed outside. Standing in the courtyard, I overheard Mishkin say to Fodor: "Those are pretty small potatoes." When the drill was over, Fodor had disappeared.

Cognitive neuroscience has grown into an important field that has attracted researchers from many areas of science, including social psychology and economics, which previously had little or no direct connection with neuroscience. What made this possible was the introduction of noninvasive methods for visualizing brain activity, in the early 1990s, especially functional magnetic resonance imaging (fMRI), which now has a spatial resolution of a few millimeters. The large fMRI data sets being generated are analyzed with new computational methods such as Independent Component Analysis (to be discussed in chapter 6).

Since the brain can't work without oxygen, and blood flow is tightly regulated at submillimeter levels, fMRI measures the blood oxygen level dependent (BOLD) signal as a surrogate for brain activity. The degree of oxygenation in the blood changes its magnetic properties, which can be monitored noninvasively with fMRI and used to produce dynamic images of brain activity with a time resolution of a few seconds, short enough to keep track of which parts of the brain are engaged during an experiment. Functional MRI has been used to explore the temporal integration time scale in different parts of the visual hierarchy.

Uri Hasson at Princeton University performed an fMRI experiment designed to probe which parts of the visual hierarchy are involved in processing movies of different lengths.[18] A Charlie Chaplin silent film was cut into segments, which were scrambled at time scales of 4, 12, and 36 seconds and presented to subjects. At 4 seconds, subjects could recognize a scene; at 12 seconds, connected actions; and at 36 seconds, a story with beginning and end. The fMRI responses in the primary visual cortex at the bottom of the hierarchy were strong and reliable regardless of the time scale, but at higher levels of the visual hierarchy, only the longer time scales evoked a reliable response, and areas of prefrontal cortex at the top of the hierarchy required the longest time interval. This is consistent with other experiments showing that working memory, our ability to hold onto information like telephone numbers and elements of a task we are working on, is also organized in a hierarchy, with the longest working memory time scales in the prefrontal cortex.

One of the most exciting areas of research in neuroscience, the study of learning in brains can be studied at many levels of investigation, from molecules to behavior.

II Many Ways to Learn

Timeline

1949—Donald Hebb publishes *The Organization of Behavior*, which introduced the Hebb rule for synaptic plasticity.

1982—John Hopfield publishes "Neural Networks and Physical Systems with Emergent Collective Computational Abilities," which introduced the Hopfield net.

1985—Geoffrey Hinton and Terry Sejnowski publish "A Learning Algorithm for Boltzmann Machines," which was a counterexample to Marvin Minsky and Seymour Papert's widely accepted belief that no learning algorithm for multilayer networks was possible.

1986—David Rumelhart and Geoffrey Hinton publish "Learning Internal Representations by Error-Propagation," which introduced the "backprop" learning algorithm now used for deep learning.

1988—Richard Sutton publishes "Learning to Predict by the Methods of Temporal Differences" in *Machine Learning*. Temporal difference learning is now believed to be the algorithm implemented in all brains for reward learning.

1995—Anthony Bell and Terrence Sejnowski publish "An Information-Maximization Approach to Blind Separation and Blind Deconvolution," describing an unsupervised algorithm for Independent Component Analysis.

2013—Geoffrey Hinton's NIPS 2012 paper "ImageNet Classification with Deep Convolutional Neural Networks" reduces the error rate for correctly classifying objects in images by 18 percent.

2017—AlphaGo, a deep learning network program, beats Ke Jie, the world champion at Go.

6   The Cocktail Party Problem

At a crowded cocktail party, it can be a challenge to hear the person in front of you when the air is filled with a cacophony of others talking around you. Having two ears helps direct your hearing in the right direction, and your memory can fill in missing snatches of conversation. Now imagine a cocktail party with 100 people in a room and 100 nondirectional microphones spread around, each picking up sounds from everyone but with different ratios of amplitudes for each person on each microphone. Is it possible to devise an algorithm that can separate each of the voices into separate output channels? To make it even more difficult, what if the sound sources were unknown—such as music, clapping, nature sounds, or even random noise? This is called the "blind source separation problem" (figure 6.1).

At the 1986 Neural Networks for Computing, AIP Conference, a precursor of the NIPS conferences, held on April 13–16 in Snowbird, Utah, there was a poster entitled "Space or Time Adaptive Signal Processing by Neural Network Models." Its authors, Jeanny Herault and Christian Jutten, used a learning algorithm to blindly separate mixtures of sine waves (which are pure frequencies) presented to a neural network model; they pointed to a new class of unsupervised learning algorithms.[1] Although it was not known at the time if there was a general solution that could blindly separate other types of signals, a decade later, Anthony Bell and I found an algorithm that could solve the general problem.[2]

Independent Component Analysis

The perceptron is a one-neuron neural network. The next simplest network architecture has more than one model neuron in the output layer; with each input neuron connected to each output neuron, it transforms patterns on the input layer into patterns on the output layer. This network

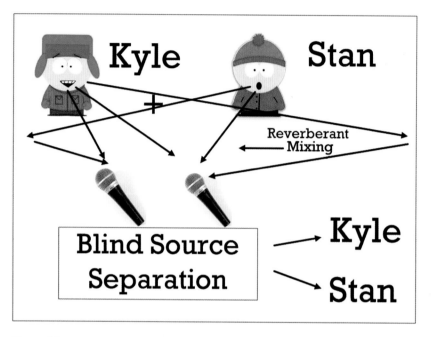

Figure 6.1
Blind source separation. Kyle and Stan are talking at the same time in a room with two microphones. Each microphone picks up signals from the speakers and reflections from the walls of the room. The challenge is to separate the two voices from each other without knowing anything about the signals. Independent component analysis (ICA) is a learning algorithm that solves this problem without knowing anything about the sources.

can do more than just classify inputs. It can learn to perform blind source separation.

An undergraduate working as a summer intern at ETH Zurich (the Swiss Federal Institute of Technology in Zurich) in 1986, Tony Bell (figure 6.2) was an early convert to neural nets and traveled down to the University of Geneva to hear four talks by neural network pioneers. After completing his doctorate at the University of Brussels, he moved to La Jolla in 1993 to join my lab as a postdoctoral fellow.

The "general infomax learning principle" maximizes the information flowing through a network.[3] Tony was working on signal transmission in dendrites, which are long thin cables that the brain's neurons use to collect information from thousands of synapses attached to the dendrites. He had an intuition that it should be possible to maximize the information coming

Figure 6.2
Anthony Bell thinking independently around 1995 when he was working on independent component analysis. Experts know many ways that fail to solve a problem, but it is often someone who is looking at a problem for the first time who sees a new approach and solves it. Tony and I discovered an iterative algorithm for solving the blind source separation problem that is now in engineering textbooks and has thousands of practical applications. Courtesy of Tony Bell.

down a dendrite by changing the densities of ion channels in the dendrite. In simplifying the problem (ignoring the dendrites), Tony and I found a new information-theoretic learning algorithm, which we called "independent component analysis" (ICA), that solved the blind source separation problem (box 6.1).[4]

Independent component analysis has since been used for thousands of applications and is now in signal processing textbooks.[5] When applied to patches from natural images of outdoor scenes, the ICA's independent components are localized, oriented edge filters (figure 6.3), similar to those of the simple cells in the visual cortex of cats and monkeys (figure 5.4).[6] With ICA, only a few of the many sources are needed to reconstruct a patch of an image; such reconstructions are called mathematically "sparse."[7]

Box 6.1
How Independent Component Analysis Works

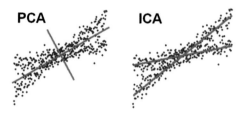

Comparison between principal component analysis (PCA) and independent component analysis (ICA). The outputs from the two microphones in figure 6.1 are plotted against each other on the vertical and horizontal axes above. The coordinates of each dot are their values at a single time point. PCA is a popular unsupervised learning technique that picks out a direction that bisects the two signals, maximally mixing them, and the PCA axes are always perpendicular to each other. ICA finds the axes that fall along the directions of the dots, representing the separated signals, which may not be perpendicular.

These results confirmed a conjecture made by Horace Barlow, a distinguished vision scientist, in the 1960s, when David Hubel and Torsten Wiesel discovered simple cells in the visual cortex. An image contains a great deal of redundancy because nearby pixels often have similar values (such as pixels in the sky). Barlow conjectured that, by reducing the redundancy in the representation of natural scenes,[8] the simple cells were able to transmit the information in the image more efficiently. It took fifty years to develop the mathematical tools to confirm his intuition.

Tony and I also showed that when independent component analysis is applied to natural sounds, the independent components are temporal filters with different frequencies and durations, similar to the filters found in the early stages of the auditory system.[9] This gave us confidence that we were on the right track to understanding fundamental principles about how the sensory signals were represented in the earliest stages of processing in the visual cortex. By extending this principle to independent feature subspaces of linear filters, it was possible to model complex cells in visual cortex.[10]

Figure 6.3
Independent component analysis filters derived from natural images. Small patches
(12×12 pixels) from images of natural scenes in the left panel were used as inputs to
an ICA network with 144 output units. The resulting independent components in
the right panel resemble the simple cells found in the primary visual cortex: They
are localized and oriented with positive regions (white) and negative regions (black),
where gray is zero. It only takes a few of the filters to represent any given patch, a
property called "sparsity." Left: courtesy of Michael Lewicki; right: from Bell and
Sejnowski, "The 'Independent Components' of Natural Scenes Are Edge Filters,"
figure 4.

The ICA network has an equal number of input and output units and
a fully connected set of weights between them. To solve the blind source
separation problem, the sounds from the microphones are played through
the input layer, one input unit for every microphone, and the ICA learning
algorithm, like the perceptron algorithm, iteratively modifies the weights
to the output layer until they converge. But, unlike the perceptron, which
is a supervised learning algorithm, independent component analysis is an
unsupervised learning algorithm that uses a measure of the independence
between the output units as a cost function; it does not know what the
output target should be. As the weights are changed to make the outputs as
independent as possible, the original sound sources become perfectly separated, or as "decorrelated" as possible if they are not independent. Unsupervised learning can discover previously unknown statistical structure in
many different types of data sets.

Independent Components in the Brain

Tony Bell's infomax ICA algorithm set off a sequence of Aha! moments, as others in my lab began to apply it to different types of recordings from the brain. Using The first electrical signals from the brain had been recorded from the scalp by Hans Berger in 1924 and was called "electroencephalography" (EEG). Neuroscientists have used these complex, oscillating signals to eavesdrop on our ever-changing brain states, which vary with our alertness and sensorimotor interactions. The electrical signal at an electrode on the scalp receives inputs from many different sources within the cerebral cortex as well as muscle and eye movement artifacts. Each scalp electrode receives a mixture of signals from the same set of sources in the brain, but with different amplitudes, which is formally the same as the cocktail party problem.

Scott Makeig, who was a staff scientist in my lab at the Salk Institute in the 1990s, used ICA to extract dozens of dipolar sources in the cortex and their time courses from EEG recordings (figure 6.4). A dipole is one of the simplest patterns a brain source can have, the simplest being a uniform pattern over the scalp, generated by a static point charge, and the second simplest, the dipole pattern generated by current moving in a straight line, which occurs in cortical pyramidal neurons. Think of the dipole as an arrow. The surface of the scalp is positive in the direction of the arrow's head and negative in the direction of its tail; the pattern covers the entire head, which is why it is so difficult to separate many brain sources that are activated at the same time. Two sources extracted from EEG, IC2 and IC3, are approximately dipolar sources in figure 6.4. Independent component analysis also separates the artifacts, such as eye movements and electrode noise, which could then be subtracted out with high accuracy (IC1 and IC 4 in figure 6.4). Many thousands of papers have since been published using ICA to analyze EEG recordings, and important discoveries have been made using ICA to analyze a wide range of brain states.

Martin McKeown, who was then a postdoctoral fellow in my lab with a background in neurology, figured out how to flip space and time to apply independent component analysis to functional magnetic resonance imaging recordings (figure 6.5).[11] Brain imaging with fMRI measures the level of blood oxygenation, which is indirectly linked to neural activity, at tens of thousands of locations within the brain. In figure 6.5, the ICA sources were brain regions that had a common time course but were spatially independent of the other sources. Sparsity in the spatial domain means that at any given time, only a few regions are highly active.

ICA Decomposition

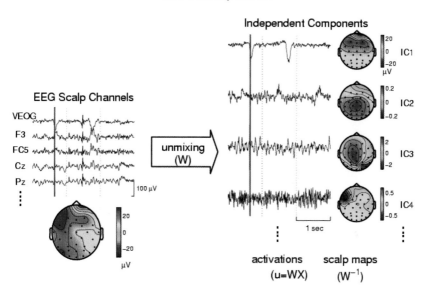

Figure 6.4

Independent component analysis applied to electroencephalographic (EEG) recordings from the scalp. Scalp maps seen from above (nose pointing up) with electrodes located at the black dots and color maps of the voltages in microvolts (μV) at one time point. The fluctuating EEG signals shown from five scalp channels shown in the left panel are contaminated with artifacts from eye blinks and muscle signals. ICA separates the brain components from artifacts, as shown in the right panel (where "IC" stands for "independent component"). IC1 is an eye blink based on the slow time course and the scalp map, which has highest values (red) over the eyes. IC4 is a muscle artifact based on the high frequency high amplitude noise and the localized source on the scalp map. IC2 and IC3 are brain sources, indicated by the dipolar pattern on the scalp (positive red region opposed to negative blue region) compared to the more complex pattern on scalp from the EEG recordings as shown on the scalp map in the left panel. Courtesy of Tzyy-Ping Jung.

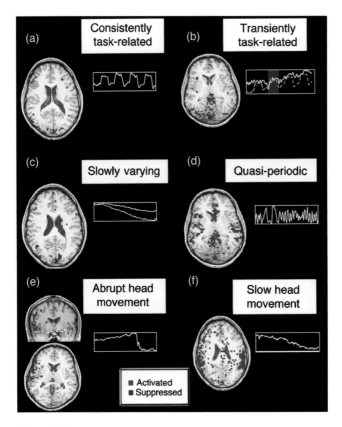

Figure 6.5
Independent component analysis applied to functional magnetic resonance imaging
(fMRI) data. A component consists of a brain activity map and a time course. This
illustrates several type of components. The task presents a visual stimulus for 5 seconds, which is picked up by task-related components. The time courses of the signals
in the boxes is around one minute and the task is repeated four times, as in panel
(a). Other components pick up artifacts such as head motions. From M. J. McKeown,
T.-P. Jung, S. Makeig, G. D. Brown, S. S. Kindermann, T.-W. Lee, and T. J. Sejnowski,
"Spatially Independent Activity Patterns in Functional MRI Data during the Stroop
Color-Naming Task," *Proceedings of the National Academy of Sciences of the United States
of America* 95, no. 3 (1998): 806, figure 1.

Because independent component analysis is unsupervised, it can reveal networks of brain areas that work together, which goes beyond supervised techniques that try to relate the activity in an area to a sensory stimulus or motor response. For example, ICA has been used to uncover multiple resting states in fMRI recordings from subjects who are simply asked to stay still in the scanner and rest.[12] We still do not yet understand what these resting states mean, but they could represent combinations of brain areas that are responsible for what happens in our brains when we daydream, have a nagging concern in the back of our mind, or are planning dinner.

The principle of maximum independence is related to principles of sparse coding. Although ICA uncovers many independent components, only a few of them were needed to reconstruct a given patch from a natural image. This principle also applies to the visual cortex, which has one hundred times more cells than the inputs coming from a retina. Each of our retinas has 1 million ganglion cells, and there are 100 million neurons in the primary visual cortex, the first of many layers in the visual hierarchy in the cortex. The compact coding of visual signals in the retinas gets expanded in the cortex to a new code that is highly distributed and highly sparse. The expansion into a space of much higher dimensionality is exploited in other coding schemes, including those found in auditory cortex and olfactory cortex, and a new class of algorithms called "compressed sensing algorithms" has generalized the principle of sparsity to improve the efficiency of storing and analyzing complex data sets.[13]

Beyond Independent Component Analysis

The story of ICA illustrates the importance of techniques in making new discoveries in science and engineering. We normally think of techniques as measuring devices like microscopes and amplifiers. But algorithms are also techniques, and they can allow new discoveries to be made with data from old instruments. EEG recordings have been around for nearly 100 years, but without independent component analysis, it wasn't possible to pin down the underlying brain sources. The brain itself is a system of interlocking algorithms, and I would not be surprised if in some part of the brain nature discovered a way to implement ICA.[14]

During the 1990s, many other advances were made in developing new learning algorithms for neural networks, many of which, like ICA, are now part of the mathematical toolbox in machine learning. These algorithms are embedded in many commonly used appliances, none of which say "neural networks inside." Take headsets or cell phones, for example. Te-Won Lee and Tzyy-Ping Jung, two former postdoctoral fellows in my lab who went on to start a company called "SoftMax," used ICA with two microphones in a Bluetooth headset to cancel background noise, making it possible for a listener to hear someone talking at a noisy restaurant or sporting event. In 2007, SoftMax was bought by Qualcomm, which designs the chips that are used in many cell phones and today ICA-like solutions are embedded in a billion cell phones. If you had a penny for every cell phone running ICA, you'd be a multimillionaire today.

Tony Bell has for many years been interested in an even more difficult problem. As human beings, we have many networks within us in which information emerges from one network level to another, from molecules, to synapses, to neurons, to neural populations, and on up to form decisions, all explained by the laws of physics and biochemistry (figure 4.4). But we have the impression that we, not physics or biochemistry, are in control. It is a mystery how internal activity emerging in neural populations in our brains leads us to make decisions, to read this book, for example, or to play tennis. Made well below the level of our consciousness, these decisions somehow bubble up from neurons interacting through synapses formed by experiences based on molecular mechanisms. But from our human perspective, it was our decisions that caused all these events to occur in our brains: introspectively, causality seems to be running in the opposite direction from physics and biochemistry. How to reconcile these two perspectives is a deep scientific question.[15]

7   The Hopfield Net and Boltzmann Machine

Computer scientist Jerome Feldman was at the University of Rochester when he embraced a connectionist network approach to artificial intelligence in the 1980s. Ever the truth teller, Jerry pointed out that the algorithms being used in AI took billions of steps to reach an often incorrect conclusion, whereas the brain could reach a usually correct conclusion in around 100 steps.[1] Feldman's "100-step rule" was not popular among AI researchers at the time, but a few, most notably Allen Newell at Carnegie Mellon, did use it as a constraint.

Jerry once rescued me when I got stranded at the airport in Rochester, New York. I was on my way back to Baltimore from a visit to the General Electric Research Laboratory in Schenectady when the pilot started telling us about the weather in Rochester. I'd gotten on the wrong plane. After we landed and I booked the earliest flight to Baltimore, which didn't leave until the next day, I bumped into Jerry, who was returning home from a committee meeting in Washington, D.C. He graciously invited me to stay with him that night. Jerry has since moved on to UC, Berkeley, but I think of him whenever I'm stranded at an airport.

Jerry distinguished between "scruffy" and "neat" connectionist models. Scruffy models, like the ones that Geoffrey Hinton and I worked on, distributed the representation of objects and concepts across many units in the network, whereas neat models, like the ones Jerry believed in, provided a computationally compact representation of objects and concepts, with one label on one unit. In a broader context, scruffy science uses approximations to get qualitative answers, whereas neat science strives to pin down exact solutions to problems. In reality, both are needed to make progress.[2] I had no problem with getting a scruffy toehold, but made every effort to reach a neater explanation, and eventually it paid off: Geoffrey and I were about to hit the "neat" jackpot.

John Hopfield

To receive a doctorate in physics, you have to solve a problem. A good physicist should be able to solve any problem, but a great physicist knows what problem to solve. John Hopfield is a great physicist. After a distinguished career in condensed matter physics, he turned his interest to biology and, in particular, to the problem of "molecular proofreading." When DNA is replicated during cell division, errors are inevitable, and these must be corrected to preserve the fidelity of the daughter cells. John figured out a clever scheme for how that could be done, and, even though the process he proposed consumes energy, subsequent experiments showed he was right. Getting anything right in biology is a spectacular achievement.

John was my doctoral advisor at Princeton when he was just getting interested in neuroscience. With growing enthusiasm, he would tell me what he had learned from the neuroscientists who spoke at meetings of the Neuroscience Research Program (NRP), based in Boston. I found the proceedings of small workshops published by the NRP invaluable since they gave me a sense of what problems were being studied and the thinking in the field at the time. I still have my copy of the proceedings of a workshop on neural coding that was organized by the legendary neuroethologist Theodore Holmes Bullock, who would one day become a colleague of mine at UC, San Diego. Ted's book with Adrian Horridge on invertebrate nervous systems is a classic.[3] I collaborated with Ted on modeling the collective behavior of coral reefs and was proud to be a coauthor on his last scientific paper in 2008.[4]

Neural networks with feedback connections to earlier layers and recurrent connections between units within a layer can have much more complex dynamics than networks that only have feedforward connections. The general case of networks with arbitrarily connected units with positive (excitatory) and negative (inhibitory) weights poses a difficult mathematical problem. Although Jack Cowan at the University of Chicago and Stephen Grossberg at Boston University had made progress in the late 1970s by showing that such networks could reproduce visual illusions[5] and visual hallucinations,[6] engineers found it hard to get the networks to solve complex computational problems.

A Network with Content-Addressable Memories

In the summer of 1983, Geoffrey Hinton, John Hopfield (figure 7.1), and I were at a workshop at the University of Rochester organized by Jerry

Figure 7.1
John Hopfield solving a problem on the waterfront at Woods Hole, Massachusetts around 1986. Hopfield had a seminal influence on neural networks in the 1980s by inventing an eponymous network that opened the door to deep learning. Courtesy of John Hopfield.

Feldman. Hopfield told us that he had solved the convergence problem for a strongly interacting network. He had proved that a particular type of nonlinear network model, now called the "Hopfield net," was guaranteed to converge to a stable state, called an "attractor" (figure 7.2; box 7.1).[7] (Highly nonlinear networks are prone to oscillate or exhibit even more chaotic behavior.) Furthermore, the weights in the network could be chosen so that the attractors were memories. The Hopfield net could thus be used to implement what is called a "content-addressable memory," whereby a stored memory could be retrieved by starting with part of the memory and letting the network complete it. This is reminiscent of how we recall memories. If we see the face of someone we know, we can recall the person's name and conversations we've had with that person.

What made the Hopfield net a major breakthrough was that it was mathematically guaranteed to converge. Researchers had thought it would

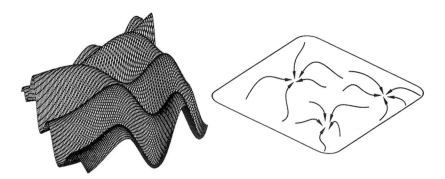

Figure 7.2
Energy landscape of a Hopfield net. (Left) The state of the network can be visualized as a point on an energy surface. (Right) Each update moves the state closer to one of the energy minima, called "attractor states." From A. Krogh, J. Hertz, and R. G. Palmer, *Introduction to the Theory of Neural Computation* (Redwood City CA: Addison-Wesley, 1991). Left: figure 2.6; Right: figure 2.2.

be impossible to analyze the general case of a highly nonlinear network. When updates are made simultaneously for all the units in such a network, the dynamics can be extremely complicated, and there is no guarantee of convergence.[8] But Hopfield showed that, when the units of the network are updated sequentially, the special case of a symmetric network in which reciprocal connections between pairs of units are equal in strength is tractable and does indeed converge.

There is increasing evidence that neural networks in the hippocampus (essential for storing long-term memories of specific events and unique objects) have attractor states like those in a Hopfield net.[9] Although the Hopfield model is highly abstracted, its qualitative behavior is similar to what is observed in the hippocampus. Hopfield nets were a bridge from physics to neuroscience that many physicists crossed in the 1980s. Surprising insights were obtained by analyzing neural networks and learning algorithms with sophisticated tools from theoretical physics. Physics, computation, and learning are profoundly linked in an area of neuroscience theory that has been successful at illuminating brain function.

John Hopfield and David Tank, who was then at Bell Laboratories, went on to show that a variant of the Hopfield net, in which the units were continuously valued between zero and one, could be used to obtain good solutions for optimization problems such as the "traveling salesman problem," where the goal is to find the shortest route that visits many cities only once.[10] This is a notoriously difficult problem in computer science.

Box 7.1

The Hopfield Net

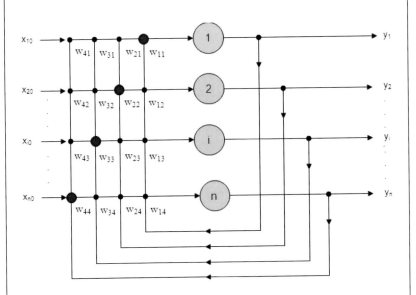

In a Hopfield net, each unit sends an output wire to all the other units in the network. The inputs are x_i and the outputs are y_j. The strengths of the connections or weights between the units are symmetric: $w_{ij} = w_{ji}$. On each time step, one of the units is updated by summing up inputs and comparing that to a threshold: If the inputs exceed the threshold, the output of the unit is 1; otherwise 0. Hopfield showed that the network has an energy function that never increases with each update of a unit in the network:

$$E = \Sigma \, w_{ij} \, x_i \, x_j$$

Eventually, the Hopfield net arrives at an "attractor state," when none of the units changes and the energy function is at a local minimum. This state corresponds to a stored memory, which can be recovered by initializing the network with a part of the stored state. This is how the Hopfield net implements a content-addressable memory. The weights of the stored vectors can be learned by Hebbian synaptic plasticity:

$$\Delta w_{ij} = \alpha \, x_i \, x_j,$$

where the left side is the change in the strength of the weight, α is the learning rate, and x_i is a stored vector.

Drawing courtesy of Dale Heath.

The energy function for the networks included the lengths of the paths and constraints on visiting each city once. After an initial transient, Hopfield and Tank's network would settle down to a state of minimum energy that represented a good tour, though not always the best tour.

Finding the Global Energy Minimum

Dana Ballard, who with Christopher Brown had written a classic book on computer vision in 1982,[11] was also at the 1983 workshop. Geoffrey Hinton and I were working with Dana on a review of a new approach to analyzing images for *Nature*.[12] The idea was that the nodes in a network model represented features in the image and the connections in the network implemented constraints between the features; compatible nodes had positive interactions and inconsistent nodes had negative interactions with one another. In vision, a consistent interpretation of all the features must be found that satisfies all the constraints.

Could the Hopfield net solve this constraint satisfaction problem? The energy function was a measure of how well the network satisfied all the constraints (See box 7.1). The vision problem required a solution that was the global energy minimum, the best solution, whereas the Hopfield net, by design, found only local minima of the energy. I had recently come across a paper in the journal *Science* by Scott Kirkpatrick, then at IBM's Thomas J. Watson Research Center in Yorktown Heights, New York, that I thought could help.[13] Kirkpatrick used a method called "simulated annealing" to get around local minima. Suppose you had a bunch of components in an electrical circuit that had to be mounted onto two circuit boards. What would be the best placement of the parts to minimize the number of wires needed to connect them?

Poor solutions are found by initially randomizing the placement of the parts, then moving them back and forth one at a time to see which placement had fewest wires because the network can easily get trapped in a local minimum when there is no improvement by moving any single component. The way to escape the local minimum is to allow random jumps to a configuration with longer wire lengths. The probability of jumping out, though high at the beginning, gradually decreases so that, by the end, it is zero. If the decrease in probability is slow enough, the final placement of the parts will have a global minimum of connecting wires. In metallurgy, this process is called "annealing"; heating up a metal and slowly cooling it produces large crystals with minimal defects, which are what make the metal brittle and prone to cracks.

Boltzmann Machines

In a Hopfield net, simulated annealing corresponds to "heating up" the updates so that the energy can go uphill as well as downhill. Because the units flip randomly at a high temperature, if the temperature is gradually lowered, there is a high probability that the Hopfield net will end up frozen in the lowest energy state when the temperature reaches zero. In practice, simulations start out at a constant temperature to allow the network to come to equilibrium, where it can visit many nearby states and explore a wide range of possible solutions.

For example, in figure 7.3, the silhouetted figure is ambiguous and, depending on what part you pay attention to, you will either see a vase or two faces, but never both at the same time. Consider the problem of deciding what part of the image is the figure and what is the background (called the "ground"). We designed a Boltzmann machine network that mimics this figure–ground decision,[14] with some units that represent the

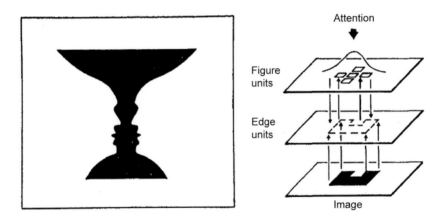

Figure 7.3
Ambiguous figure–ground problem. (Left) When you focus your attention on the black figure, you see a vase and the white is ground. But when you focus on the white areas, you can see two faces looking at each other. You can flip back and forth but you cannot see both interpretations at the same time. (Right) Figure–ground network model. Two types of units representing the edges of an object (line segments) and whether a pixel is part of the figure or part of the ground (squares). Image inputs are bottom up, and attention input is top down. Attention is implemented as a bias to the region that should be filled in as the figure. From P. K. Kienker, T. J. Sejnowski, G. E. Hinton, and L. E. Schumacher, "Separating Figure from Ground with a Parallel Network," *Perception* 15 (1986): 197–216. Left: figure 1; right: figure 2.

Box 7.2
The Boltzmann Machine

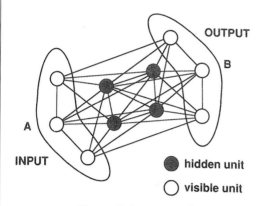

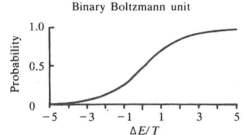

All connections in a Boltzmann machine are symmetric, as they are in the Hopfield net, and the binary units are updated one a time by setting $s_i = 1$ with a probability given by the above sigmoid function, where the inputs ΔE are scaled by temperature T. The input layer and the output layer are "visible," in the sense that they interact with the outside world. The "hidden units" represent features having internal degrees of freedom that can affect the visible units. The Boltzmann machine learning algorithm has two phases: in the "wake" phase, the inputs and outputs are clamped and after the network comes to equilibrium the average correlation between pairs of units is computed; in the "sleep" phase, the correlations are again computed with the inputs and outputs unclamped. Then the weights are incrementally updated:

$$\Delta w_{ij} = \varepsilon \left(<s_i s_j>^{wake} - <s_i s_j>^{sleep} \right)$$

figure when they are activated and others that represent the edges. We have already seen that there are simple cells in the visual cortex that are activated by edges, but the figure could lie on either side of an edge. This was implemented in our Boltzmann machine network by having two edge units, each supporting the figure on either side. Such neurons were subsequently discovered in the visual cortex and are called "border-ownerships cells."[15]

The weights in the Boltzmann network were handcrafted to implement the constraints (figure 7.4). There are excitatory connections between the figure units and inhibitory connections between the edge units. The edge units have excitatory connections with the figure units they point to, supporting the figure, and inhibitory connections with the figure units in the opposite direction. Attention was implemented by a bias to some of the figure units. When the Boltzmann network uses the Hopfield update rule for the units, it falls into local energy minima that are consistent in local patches but inconsistent globally. When noise was added to the updates, the Boltzmann network jumped out of the local minima, and, by slowly annealing the temperature of the noise, the network relaxed to a globally consistent solution at the global energy minimum (figure 7.4). Because the updates are asynchronous and independent, the network can be implemented by a computer with millions of units working together in parallel and can converge to solutions much faster than a digital computer that performs one operation at a time, in sequence.

I had by this time finished my postdoctoral fellowship at Harvard Medical School with Stephen Kuffler and moved to my first job in the Department of Biophysics at Johns Hopkins; Geoffrey Hinton had taken a faculty position in the Computer Science Department at Carnegie Mellon, where he was fortunate to have the support of Allen Newell, who was open to new directions in artificial intelligence. Pittsburgh and Baltimore are close enough so that Geoffrey and I could visit each other on weekends. We called our new version of the Hopfield net the "Boltzmann machine" after Ludwig Boltzmann, the nineteenth-century physicist who was a founder of statistical mechanics, the source of the tools that we were using to analyze our fluctuating neural network model, which, we were about to discover, was also a powerful learning machine.

Kept at a constant "temperature," a Boltzmann machine will come to equilibrium. Something magical happens at equilibrium that would open a door that everyone thought was closed for good: multilayer neural network learning. One day, Geoffrey called to say he had just derived a simple learning algorithm for the Boltzmann machine. The goal of the algorithm was to perform a mapping from input units to output units, but, unlike the

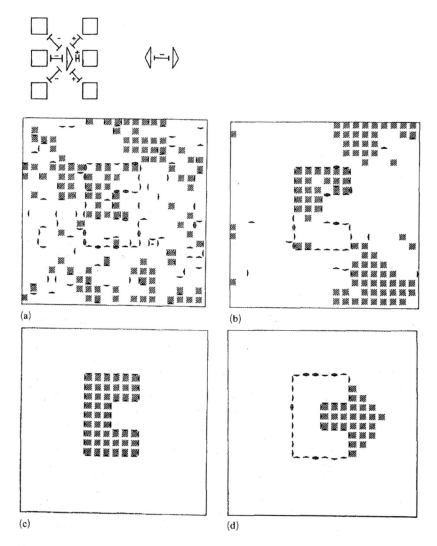

Figure 7.4

Separating figure from ground with a Boltzmann machine. (Above) The square units in the network identify the figure and the triangular edge units identify the outline, with the signs of the connections indicated. Edge units can point toward or away from the figure. (Below) (a) Snapshot of a network with attention on the inside of the "C." The temperature starts out high so that the units are fluctuating between on and off. (b) As the temperature drops, units on the inside of the "C" begin to coalesce, with support from the boundary units that point to the inside. Units on the outside that do not have attention or edge input disappear as the temperature is decreased. (c) The figure is filled in when attending the inside when the temperature reaches zero. (d) The outside is filled in when the process is repeated while attending the outside. From P. K. Kienker, T. J. Sejnowski, G. E. Hinton, and L. E. Schumacher, "Separating Figure from Ground with a Parallel Network," *Perception* 15 (1986): 197–216, Below: figure 6; above: figure 3.

perceptron, the Boltzmann machine also had units in between, which we called "hidden units" (box 7.2). By presenting input-output pairs and applying the learning algorithm, the Boltzmann network learned the desired mapping. But the goal was not just to memorize the pairs; it was also to correctly categorize new inputs that were not used to train the network. Also, because it is always fluctuating, the Boltzmann machine is learning the probability distribution—how often each output state is visited for a given input pattern—which makes it generative: after learning, it can generate new input samples by clamping each output category.

Hebbian Synaptic Plasticity

The surprise was that the Boltzmann machine learning algorithm turned out to have a long history in neuroscience, going back to the psychologist Donald O. Hebb, who in his book *The Organization of Behavior* postulated that when two neurons fired together, the synapse between them should strengthen:

> Let us assume that the persistence or repetition of a reverberatory activity (or "trace") tends to induce lasting cellular changes that add to its stability. When an axon of cell A is near enough to excite a cell B and repeatedly or persistently takes part in firing it, some growth process or metabolic change takes place in one or both cells such that A's efficiency, as one of the cells firing B, is increased.[16]

This may be the most famous prediction in all of neuroscience. Hebbian synaptic plasticity was later discovered in the hippocampus, an important brain area for long-term memory. When a hippocampal pyramidal cell receives a strong input at the same time the neuron is spiking, the strength of the synapse is increased. Subsequent experiments showed that the strengthening was based on the conjunction of transmitter release from the synapse and elevation of the voltage in the recipient neuron. Moreover, this conjunctive occurrence was recognized by a special receptor, the NMDA (N-methyl-D-aspartate) glutamate receptor that triggers long-term potentiation (LTP), which is rapid in onset and long lasting, a good candidate for the substrate of long-term memory. Hebbian plasticity at a synapse is governed by coincidences between inputs and outputs, just like the Boltzmann machine learning algorithm (see box 7.2).

Even more amazing, the Boltzmann machine had to go to sleep to be able to learn. Its learning algorithm had two phases. In the first or "wake" phase, with the input and output patterns were clamped to the desired mapping, the units in the network were updated many times to settle down to an equilibrium, and the fraction of time each pair of units were on together was counted. In the second or "sleep" phase, the input and output units were set free, and the fraction of time each pair of units were on together was counted in a free running condition. Each connection strength was then updated in proportion to the difference between the coincidence rates in the wake and sleep phases (box 7.2). The computational reason for the sleep phase is to determine which part of the clamped correlations was due to external causes. Without subtracting the internally generated correlations, the network would strengthen the internal patterns of activity and would learn to ignore outside influences, a network version of folie à deux. Interestingly, extreme sleep deprivation in humans leads to delusional states, a common problem in intensive care units in hospitals that have no windows and constant lighting. Patients with schizophrenia often have sleep disorders that can contribute to their delusional ideation. We were convinced that we were on the right track to understanding how the brain worked.

Learning Mirror Symmetries

A problem the Boltzmann machine could solve but a perceptron could not is how to learn mirror symmetries.[17] The human body is bilaterally symmetric along a vertical axis. We can generate a large number of random patterns with this axis of symmetry, as shown in figure 7.5, and also with horizontal and diagonal axes of symmetry. In our Boltzmann machine network, 10×10 blocks of binary inputs projected to sixteen hidden units, which in turn projected to three output units, one for each of the three possible axes of symmetry. The Boltzmann machine was 90 percent successful at classifying the axis of symmetry of novel inputs after being trained on 6,000 symmetric input patterns. A perceptron can do no better than chance because a single input carries no information about the symmetry of the pattern; the correlations between pairs of inputs must be interrogated. What is remarkable is that the array of inputs a human observer sees is not what the Boltzmann machine sees since each hidden unit receives inputs from the whole array in no particular order. The equivalent problem for an observer would be to randomize the locations of the input units in the array, which would make the array look random to the observer even though there is a hidden symmetry.

One day, I was watching the display and calling the symmetry of each input pattern at a rate of two per second. Neal Cohen, then a colleague in the Psychology Department at Johns Hopkins, was also watching the

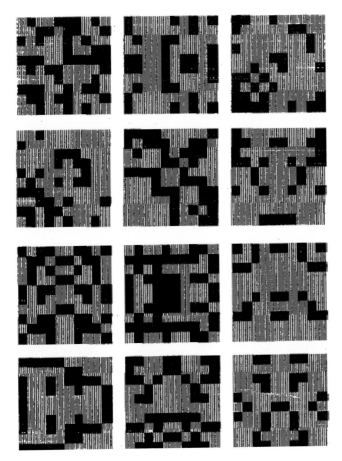

Figure 7.5
Symmetric random patterns. Each 10×10 array has a vertical, horizontal, or diagonal axis of mirror symmetry. The goal of the network model is to learn how to classify the axis of the symmetry in new patterns not used to train the network model. From T. J. Sejnowski, P. K. Kienker, and G. E. Hinton, "Learning Symmetry Groups with Hidden Units: Beyond the Perceptron," *Physica* 22D (1986): 260–275, figure 4.

display but could not categorize the symmetries without scrutinizing the patterns and was amazed that I could. Watching the display for days as the Boltzmann machine learned had trained my visual system to detect the symmetry automatically, without having to look around the display. Neal and I designed an experiment with undergraduates as naive subjects and followed their progress.[18] At the beginning, it took them many seconds to get the right symmetry, but after a few days of training, they were much faster, and by the end of the experiment, they could detect the symmetries so quickly and effortlessly they could talk with us during the task and still get all of them right. This was remarkably fast perceptual learning.

I taught "The Biophysics of Computation" at Johns Hopkins, a course that attracted several talented students and researchers. Ben Yuhas was a graduate student in the Department of Electrical Engineering who worked with me and for his doctoral dissertation, he trained a neural network to read lips.[19] There is information on the sound of a voice in the movement of a person's mouth. Ben's network transformed images of mouths into the corresponding frequency spectrum of the sound being generated at each time step. This could then be added to the noisy sound spectrum to improve speech recognition. His fellow graduate student Andreas Andreou, a Greek Cypriot with a booming voice, was building analog VLSI (very large-scale integration) chips in the basement of Barton Hall. (These chips are featured in chapter 14.) In the 1980s, there was hostility from faculty in their department toward neural networks, which was common at many institutions, but this did not deter either Ben or Andreas. Indeed, Andreas would go on to become a full professor at Hopkins and to cofound the Johns Hopkins University Center for Language and Speech Processing. Ben has a consulting group on data science for political and corporate clients.

Learning to Recognize Handwritten Zip Codes

More recently, Geoffrey Hinton and his students at the University of Toronto trained a Boltzmann machine with three layers of hidden units to classify handwritten zip codes with high accuracy (figure 7.6).[20] Because the Boltzmann network had feedback as well as feedforward connections, it was possible to run the network in reverse, clamping one of the output units and generating input patterns that corresponded to the clamped output unit (figure 7.7). Generative networks capture the statistical structure of the training set and the samples they generate inherit these properties. It is as if these networks go to sleep and activity at the highest level of the networks generates sequences of dreamlike states on the input layer.

Although the rise of neural networks in physics and engineering was swift, traditional cognitive scientists were slow to accept it as a formalism

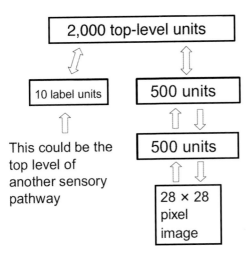

Figure 7.6
Multilayer Boltzmann machine for handwritten digit recognition and generation.
The image has 28 × 28 = 784 pixels, which can be white or black. The goal is to
classify the digit based on the ten output units (0–9). From G. E. Hinton, "Learning
Multiple Layers of Representation." *Trends in Cognitive Sciences* 11 (2007): 428-434,
figure 1.

Figure 7.7
Input layer patterns generated by a multilayer Boltzmann machine trained to recognize handwritten digits. Each line was generated by clamping one of the ten output
units (figure 7.6), and the input layer continuously morphed between the examples
shown above. None of these digits were in the training set—they were "hallucinated"
by the internal structure of the trained network. From G. E. Hinton, S. Osindero,
and Y. Teh, "A Fast Learning Algorithm for Deep Belief Nets." *Neural Computation* 18
(2006): 1527–1554 figure 8.

to understand memory and language processing. Except for the Parallel Distributed Processing (PDP) Group in La Jolla and a few isolated outposts, symbol processing was still the only game in town. At a 1983 Cognitive Science Society symposium that Geoffrey and I attended, Zenon Pylyshyn, a psychologist who studies short-term memory and imagery, showed his disdain for the Boltzmann machine by pouring a glass of water on the stage and shouting, "This is not computation!" Others dismissed the whole enterprise as mere "statistics." But not Jerome Lettvin, who told us that he really liked what we were doing. Lettvin had written the classic 1959 paper "What the Frog's Eye Tells the Frog's Brain" with Humberto Maturana, Warren McCulloch, and Walter Pitts,[21] which reported evidence for bug detector neurons in the frog retina that responded best to small dark spots, an idea that was highly influential in systems neuroscience. His support for our fledgling neural network model was an important link to an earlier era.

Unsupervised Learning and Cortical Development

The Boltzmann machine can be used either in its supervised version, where both inputs and outputs are clamped, or in its unsupervised version, where only the inputs are clamped. Geoffrey Hinton used the unsupervised version to build up a deep Boltzmann machine one layer at a time.[22] Starting with a layer of hidden units connected to the input units, called a restricted Boltzmann machine, Geoffrey trained these on unlabeled data, which are a lot easier to come by than labeled data (there are billions of unlabeled images and audio recordings on the Internet), and learning is much faster. The first step in unsupervised learning is to extract from the data statistical regularities that are common to all the data, but the first layer of hidden units can only extract simple features, features that a perceptron can represent. The next step is to freeze the weights to the first layer and add a second layer of units on top. More unsupervised Boltzmann learning leads to a more complex set of features, and this process can be repeated to create a network that is many layers deep.

Because the units in the upper layers incorporate more nonlinear combinations of low-level features, making it possible for them as a population to abstract what is general from what is specific, classification becomes much easier in the upper layers, requiring many fewer training examples to reach convergence at a higher level of performance. Although it is still an open problem to describe the mathematics of this disentangling, new geometrical tools are being brought to bear on these deep networks.[23]

The cortex also seems to develop layer by layer. At early stages in the development of the visual system, neurons in the primary visual cortex, the first to receive inputs from the eyes, are highly plastic and can easily be rewired by the stream of visual input, which ends when the critical period does. (This was described in chapter 5.) The hierarchy of visual areas and other sensory streams in the back of the brain mature first; cortical areas closer to the front of the brain take much longer. The prefrontal cortex, the part that is furthest forward, may not reach full maturity until early adulthood. Thus there is a gradual wave of development with overlapping critical periods when the connections in a cortical area are the most influenced by neural activity. Working with other colleagues, cognitive scientists Jeffrey Elman and Elizabeth Bates at UC, San Diego developed connectionist network explanations for how the progressive development of the cortex could account for the new abilities that emerge as a child learns more about the world.[24] This opened a new research direction into how our long childhood has made it possible for humans to become champion learners, and it put previous claims for the innateness of some behaviors into a new perspective.

In *Liars, Lovers and Heroes*,[25] which I coauthored with Steven Quartz, a former postdoctoral fellow in my lab who is now on the faculty at Caltech, we wrote that, during the extended period of brain development in childhood and adolescence, experience can profoundly influence the expression of genes in neurons, and thereby alter the neural circuits that are responsible for behavior. The interplay between genetic differences and environmental influences is an active area of research that is shedding new light on the complexity of brain development, an area that goes beyond the nature versus nurture debate and reframes it in terms of cultural biology. Our biology both produces human culture and, in turn, is molded by it.[26] A new chapter in this story was opened by a recent discovery: when there is a rapid increase in the formation of synapses between neurons during early development, the DNA inside neurons is modified epigenetically after birth by a form of methylation that regulates gene expression and is unique to the brain.[27] This epigenetic modification could be the link between genes and experience that Steve Quartz and I had envisioned.

By the 1990s, the neural network revolution was well under way. Cognitive neuroscience was expanding, and computers were getting faster—but not fast enough. The Boltzmann machine was technically sweet but terribly slow to simulate. What really helped us make progress was a faster learning algorithm, which fell out of the sky just when we most needed it.

8 Backpropagating Errors

The University of California, San Diego, founded in 1960, has grown into a major center for biomedical research. It inaugurated a Department of Cognitive Science in 1986, the first of its kind in the world.[1] David Rumelhart (figure 8.1) was already a distinguished mathematical and cognitive psychologist who had worked within the symbolic, rule-based tradition that was dominant in artificial intelligence research during the 1970s. When I first met David in 1979 at the workshop organized by Geoffrey Hinton at UC, San Diego, he was pioneering a new approach to human psychology that he and James McClelland called "parallel distributed processing" (PDP). David thought deeply about problems and often made insightful comments.

The Boltzmann machine learning algorithm could provably learn how to solve problems that required hidden units, showing that, contrary to the opinion of Marvin Minsky and Seymour Papert and most everyone else in the field, it was possible to train a multilayer network and overcome the limitations of the perceptron. There was no limit either to the number of layers in a network or to the connectivity within any given layer. But there was one problem: coming to equilibrium and collecting statistics became increasingly slow to simulate, and larger networks took much longer to reach equilibrium.

In principle, it is possible to build a computer with a massively parallel architecture that is much faster than one with a traditional von Neumann architecture that makes one update at a time. Digital computers in the 1980s could perform only a million operations per second. Today's computers perform billions of operations per second, and, by linking together many thousands of cores, high-performance computers are a million times faster than before—an unprecedented increase in technological power.

The Manhattan Project was a $26 billion dollar bet, in 2016 dollars, made by the United States without any assurance that the atomic bomb

Figure 8.1
David Rumelhart at the University of California, San Diego, around the time the
two volumes of *Parallel Distributed Processing* were published in 1986. Rumelhart was
influential in the technical development of learning algorithms for multilayer networks models and used them to help us understand the psychology of language and
thinking. Courtesy of David Rumelhart.

would work, and the biggest secret was that it did work. Once the secret
that multilayer networks could be trained using a Boltzmann machine
was out, there was an explosion of new learning algorithms. At the same
time that Geoffrey Hinton and I were working on the Boltzmann machine,
David Rumelhart had developed another learning algorithm for multilayer
networks that proved to be even more productive.[2]

Optimization

Optimization is a key mathematical concept in machine learning: for many
problems, a cost function can be found for which the solution is the state

Box 8.1
Error Backpropagation

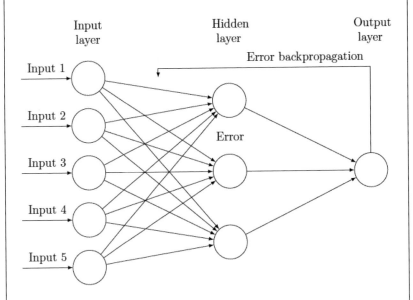

Inputs to the backprop network are propagated feedforward: In the diagram above, the inputs on the left propagate forward through the connections (arrows) to the hidden layer of units, which in turn project to the output layer. The output is compared with the value given by a trainer, and the difference is used to update the weights to the output unit to reduce the error. The weights between the input units and the hidden layer are then updated based on backpropagating the error according to how much each weight contributes to the error. By training on many examples, the hidden units develop selective features that can be used to distinguish between different input patterns so that they can be separated into different categories in the output layer. This is called "representation learning."
Courtesy of Dr. Mahmoud.

of the system with the lowest cost. In the case of the Hopfield net, the cost function is the energy, and the goal is to find a state of the network that minimizes it (as described in chapter 6). For a feedforward network, a popular cost function for learning is the summed squared error on the output layer of the training set. "Gradient descent" is a general procedure that minimizes a cost function by making incremental changes to the weights in the networks in the direction of greatest reduction to the cost.[3] Think of the cost function as a mountain range and gradient descent as the path you take to ski the fastest way down a slope.

Rumelhart discovered how to calculate the gradient for each weight in the network by a process called the "backpropagation of errors," or "backprop" for short (box 8.1). Starting on the output layer, where the error is known, it is easy to calculate the gradient on the input weights to the output units. The next step is to use the output layer gradients to calculate the gradients on the previous layer of weights, and so on, layer by layer, all the way back to the input layer. This is a highly efficient way to compute error gradients.

Although it has neither the elegance nor the deep roots in physics that the Boltzmann machine learning algorithm has, backprop is more efficient, and it has made possible much more rapid progress. The classic backprop paper, coauthored by David Rumelart, Geoffrey Hinton, and Ronald Williams, appeared in *Nature* in 1986,[4] and since then, it has been cited more than 40,000 times in other research papers. (Half the papers published never get a single citation, not even from their authors; a paper that receives even 100 citations has made a significant impact on a field, so the backprop paper was clearly a blockbuster.)

NETtalk

At Princeton in 1984, I heard a talk by a graduate student, Charles Rosenberg, on the Boltzmann machine. Although usually the one giving this talk, I was impressed. Charlie asked if he could visit my lab to work on a summer project. By the time he arrived in Baltimore, we had switched to backprop, which made it possible for us to think about working on a real-world problem rather than the toy demonstration problems I had worked on previously. Since Charlie was a student of George Miller, a legendary language expert, we looked around for a Goldilocks problem in language, one that was neither so difficult that we could not make headway on it nor so easy that known methods could solve the problem. Linguistics is a vast field with many subdisciplines: phonology, which concerns the pronunciation of words; syntax, which studies how words are arranged in a sentence; semantics, which is about the meaning of words and sentences; and pragmatics, which studies how context contributes to the meaning of language—to name just a few. We decided to start with phonology and work our way up.

English is a particularly difficult language to pronounce because the rules are complex and have many exceptions. For example, vowels are mostly long if the final consonant of a word is followed by a silent "e," such as "gave," and "brave," but there are exceptions, such as "have," which behaves irregularly. I went to the library and found a book in which phonologists had compiled hundreds of pages of these rules and exceptions. There were often rules within the exceptions and sometimes exceptions to these exceptional rules. In short, for linguists, it was rules "all the way down."[5] To make matters worse, not everyone pronounces a word the same way. There are many dialects, each with its own set of rules.

Geoffrey Hinton visited Charlie and me at Johns Hopkins during this early planning period and told us he thought that English pronunciation would be too hard to tackle. So we scaled back our ambitions and found a children's first reading book that had a hundred words in it. The network we designed had a window of seven letters, each represented by twenty-nine units including space and punctuation, for a total of 203 input units. The goal was to predict the sound of the middle letter in the window. The input units were connected to eighty hidden units, and the hidden units projected to twenty-six output units, one for each of the elementary sounds, called "phonemes," that are found in English. We called our letter-to-sound network "NETtalk" (figure 8.2).[6] There were 18,629 weights in the network, a large number by the standards of 1986, and impossibly large by the standards of mathematical statistics of the time. With that many parameters, we were told that we would overfit the training set, and the network would not be able to generalize.

As the words marched through the seven-letter window, one letter at a time, the network assigned a phoneme to the middle letter in the window. The part of the project that took the longest time was manually aligning the phoneme with the right letter since the number of letters was not the same as the number of phonemes in each word. In contrast, the learning took place before our eyes, getting better and better as the sentences cycled through the window, and when the learning converged, the performance of the network was almost perfect on the 100 word training set. Testing on new words was poor, but because generalization was expected to be

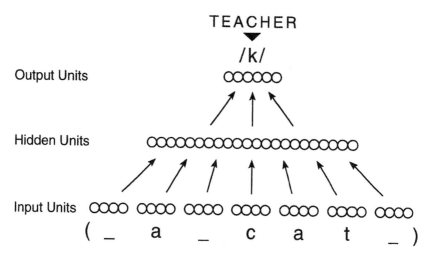

Figure 8.2

NETtalk feedforward network model. The seven groups of units on the bottom layer represent letters in a moving window through the text, one letter at a time. The goal of the network is to predict correctly the sound of the middle letter, which in this example is the hard "c" phoneme. Each unit on the input layer makes a connection with all of the hidden units, which in turn project to all of the units on the output layer. The backprop learning algorithm was used to train the weights using feedback from a teacher. The correct output pattern is compared with the output of the network, which in this case is the incorrect "k" phoneme. Errors are backpropagated to the weights on earlier layers.

low on such a small training set, this preliminary result was nonetheless encouraging.

We then used the 20,000-word Brown Corpus[7] and assigned phonemes, as well as stress marks, to each of letters. The alignment of the letters and sounds took weeks, but, once the learning started, the network absorbed the whole corpus in a single night. But how well would it generalize? Beautifully, it turned out. The network had discovered the regularities of English pronunciation and could recognize the exceptions, all with the same architecture and learning algorithm. Tiny by today's standards, our network was a testament to how efficiently a backprop network could represent English phonology. This was our first hint that how neural networks learned language—the poster child for symbolic representations—dovetailed with how humans did.

As it acquired its ability to read aloud, NETtalk first went through a babbling phase, in which it recognized the difference between consonants and vowels, but assigned the phoneme "b" to all the consonants and the phoneme "a" to all the vowels. It sounded like "ba ba" and then after more learning, it shifted to "ba ga da." This was eerily similar to the way babies babble. Then it started to get small words right, and finally, toward the end of training, we could understand most words.

To test NETtalk on dialect, we found a phonological transcription of an interview with a young Latino boy from a barrio in Los Angeles. The trained network re-created the Spanish-accented English of the boy talking about how, when visiting his grandmother, he would sometimes get candy. I recorded segments during successive stages of learning by playing the output of NETtalk into a speech synthesizer called "DECtalk" that converted a string of phoneme labels into audible speech. When I played this tape during a lecture, the audience was stunned—the network literally spoke for itself.[8] This summer project exceeded all our expectations and stood out as the first real-world application of neural network learning. I appeared with NETtalk on the *Today* show in 1986, which was seen by a surprisingly large audience. Up to this point, neural networks had been an arcane academic subject. I still meet people who heard about neural networks for the first time when they watched the show.

Although NETtalk was a powerful demonstration of how a network could represent some aspects of language, it was not a good model for how humans acquire reading skills. First, we learn to talk before we learn to read. Second, we are given a few phonetic rules to help us jumpstart the difficult task of becoming proficient at reading out loud. But reading aloud quickly becomes fast pattern recognition, without the need for conscious effort to apply rules. Most English speakers will pronounce nonsense words like "brillig," "slithy," and "toves" from Lewis Carroll's "Jabberwocky" without effort, the same way they would normal words, as will NETtalk. These pseudowords aren't in any dictionary but trigger phonemes formed from related letter patterns in English.

NETtalk made a deep impression on audiences, but now Charlie Rosenberg and I needed to analyze the network to figure out how it worked. To do that, we applied cluster analysis to the activity patterns in the hidden units and discovered that NETtalk had discovered the same grouping of similar vowels and consonants that linguists had identified. Mark Seidenberg and James McClelland used a similar approach as a starting point for a detailed comparison with the sequence of stages that children go through when they learn how to read.[9]

NETtalk had an impact on the world in ways that no one could have anticipated. As a faculty member of the Thomas C. Jenkins Department of Biophysics at the Johns Hopkins University, I became interested in the problem of protein folding. Proteins are string of amino acids that fold up into complex shapes, endowing them with a wide range of functions, such as hemoglobin, which binds to oxygen in your red blood cells. Predicting the 3D shape of a protein from its amino acid sequence is a difficult computational problem that is unsolved for most proteins even with the most powerful computers. However, there are motifs that are more predictable, called secondary structures, in which the amino acids wind up in the shape of a helix, a flat sheet, or a random coil. The algorithms being used by biophysicists took into account the chemical nature of the different amino acids, but their predictions were not good enough to help with the 3D folding problem.

Ning Qian was a first year graduate student in my lab who was one of the few chosen from all the physics students in China to come to the US for graduate studies in 1980. We wondered whether NETtalk could be used to take a string of amino acids and predict protein secondary structures, assigning alpha helix, a beta sheet, or a random coil to each amino acid. This is an important problem because the 3D structure of a protein determines its function. Instead of a string of letters, the input was a string of amino acids, and instead of predicting phonemes, the network predicted the secondary structure. The training set was 3D structures determined by x-ray crystallography. To our surprise, the secondary structure predictions for new proteins were far better than the best methods based on biophysics.[10] This landmark study was the first application of machine learning to molecular sequences, a field that is now called bioinformatics.

Another network that learned how to form the past tense of English verbs became a cause célèbre in the world of cognitive psychology as the rule-based old guard battled it out with the avant-garde PDP Group.[11] The regular way to form the past tense of an English verb is to add the suffix "ed," as in forming "trained" from "train." But there are irregular exceptions, such as "ran" from "run." Neural networks have no problem accommodating both the rules and the exceptions. Although this is no longer an active debate, the fundamental question about the role of explicit representation of rules in the brain remains open. Recent experiments on neural network learning of language support the gradual acquisition of inflectional morphology, consistent with human learning.[12] The success of deep learning with Google Translate and other natural language applications in capturing the nuances of language further supports the possibility that brains do not need to use explicit rules for language, even though behavior might suggest that they do.

Geoffrey Hinton, David Touretzky, and I organized the first Connectionist Summer School at Carnegie Mellon in 1986 (figure 8.3), at a time when

Figure 8.3
Students at the 1986 Connectionist Summer School at Carnegie Mellon University. Geoffrey Hinton is in the first row, third from right, flanked by Terry Sejnowski and James McClelland. This photo is a who's who in neural computing today. Neural networks in the 1980s were a bit of twenty-first-century science in the twentieth century. Courtesy of Geoffrey Hinton.

only a few universities had faculty who offered courses on neural networks. In a skit based on NETtalk, the students lined up in layers, with each student representing a unit in the network (although they registered an error when they propagated the "j" in "Sejnowski" since it is pronounced like "y" and does not follow the English pattern). Many of those students went on to make important discoveries of their own and to forge major careers. A second summer school was held at Carnegie Mellon in 1988 and a third at UC, San Diego, in 1990. It takes a generation for new ideas to get into the mainstream. These summer schools were intense experiences and the best investment we could make in the early days to promote the field.

Neural Networks Reborn

The two volumes of *Parallel Distributed Processing* (PDP), the now classic book edited by Rumelhart and McClelland, were published in 1986. It was the first book to lay out the implications of neural networks and multilayer learning algorithms for understanding mental and behavioral phenomena. It sold more than 50,000 copies, a best seller by academic standards. Not only did neural networks trained by backprop have hidden units with properties resembling those of cortical neurons in the visual system;[13] the breakdown patterns exhibited by these networks also had much in common with human deficits following brain damage.[14]

Francis Crick was a member of the PDP Group and came to most of the group's meetings and seminars. In the debate on how "biological" the parallel distributed processing models were, he took the position that they should be considered demonstrations rather than literal models of the brain. He wrote a chapter for the PDP book on what was then known about the cerebral cortex. I wrote a chapter that summarized what we did not know about the cerebral cortex. If those chapters were written today, both would be much longer.

There are success stories from the 1980s that are not generally known. One of the most profitable companies based on neural networks was HNC Software, Inc., founded by Robert Hecht-Nielsen, which used neural networks to prevent credit card fraud. Hecht-Nielsen was in the Electrical and Computer Engineering Department at UC, San Diego, and taught a popular course on practical applications of neural networks. Every day, credit cards are compromised by cybercriminals across the globe. Credit card transactions feed into a roaring river of data, and picking out the suspicious ones is a daunting task. In the 1980s, humans made the time-sensitive decisions of whether to approve or deny a given credit card transaction. This led to more than $150 billion of fraudulent transactions per year. HNC Software Inc. used neural network learning algorithms to detect credit card fraud with much better accuracy than humans, saving credit card companies many billions of dollars per year. HNC was acquired for $1 billion by Fair Isaac and Company (FICO) in 2002, famous for issuing credit scores.

There is something magical about watching a network learn as it gets better and better by taking small steps. It can be a slow process, but if there are enough training examples and the network is big enough, learning algorithms can find a good representation that generalizes well to new inputs. When the process is repeated from a randomly chosen set of initial weights, a different network is learned each time, but all with similar performances. Many networks can solve the same problem; this has implications for what we should expect when we are able to reconstruct the complete set of connections for the brains of different individuals. If many networks yield the same behavior, the key to understanding them is the learning algorithms used by brains, which should be easier to discover.

Understanding Deep Learning

Whereas, in convex optimization problems, there are no local minima and convergence is guaranteed to the global minimum, in nonconvex optimization problems, this is not the case. We were told by optimization experts that, because learning in networks with hidden units was a nonconvex optimization problem, we were wasting our time—our network would get trapped in local minima (figure 8.4). Empirical evidence suggested that they were wrong. But why? We now know that, in very high-dimensional spaces, local minima of the cost function are rare until the final stages of learning. At early stages, almost all directions are downhill, and, on the way down, there are saddle points, where some directions point up in error and other dimensions point down. The intuition that networks would get stuck in local minima is based on solving problems in low-dimensional spaces where there are fewer directions to escape.

Current deep network models have millions of units and billions of weights. For statisticians, who traditionally analyze simple models with only a few parameters so they can prove theorems using small data sets, a billion-dimensional space was a nightmare. They assured us that, with so many parameters, we would hopelessly overfit the data: our network would simply memorize the training data and fail to generalize to new test inputs. But using regularization techniques, like forcing the weights to decay when they weren't doing anything useful, we were able to alleviate overfitting.

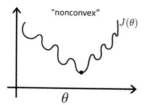
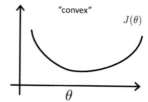

Figure 8.4

Nonconvex and convex cost functions. These graphs plot cost functions, $J(\theta)$, as a function of a parameter θ. A convex function has only one minimum (right), a global minimum that can be reached by moving downhill from any location on the surface. Imagine you are a skier and always point your skis in the steepest downhill direction. You are guaranteed to get to the bottom. In contrast, a nonconvex cost function can have local minima (left), which are traps that prevent the global minimum from being found by going downhill. As a consequence, nonconvex cost functions are difficult to optimize. However, this one-dimensional example is misleading. When there are many parameters (typically millions in a neural network), there can be saddle points, which are convex up in some dimensions and concave down in others. When you are at a saddle, there is always a direction to go downhill.

One particularly clever regularization technique, called "dropout," was invented by Geoffrey Hinton.[15] On every learning epoch, when the gradient is estimated from a number of training examples and a step is made in weight space, half the units are randomly cut out from the network—which means that a different network is trained on every epoch. As a consequence, there are fewer parameters to train on each epoch, and the resulting network has fewer dependencies between units than would be the case if the same large network were trained on every epoch. Dropout decreases the error rate in deep learning networks by 10 percent, which is a large improvement. In 2009, Netflix conducted an open competition, offering a prize of $1 million to the first person who could reduce the error of their recommender system by 10 percent.[16] Almost every graduate student in machine learning entered the competition. Netflix probably inspired $10 million of research for the cost of the prize. And deep networks are now a core technology for online streaming.[17]

Intriguingly, cortical synapses drop out at a high rate. On every spike along an input, the typical excitatory synapse in the cortex has a 90 percent failure rate.[18] This is like a baseball team where almost all the players are batting .100. How can the brain function reliably with such unreliable cortical synapses? When there are thousands of probabilistic synapses on a neuron, the variability of their summed activity is relatively low,[19] which means performance may not be degraded as much as you might imagine. The benefit for learning with dropout at the level of synapses may outweigh the cost in reduced accuracy. And since synapses take a lot of energy to operate, dropout also saves energy. Finally, because the cortex uses probabilities to compute likely—not certain—outcomes, using probabilistic components is an efficient way to represent a probability.

However unreliable they may be, cortical synapses are surprisingly precise in their strength. The sizes of cortical synapses and their corresponding strengths vary over a factor of 100, and the strengths of single synapses can be increased or decreased within this range. Working with Kristen Harris, a neuroanatomist at the University of Texas at Austin, my lab recently reconstructed a small piece of the rat hippocampus, a brain area needed for forming long-term memories, which contained 450 synapses. Most axon formed a single synapse on a dendritic branch, but in a handful of cases, two synapses from a single axon contacted the same dendrite. To our surprise, these were nearly identical in size; from previous studies, we knew this meant they had the same strength. Much is known about the conditions that lead to changes in the strengths of these synapses, which depend on the history of input spikes and the corresponding electrical activity of the dendrite, which was the same for the pair of synapses from the same axon on the same dendrite. From these observations, we inferred that the precision with which information is stored in the strengths of synapses is high, enough to store at least five bits of information.[20] That learning algorithms for deep recurrent networks need only five bits to achieve high levels of performance may not be a coincidence.[21]

The dimensionality of networks in the brain is so high that we do not even have a good estimate of how high. The total number of synapses in the cerebral cortex is around a hundred trillion, an astronomically high upper bound. A human lifetime is no more than a few billions seconds long. At that rate, you could afford to dedicate a hundred thousand synapses to each second of your life. In practice, neurons tend to have clustered local connections, such as those within a cortical column of one hundred thousand neurons connected by a billion synapses. Although this is still a large number, it is not an astronomical one. Long-range connections are much less common than local connections because neural wires take up precious volume and consume a lot of energy.

The number of neurons that represent an object or concept in the cortex is an important number to pin down. A rough estimate for the number of synapses needed is about a billion, and the number of neurons needed is about one hundred thousand, distributed in ten cortical areas,[22] allowing some 100,000 separate, noninterfering classes of objects and concepts to be stored in 100 trillion synapses. In practice, the populations of neurons representing similar objects are overlapping, which can greatly increase the capacity of the cortex to represent related objects and relationships between objects. This capacity is much greater in humans than in other mammals because of the extraordinary expansion of the associative cortex (at the top of the sensory and motor hierarchies) in the human brain over the course of evolution.

The study of probability distributions in high-dimensional spaces was a relatively unexplored area of statistics in the 1980s. There were a few statisticians who studied the statistical issues that arise when navigating high-dimensional spaces and high-dimensional data sets, like Leo Breiman from Stanford, who found a home in the Neural Information Processing Systems (NIPS) community. And some from that community, like Michael Jordan at UC, Berkeley, were recruited to statistics departments. But, for the most part, machine learning in the era of big data has trod where statisticians feared to go. But it is not enough that we can train large networks to do amazing things; we also need to analyze and understand how they do these things. Physicists have taken the lead on this front, using methods from statistical physics to analyze the properties of learning as the number of neurons and synapses becomes ever larger.

At the 2017 NIPS Conference in Long Beach, the Test of Time award was given to Benjamin Recht at UC Berkeley and Ali Rahimi at Google for their 2007 NIPS paper,[23] which showed that random features can be an effective way to improve the performance of networks with one layer of learned weights, something that Frank Rosenblatt knew empirically for the perceptron in 1960. The presentation after the award given by Rahimi was an impassioned defense of rigor in machine learning, and he lamented the lack of rigor in deep learning, which he derisively referred to as "alchemy." I was sitting next to Yann LeCun, who was fuming. In a blog after the talk Yann wrote: "Criticizing an entire community (and an incredibly successful one at that) for practicing 'alchemy,' simply because our current theoretical tools haven't caught up with our practice is dangerous. Why dangerous? It's exactly this kind of attitude that lead the ML community to abandon neural nets for over 10 years, *despite* ample empirical evidence that they worked very well in many situations."[24] This is a classic scrimmage between the scruffy and neat approaches to science. Both are needed to make progress.

Limitations of Neural Networks

Although they may give the right answer to a problem, currently, there is no way to explain how neural networks arrive at that answer. For example, suppose that a female patient presents in an emergency room with a sharp pain in her chest. Is this a myocardial infarction, in which case immediate intervention is needed, or simply a bad case of indigestion? A network trained to make a diagnosis might be more accurate than the admitting doctor, but without an explanation for how the network made the decision, we would be justifiably reluctant to trust it. Doctors also are trained to follow what amounts to algorithms, series of tests and decision points that guide them through routine cases. The problem is that there are rare cases that fall outside the scope of their "algorithms," whereas a neural network trained on many more cases, far more than the average doctor will ever see in a lifetime, might well catch those rare cases. But would you trust the statistically stronger diagnosis of a neural network with no explanation over a doctor's diagnosis with a plausible one? In fact, those doctors who are highly accurate in making a rare diagnosis have had broad experience, and most use pattern recognition rather than algorithms.[25] This is probably so for the highest-level experts in all fields.

Just as it is possible to train networks to give expert diagnosis, would it be possible to train networks to give explanations by making them part of their training sets? This might even improve the diagnosis. The reason this is problematic is that many of the explanations doctors give are incomplete, oversimplified, or wrong. Medical practice changes dramatically from one generation to the next because the complexity of the body greatly exceeds our current understanding. If we could analyze the internal states of network models to extract causal explanations, this could lead to new insights and hypotheses that could be tested to advance medicine.

The objection that a neural network is a black box whose conclusions cannot be understood can also be made of brains, and, indeed, there is great variability in the decisions made by individuals given the same data. We really don't know yet how brains draw inferences from experience. As shown in chapter 3, conclusions are not always based on logic, and there are cognitive biases.[26] Moreover, the explanations we accept are often nothing more than rationalizations or plausible stories. We cannot exclude the possibility that some very large generative network will someday start talking, and we can ask it for explanations. Should we expect better stories and rationalizations from such a network than those we receive from humans? Recall that consciousness does not have access to the inner workings of brains. Deep learning networks typically provide not one but several leading predictions in rank order, which gives us some information about the confidence of a conclusion. Supervised neural networks can only solve problems that fall within the range of data that were used to train the network. If it has been trained on similar cases or examples, a neural network should do a fine job at interpolating to novel cases. But if a novel input is outside the range of training data, extrapolation is perilous. This should come as no surprise since the same limitation applies to humans; an expert in physics should not be expected to give good advice on political issues, or even in an area of physics outside the expert's expertise. But, as long as the data set is big enough to encompass the full range of potential inputs, a network's generalization to new inputs should be good. In practice, humans tend to use analogies to extrapolate from an understood domain to a new domain, but these can turn out to be false analogies if the two domains are fundamentally different.

All neural networks that classify inputs are biased. First, the choice of classification categories introduces a bias that reflects human bias in how we chop up the world. For example, it would be useful to train a network to detect weeds in lawns. But what is weed? One man's weed is another man's wildflower. Classification is a much broader problem that reflects cultural biases. This ambiguity is compounded by the data sets that are used to train the network. For example, several companies provide law enforcement agencies with systems that identify criminals based on facial recognition. There are more false positives among the black faces than white faces because the databases used to train the networks have many more white faces, and the more data you have the more accurate you can be.[27] Database biases can be corrected by rebalancing the data, but there are inevitably hidden biases depending on where the data are obtained and what they are used to decide.[28]

Another objection to reliance on neural networks is that they may optimize profits at the expense of fairness. For example, suppose that an underrepresented minority applies for a home mortgage and is denied the loan by a neural network that has been trained on millions of applications. Inputs to the network include current address and other information that are highly correlated with being a minority. So even though there is a law against explicitly discriminating against minorities, the network may be using this information to implicitly discriminate against them. The problem here is not with the neural network, but with the cost function we gave it to optimize. If profit is the only goal, the network will use whatever information it is given to maximize profit. The solution to this problem is to incorporate fairness as another term in the cost function. Although the optimal solution would be a judicious balance between profit and fairness, the trade-off must be made explicit in the cost function, which requires that someone decide how to weight each goal. The ethical perspective of those in the humanities and social sciences should inform these trade-offs. But we must always keep in mind that choosing a cost function that seems fair may have unintended consequences.[29]

Calls to regulate the use of AI have come from Elon Musk and Stephen Hawking as well as legislators and researchers. An open letter signed by 3,722 AI and robotics researchers in 2015 called for a ban on autonomous weapons:

> In summary, we believe that AI has great potential to benefit humanity in many ways, and that the goal of the field should be to do so. Starting a military AI arms race is a bad idea, and should be prevented by a ban on offensive autonomous weapons beyond meaningful human control.[30]

This call for a ban was well meaning but could boomerang. Not all nations may buy into the ban. Russian President Vladimir Putin is on record:

> Artificial intelligence is the future, not only for Russia, but for all humankind. It comes with colossal opportunities, but also threats that are difficult to predict. Whoever becomes the leader in this sphere will become the ruler of the world.[31]

The problem with wholesale bans is that AI is not a monolithic field, but one that has many diverse tools and applications, each of which has its own consequences. For example, the automation of credit scoring was an early application of machine learning in the 1980s. There were concerns that individuals would be unfairly scored if they happened to live in the wrong zip code. This led to legislation to put limits on what information was used to compute the scores and companies were required to inform an individual on ways to improve their score. Each application will have a different set of issues that are best handled on a case-by-case basis rather than a blanket ban on research.[32]

Passages

While on sabbatical at Caltech in 1987 as the Cornelis Wiersma Visiting Professor of Neurobiology, I visited Francis Crick at the Salk Institute. Francis was building a research group that was especially strong in vision, one of my special interests. I played my NETtalk demo tape at a faculty lunch, which opened up a lively discussion. My move to La Jolla in 1989 marked an exciting transition from junior faculty at Johns Hopkins to senior faculty at the Salk Institute, and almost overnight many opportunities opened up, including an appointment with the Howard Hughes Medical Institute, which provided generous support for my research for twenty-six years.

When I moved to UC, San Diego, in 1989, I was sorry that David Rumelhart, who taught us how to backpropagate, had already left for Stanford, and I only saw him sporadically after that. Over the years, I noticed that David's behavior changed in ways that were disturbing. Eventually, he was diagnosed with frontotemporal dementia, a progressive loss of neurons in the frontal cortex that affects personality, behavior, and language. Rumelhart died in 2011 at age 68, no longer able to recognize family or friends.

9 Convolutional Learning

By 2000, the neural network fever from the 1980s had broken, and neural networks became normal science again. Thomas Kuhn once characterized the time between scientific revolutions as the normal work of scientists theorizing, observing, and experimenting within a settled paradigm or explanatory framework.[1] Geoffrey Hinton moved to the University of Toronto in 1987 and continued with a steady stream of incremental improvements, although none of them had the magic that the Boltzmann machine once held for us. Hinton became the leader of the Neural Computation and Adaptive Perception (NCAP) Program at the Canadian Institute for Advanced Research (CIFAR) in the first decade of the new century, which consisted of around twenty-five researchers from Canada and other countries who were focused on solving difficult problems with machine learning. I was a member of the NCAP Advisory Board, chaired by Yann LeCun, and attended the program's annual meetings just before the NIPS conferences. Making slow but steady progress, the neural network pioneers explored many new strategies for machine learning. Although their networks had many useful applications, the high expectations for the field in the 1980s had not been fulfilled. This did not deter the pioneers from keeping the faith, however. In retrospect, they were setting the stage for a dramatic breakthrough.

Steady Progress in Machine Learning

The NIPS conferences were the incubator for neural networks in the 1980s and opened the door for other algorithms that could handle large, high-dimensional data sets. Vladimir Vapnik's Support Vector Machine (SVM) burst on the scene in 1995 to open up a new chapter in perceptron networks, left for dead in the 1960s. What made the SVM a powerful classifier, now in every networker's toolkit, was the "kernel trick," a mathematical transformation that is the equivalent of jumping from data space to hyperspace, where the data points are remapped to make them easier to separate. Tomaso Poggio had developed a hierarchical network called "HMAX" that could classify a limited number of objects.[2] This suggested that performance would improve with deeper networks.

In the first years of the new century, graphical models were developed that made contact with a rich vein of probabilistic models called "Bayes networks," based on a theorem formulated by the eighteenth-century British mathematician Thomas Bayes that allows new evidence to update prior beliefs. Judea Pearl at the University of California, Los Angeles, had earlier introduced "belief networks"[3] to artificial intelligence based on Bayesian analysis, which were strengthened and extended by developing methods for learning the probabilities in the networks from data. The algorithms of these and other networks built up a powerful armamentarium for machine learning researchers.

As the processing capability of computers continued to rise exponentially, it became possible to train ever larger networks. It was generally thought that wider neural networks with a greater number of hidden units were more effective than deeper networks with a greater number of layers, but this was shown not to be the case for networks trained layer by layer,[4] and the vanishing error gradient problem was identified, which slowed down learning near the input layer.[5] When this problem was eventually overcome, however, it became possible to train deep backprop networks that performed favorably on benchmarks.[6] And, as deep backprop networks began to challenge traditional approaches in computer vision, the word at the 2012 NIPS Conference was that the "Neural" was back in "Neural Information Processing Systems."

In computer vision, steady progress in recognizing objects in images over the last decade of the previous century and the first decade of the current one had improved performance on benchmarks (used to compare different methods) by a fraction of a percent per year. Methods improved slowly because each new category of objects requires a domain expert to identify the pose-invariant features needed to distinguish them from other objects. Then, in 2012, Geoffrey Hinton and two students, Alex Krizhevsky and Ilya Sutskever, submitted a paper to the NIPS conference on object recognition in images that used deep learning to train AlexNet, a deep convolutional network that will be the focus of this chapter.[7] Using the ImageNet database of more than 15 million labeled high-resolution images in more than 22,000 categories as benchmark, AlexNet achieved an unprecedented reduction in the error rate of 18 percent.[8] This leap forward in performance sent a shock wave through the computer vision community, setting development of ever larger networks on a course of accelerated progress that is now reaching human levels of performance. By 2015, the error rate on the ImageNet database had fallen to 3.6 percent.[9] The deep learning network that Kaiming He and colleagues used to achieve this low rate in many ways resembles the visual cortex; it was introduced by Yann LeCun, who originally called it "Le Net."

A student in France when Geoffrey Hinton and I first met him in the 1980s, Yann LeCun (figure 9.1, right) was inspired by HAL 9000, the mission computer in the epic 1968 science fiction film *2001: A Space Odyssey*, to pursue artificial intelligence when he was nine years old. He had independently discovered a version of backpropagation for his doctoral dissertation in 1987,[10] after which he moved to Toronto, to work with Geoffrey. He later moved to AT&T Bell Laboratories in Holmdel, New Jersey, where he trained a network that could read handwritten zip codes on letters, using the Modified National Institute of Standards and Technology (MNIST)

Figure 9.1
Geoffrey Hinton and Yann LeCun have mastered deep learning. This photo was taken at a meeting of the Neural Computation and Adaptive Perception Program of the Canadian Institute for Advanced Research around 2000, a program that was an incubator for what became the field of deep learning. Courtesy of Geoffrey Hinton.

database, a labeled data benchmark. Millions of letters each day have to be routed to mailboxes; today this is fully automated. The same technology also made it possible to read automatically the amount on your bank check at ATM machines. Interestingly, the hardest part is locating where on the check the numbers are written since each check has a different format. It was already apparent back in the 1980s that Yann had an extraordinary talent for taking proofs of principle (something academics are good at) and making them work in the real world. This requires the products to be battle tested and robust.

Convolutional Neural Networks

When Yann LeCun moved to New York University in 2003, he continued to evolve his vision network, which is now known as the "ConvNet" (figure 9.2). The fundamental building block of the network is based on convolution, which can be thought of as a small sliding filter that is passed over the image, creating a layer of features across the image. For example, the filter could be an oriented edge detector such as those introduced in chapter 5, which has a large output only when the window is over an edge of an object in an image in the correct orientation or texture with that orientation within an object. Although the window on the first layer is only a small patch of the image, since there can be many filters, many features can be represented in every patch. The filters in the first layer that is convolved with the image are similar to what David Hubel and Torsten Wiesel called "simple cells" in the primary visual cortex (figure 9.3).[11] The filters in higher layers respond to even more complex features.[12]

In early versions of ConvNet, the output of each filter was passed through a nonlinearity, called a "sigmoid function," that smoothly increased from 0 to 1, suppressing the output of weakly activated units (see the sigmoid function in box 7.2). The window in the second layer that received inputs from the first layer covered a larger region of the visual field, so that after several more layers, there were units that received inputs from the entire image. This top layer was analogous to the top of the visual hierarchy, which in primates is called the "inferotemporal cortex" and has receptive fields that cover most of the visual field. The top layer was then fed into a classification layer, connected all-to-all, which was used to train the entire network to classify an object in the image using backprop.

Many incremental improvements were made to ConvNet over the years. An important addition was to aggregate each feature over a region, called "pooling." This provides a measure of translation invariance and is similar

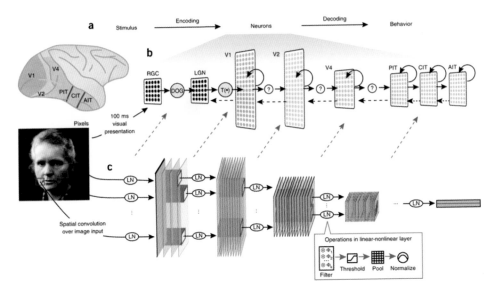

Figure 9.2

Visual cortex compared with a convolutional network for object recognition in images. (Top) (a, b) Hierarchy of layers in the visual cortex starting with inputs to primary visual cortex (V1) from the retina and thalamus (RGC, LGN) to the inferior temporal cortex (PIT, CIT, AIT) showing a correspondence between cortical areas and the layers of convolutional network. (Bottom) (c) Inputs from the image on the left project to the first convolutional layer, which consists of several feature planes, each representing a filter like the oriented simple cells found in the visual cortex. The filters are thresholded and pooled across the first layer and normalized to produce invariant responses across the patch similar to the complex cells in the visual cortex (box: Operations in linear-nonlinear layer). This operation is repeated on each convolutional layer of the network. The output layer has all-to-all connectivity with inputs from last convolutional layer. From Yamins and DiCarlo, "Using Goal-Driven Deep Learning Models to Understand Sensory Cortex," figure 1.

to the complex cells discovered by Hubel and Wiesel in the primary visual cortex, which respond to lines with the same orientation throughout a patch of the visual field. Another useful operation was gain normalization, which adjusts the amplification of the inputs so that each unit is working within its operating range, something that is implemented in the cortex by feedback inhibition. The sigmoid output function also was replaced by rectified linear units (ReLUs), which have zero output up to a sharp threshold and increase linearly above threshold. This has the advantage that units

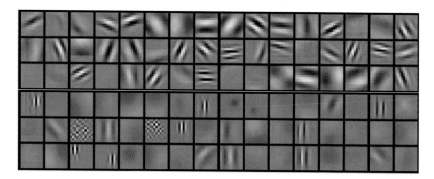

Figure 9.3

Filters from the first layer of a convolutional network. Each filter is localized to a patch in the visual field. The preferred stimuli of the filters in the top three rows are oriented like simple cells in the visual cortex. The preferred stimuli on the second layer shown in the bottom three rows are more extended and have complex shapes. From Krizhevsky, Sutskever, and Hinton, "ImageNet Classification with Deep Convolutional Neural Networks," figure 3.

below threshold are effectively cut out of the network, which is closer to how the threshold of a real neuron works.

Each of the changes to ConvNet had a computational justification that improved the performance of the network in ways that an engineer could understand, but with these changes, it came to resemble more and more closely what we knew about the architecture of the visual cortex in the 1960s, even though at the time we could only guess what the functions of simple and complex cells were, or what the distributed representations at the top of the hierarchy were meant to accomplish. This illustrates the potential for fruitful symbiotic relationships between biology and deep learning.

Deep Learning Meets the Visual Hierarchy

A philosopher of the mind, Patricia Churchland specializes in neurophilosophy at UC, San Diego.[13] That knowledge ultimately depends on how the brain represents knowledge clearly has not stopped philosophers from thinking about knowledge as, in the words of Immanuel Kant, a "Ding an sich" (thing in itself), something independent of the world. But, just as clearly, grounded knowledge is essential if we (among other animals) are to survive in the real world. Motivated by the remarkable similarity in the patterns of activity among the hidden units of a trained multilayer neural network and those recorded from populations of biological neurons recorded one at a time, Patricia and I wrote *The Computational Brain* in 1992 to develop a conceptual framework for neuroscience based on large populations of neurons.[14] (Now in its second edition, our book is a good primer if you want to learn more about brain-style computing.) James DiCarlo at MIT recently compared the responses of neurons at different levels of the visual cortex hierarchy of monkeys trained to recognize images of objects with the responses of units in a deep learning neural network that could recognize the same images (figure 9.2).[15] He concluded that the statistical properties of the neurons in each layer of the deep learning network matched quite closely those of neurons in the cortical hierarchy.

The similarity between the performances of units in a deep learning network and those of neurons in the monkey's visual cortex is a puzzle, especially because the monkey's brain is unlikely to be using backprop for learning. Backprop requires the feedback of detailed error signals to each neuron in each layer of a neural network with much greater precision than that found in known feedback connections of biological neurons. But other learning algorithms are more biologically plausible, such as the Boltzmann machine learning algorithm, which uses Hebbian synaptic plasticity that has been found in the cortex. This raises an interesting question of whether there is a mathematical theory of deep learning that applies to a large class of learning algorithms including those in the cortex. In chapter 7, I alluded to the disentangling of classification surfaces in the upper layers of the visual hierarchy, where the decision surfaces are flatter than those in lower layers. A geometric analysis of the decision surface may lead to a deeper mathematical understanding of both deep learning networks and the brain.

One of the advantages of a deep learning neural network is that we can "record" from every unit in the network and follow the flow of information as it is transformed from layer to layer. Strategies for the analysis of such a network could then be applied to analyzing neurons in the brain. One of the wonderful things about a technology that works is that there usually is both a good explanation behind the technology and a strong incentive to figure that explanation out. The first steam engines were built by engineers following their intuitions; the theory of thermodynamics that explained how the engines worked came later, along with improvements in their efficiency. The analysis of deep learning networks by physicists and mathematicians is well under way.

Working Memory and Persistence of Activity

Neuroscience has come a long way since the 1960s, and much can be gained from our current knowledge of the brain. In 1990, Patricia Goldman-Rakic taught a monkey to remember a location that was briefly cued with a light and to make an eye movement to the remembered location after a delay period.[16] Recording from the monkey prefrontal cortex, she reported that some neurons that initially responded to the cue maintained their activity during the delay period. Psychologists call this "working memory" in humans, which is how we can keep 7 ± 2 items in mind while we are in the middle of performing a task, like dialing a phone number.

The traditional feedforward network propagates inputs up the network, one layer at a time. Incorporating working memory would make it possible for a later input to interact with the trace left behind from a previous input to the network. For example, when translating a French sentence into English, the first French word into the network influences the order of subsequent English words. The simplest way to implement working memory in a network is to add recurrent connections, which are common in the human cortex. Recurrent connections in neural networks within a layer and feedback connections to previous layers allow temporal sequences of inputs to be temporally integrated. Such networks were explored in the 1980s and are used extensively in speech recognition.[17] In practice, this works well for short-range dependencies, but poorly when the gap between inputs is large since the influence of an input tends to decay with time.

In 1997, Sepp Hochreiter and Jürgen Schmidhuber found a way to overcome the decay problem, which they called "long short-term memory" (LSTM).[18] LSTM passes the activity into the future without decay as a default, which is what happens during the delay period in the monkey prefrontal cortex, and it also has a complex scheme for deciding how to integrate the new incoming information with the old information. As a consequence, long-range dependencies are preserved selectively. This version of working memory in neural networks lay dormant for twenty years until it was awakened and implemented in deep learning networks, where it has been spectacularly successful in many domains that depend on learning sequences of inputs and outputs, such as movies, music, movements, and language.

Schmidhuber is a codirector of the Dalle Molle Institute for Artificial Intelligence Research in Manno, a tiny town located in the Ticino district of southern Switzerland, near some of the best hikes in the Alps.[19] This creative and idiosyncratic Rodney Dangerfield of neural networks is convinced he doesn't get enough credit for his creativity. Thus, at a panel discussion at the 2015 NIPS Conference in Montreal, he introduced himself from the audience as "You again, Schmidhuber," and, at the 2016 NIPS Conference in Barcelona, he harassed a tutorial speaker for five minutes for not paying enough attention to his ideas.

In 2015, Kelvin Xu and colleagues coupled a deep learning network for identifying objects in images with a long short-term memory recurrent network to caption pictures. Using a first pass from a deep learning network that identified all the objects in the scene as input, they trained the recurrent LSTM network to output a string of English words that described the scene in a caption (figure 9.4). And they also trained the LSTM network to identify the location in the image corresponding to each word in the caption.[20] What makes this application impressive is that the long short-term memory network was never trained to understand the meaning of the sentence in the caption, only to output a syntactically correct string of words based on the objects and their locations in the image. Together with the earlier NETtalk example in chapter 8, this is more evidence that neural networks seem to have an affinity for language for reasons we do not yet understand. Perhaps a new theory of language will emerge from analyzing LSTM networks that will illuminate both how the networks work and the nature of natural language.

Generative Adversarial Networks

In chapter 7, the Boltzmann machine was presented as a generative model that can produce new input samples when the output is clamped to a category that it has been trained to recognize and the activity patterns percolate down to the input layer. Ian Goodfellow, Yoshua Bengio and their colleagues at the University of Montreal showed that it was possible to train feedforward networks to generate even better samples in an adversarial context.[21] A generative convolutional network can be trained to produce good image samples by trying to fool another convolutional network that has to decide whether an input is a real image or a fake one. The output of the generative network is given as input to a discriminative convolutional network that is trained to give a single output: 1 if the input is a real image, and 0 if it is a fake image. These two networks compete against each other. The generative network tries to increase the error

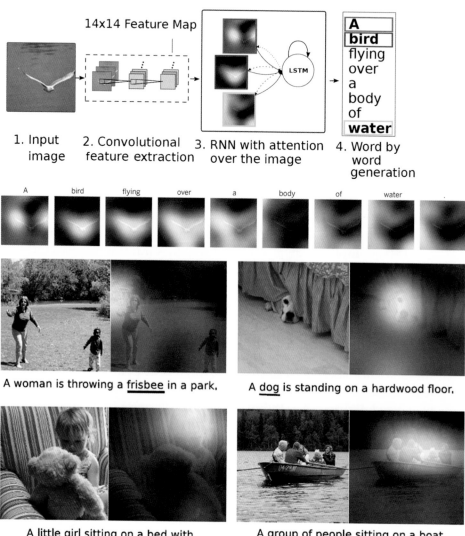

Figure 9.4

Picture captioning with deep learning. The upper panel illustrates the procedure that analyzes the photo. The ConvNet (CNN) in the first step labels the objects in the photo and passes this on to the recurrent neural network (RNN). The RNN was trained to output an appropriate string of English words. The bottom four panels illustrate a further refinement that uses attention (white cloud) to indicate the referent of the word in the photo. Top: From M. I. Jordan and T. M. Mitchell, "Machine Learning: Trends, Perspectives, and Prospects," *Science* 349, no. 6245 (2015): 255–260, figure 2. Courtesy of Tom Mitchell. Bottom: From Xu et al., "Show, Attend and Tell," 2015, rev. 2016, figures 1 and 3, https://arxiv.org/pdf/1502.03044.pdf. Courtesy of Kelvin Xu.

rate of the discriminative network, which is trying to reduce its error rate. The tension between these two goals produces astonishing photorealistic images (figure 9.5).[22]

Keep in mind that these generated images are synthetic and the objects in them never existed. They are generalized versions of the unlabeled images in the training set. Note that generative adversarial networks are unsupervised, which makes it possible for them to use unlimited data. There are many other applications for these networks ranging from cleaning up noise in astronomical images of galaxies with superresolution[23] to learning representations of emotional speech.[24]

By slowly changing the input vector of the generative network, it is possible to gradually shift the image, so that parts and pieces, like windows, gradually appear or morph into other objects, like cabinets.[25] Even more remarkably, it is possible to add and subtract vectors representing the state of the network to obtain mixtures of objects in the image, as illustrated in figure 9.6. The implication of these experiments is that the representations of images in the generative network represent rooms much the way we would describe the parts of scenes. This technology is advancing rapidly, and its next frontier is to generate realistic movies. By training a recurrent generative adversarial network against movies of an actor like Marilyn Monroe, it should be possible to create new performances of actors no longer alive.

It is fashion week in Milan and models with otherworldly expressions are on the runways with striking struts (figure 9.7). Something is stirring in the fashion world: "'Many jobs are vanishing,' Silvia Venturini Fendi said before her show: 'Androids will take the old jobs, but the only thing that they can't replace is our creativity and our minds.'"[26] Now imagine generative adversarial networks that have been trained to generate new styles and haute couture with almost endless variety. The world of fashion may be on the brink of a new era, along with many other businesses that depend on creativity.

It's All about Scaling

Most of the current learning algorithms were discovered more than twenty-five years ago, so why did it take so long for them to have an impact on the real world? With the computers and labeled data that were available to researchers in the 1980s, it was only possible to demonstrate proof of principle on toy problems. Despite some promising results, we did not know how well network learning and performance would scale as

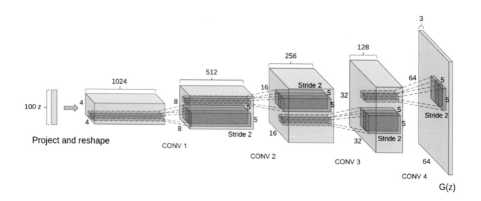

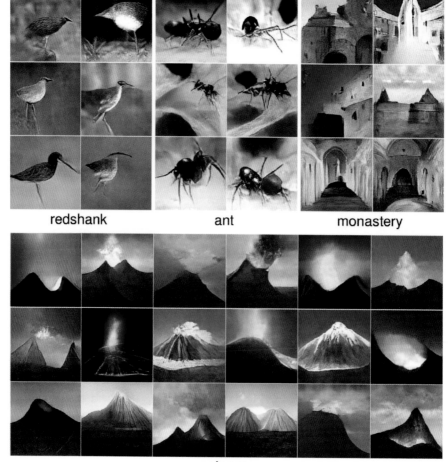

redshank   ant   monastery

volcano

Figure 9.5

Generative adversarial networks (GANs). The top panel illustrates a convolutional network used to generate a sample of images trained to fool the discriminative convolutional network. The input on the left are 100-dimensional continuously valued vectors that are chosen randomly to generate different images; the input vector then activates layers of filters with a larger and larger spatial scale. The lower panels display sample images produced by training a GAN on photos from single categories. Top: From A. Radford, L. Metz, and S. Chintala, "Unsupervised Representation Learning with Deep Convolutional Generative Adversarial Networks," figure 1, arXiv:1511.06434, https://arxiv.org/pdf/1511.06434.pdf. Courtesy of Soumith Chintala. Bottom: From A. Nguyen, J. Yosinski, Y. Bengio, A. Dosovitskiy, and J. Clune, "Plug & Play Generative Networks: Conditional Iterative Generation of Images in Latent Space," figure 1, https://arxiv.org/pdf/1612.00005.pdf. Courtesy of Ahn Nguyen.

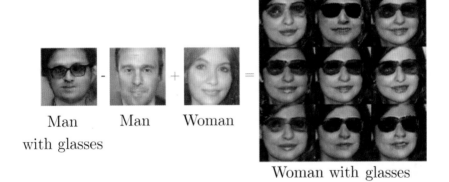

Man   Man   Woman

with glasses

Woman with glasses

Figure 9.6

Vector arithmetic in generative adversarial networks. Mixtures of inputs to a generative network trained on faces produced the outputs on the left, which were then used to create the blends on the right by adding and subtracting the chosen input vectors. Because the blends are done at the highest representational level, parts and poses are seamlessly combined, rather than averaged as occurs in morphing. Adapted from A. Radford, L. Metz, and S. Chintala, "Unsupervised Representation Learning with Deep Convolutional Generative Adversarial Networks," figure 7, arXiv:1511.06434, https://arxiv.org/pdf/1511.06434/.

Figure 9.7
Spring/summer 2018 men's wear show for Giorgio Armani, in Milan.

the number of units and connections increased to match the complexity of real-world problems. Most algorithms in AI scale badly and never went beyond solving toy problems. We now know that neural network learning scales well and that performance continues to increase with the size of the network and the number of layers. Backprop, in particular, scales extremely well.

Should we be surprised? The cerebral cortex is a mammalian invention that mushroomed in primates and especially in humans. And as it expanded, more capacity became available and more layers were added in association areas for higher-order representations. There are few complex systems that scale this well. The Internet is one of the few engineered systems whose size has also been scaled up by a million times. The Internet evolved once the protocols were established for communicating packets, much like the genetic code for DNA made it possible for cells to evolve.

Training many deep learning networks with the same set of data results in a large number of different networks that have roughly the same average level of performance. What we would like to know is what all these equally good networks have in common, but analyzing a single network will not reveal this. Another approach to understanding the principles behind deep learning is to further explore the space of learning algorithms; we have only sampled a few locations in the space of all learning algorithms. What could emerge from a much broader exploration is a computational theory of learning as profound as theories in other areas of science,[27] one that could shed much welcome light on the learning algorithms discovered by nature.

Yoshua Bengio[28] (figure 9.8) at the University of Montreal and Yann LeCun succeeded Geoffrey Hinton as the directors of CIFAR's Neural Computation and Adaptive Perception (NCAP) Program when it passed its ten-year review and was renamed "Learning in Machines and Brains." Yoshua led a team at the University of Montreal that applied deep learning to natural language, which will be a new focus for the Learning in Machines and Brains program. In meetings over ten years, this small group of around two dozen faculty and fellows gave birth to deep learning. The substantial progress in the last five years in the application of deep learning to many problems that had previously been intractable can be traced to them, but of course they are a small part of a much larger community (one that will be explored in chapter 11).

Even though deep learning networks have proven themselves in many applications, they would never survive on their own in the real world.[29]

Figure 9.8
Yoshua Bengio is the codirector of the CIFAR Learning in Machines and Brains Program. A French-born Canadian computer scientist, Yoshua has been a leader in applying deep learning to problems in natural language. Advances made by Geoffrey Hinton, Yann LeCun, and Yoshua Bengio were seminal for the successes of deep learning. Courtesy of Yoshua Bengio.

They are coddled by researchers who feed them data, who tweak their hyperparameters like learning rate, number of layers, and number of units in each layer to improve convergence, and who provide them with vast computing resources. On the other hand, neither would the cerebral cortex survive in the real world without the rest of the brain and body to provide support and autonomy, which, in an uncertain world, is a much more difficult problem than pattern recognition. Chapter 10 will introduce an ancient learning algorithm that that helped us survive in nature by motivating us to seek rewarding experiences.

According to a story going back to the Middle Ages, the inventor of the game of chess was offered a field of wheat from a grateful ruler. The inventor instead requested one grain of wheat on the first square, two on the second, four on the third, and so on, doubling the number of grains on each successive square until all sixty-four squares of the chess board were covered with grains of wheat. Thinking this a modest request, the ruler readily agreed. In reality, however, to grant that request, he would have had to have given the inventor not just all the wheat in his kingdom, but all the wheat in the entire world for many centuries to come since the number of wheat grains on the sixty-fourth square would have been 2^{64} (roughly 10^{19}).[1] This is called "exponential growth." The number of board positions in games like chess and Go grows even faster than the number of wheat grains in our story. At every move, there are on average thirty-five possible moves in a chess game, and, for Go, the branching factor is 250. This makes the exponential growth much more rapid.

Learning How to Play Backgammon

Games have the advantage that the rules are well defined, the players have perfect knowledge of the board and the decisions not as complex as those in the real world, but sufficiently complex to be challenging. In 1959, Arthur Samuel, a machine learning pioneer at IBM in the early days of commercial digital computers, wrote a program that could play checkers so successfully that on the day it was announced, IBM's stock scored a major gain. Checkers is a relatively easy game, but Samuel's program, based on a cost function to assess the strengths of different game positions, much like previous game programs, and run on IBM's first commercial computer, the IBM 701, which used vacuum tubes, was impressive in one novel respect: it learned by playing itself.

Before moving on to IBM's Thomas J. Watson Research Center in York-town Heights, New York, Gerald Tesauro worked with me when he was at the Center for Complex Systems Research at the University of Illinois in Urbana-Champaign on the problem of teaching a neural network to play backgammon (figure 10.1).[2] Our approach used expert supervision to train networks with backprop to evaluate game positions and possible moves. The flaw in this approach was that the program could never get better than our experts, who were not at world-championship level. But, with self-play, it might be possible to do better. The problem with self-play at that time was that the only learning signal was win or lose at the end of the game. But when one side won, which of the many moves were responsible? This is called the "temporal credit assignment problem."

A learning algorithm that can solve this temporal credit assignment problem was invented in 1988 by Richard Sutton,[3] who had been work-ing closely with Andrew Barto, his doctoral advisor, at the University of Massachusetts at Amherst, on difficult problems in reinforcement learn-ing, a branch of machine learning inspired by associative learning in ani-mal experiments (figure 10.2). Unlike a deep learning network, whose only job is to transform inputs into outputs, a reinforcement network interacts in a closed loop with the environment, receiving sensory input, making

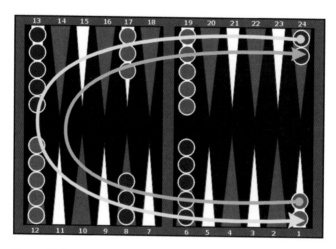

Figure 10.1
Backgammon board. Backgammon is a race to the finish, with the red pieces moving in the opposite direction of the black pieces (arrows). The starting position is shown. Two dice are rolled, and the two numbers indicate how far two pieces can be moved ahead.

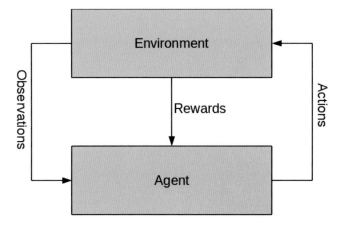

Figure 10.2
Reinforcement learning scenario. The agent actively explores the environment by taking actions and making observations. If an action is successful, the agent receives a reward. The goal is to learn actions that maximize future rewards.

decisions, and taking actions. Reinforcement learning is based on the observation that animals solve difficult problems in uncertain conditions by exploring the various options in the environment and learning from their outcomes. As learning improves, the exploration decreases, eventually leading to pure exploitation of the best strategy found during learning.

Suppose you have to make a series of decisions to reach a goal. If you already know all the possible choices and each of their expected future rewards, you can use a search algorithm—specifically, Richard Bellman's algorithm for dynamic programming[4]—to figure out the set of choices that maximizes future rewards, but, as the number of possible choices grows, the size of the problem grows exponentially, which has been called the "curse of dimensionality," and was illustrated at the beginning of this chapter. But, if you don't have all the information about the outcomes of the choices ahead of time, you have to learn to make the best choices you can as you go along. This is called "online learning."

The online learning algorithm that Richard Sutton (figure 10.3) developed depended on differences between expected and received rewards (box 10.1). In temporal difference learning, you compare your estimated long-range reward for making a move in a current state, with a better estimator based on the actual reward you got, and the estimated long-range reward of the next state. By changing the previous estimate to be more like the improved estimate, the decisions that you make on moves will get better

Figure 10.3
Richard Sutton at the University of Alberta in Edmonton in 2006. He taught us how to learn the route to future rewards. Rich is a cancer survivor who has remained a leader in reinforcement learning and continues to develop innovative algorithms. He is generous with his time and insights, which everyone in the field greatly values. His book with Andrew Barto, *Reinforcement Learning: An Introduction*, is a classic in the field. The second edition is freely available on the Internet. Courtesy of Richard Sutton.

and better. The update is made to a value network that estimates the future expected reward for each board position and is used to decide on the next move. The temporal difference algorithm converges to the optimal rule for making decisions in a given state after you have had enough time to explore the possibilities. The curse of dimensionality is avoided because only a small fraction of all possible board positions are actually visited, but this is enough to develop good strategies for similar board positions that are likely to arise in new games.

Gerry Tesauro's program, called "TD-Gammon," had important features of the backgammon board and rules built into it, but it had no knowledge of what was a good move to make. At the beginning of the learning, the moves were random, but eventually one side won and got the final reward.

Box 10.1

Temporal Difference Learning

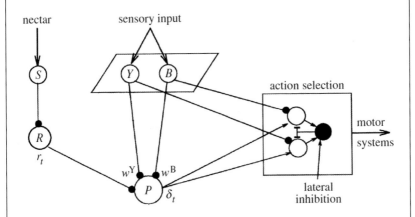

In this model of the honeybee brain, actions are chosen (such as landing on a flower) that maximize all future discounted rewards:

$$R(t) = r_{t+1} + \gamma r_{t+2} + \gamma^2 r_{t+3} + \ldots,$$

where r_{t+1} is the reward at time $t+1$ and $0 < \gamma < 1$ is a discount factor. The predicted future reward based on current sensory inputs $s(t)$ is computed by neuron P:

$$P_t(s) = w^y s^y + w^b s^b,$$

where the sensory input from yellow (Y) and blue (B) flowers are weighted by w^y and w^b. The reward prediction error $\delta(t)$ at time t is given by

$$\delta_t = r_t + \gamma P_t(s_t) - P_t(s_{t-1}),$$

where r_t is the current reward. The change in each weight is given by:

$$\delta w_t = \alpha\, \delta_t\, s_{t-1},$$

where α is the learning rate. If the current reward is greater than the predicted reward, and δ_t is positive, the weight is increased on the sensory input that was present before the reward, but if the current reward is less than expected, and δ_t is negative, the weight is decreased.

Adapted from Montague, P. R. and Sejnowski, T. J., *The Predictive Brain: Temporal Coincidence and Temporal Order in Synaptic Learning Mechanisms*, figure 6A.

The winner in backgammon is the first player to "bear off" all of the pieces from the game board.

Since the only actual reward occurs at the end of a game, you might reasonably expect that TD-Gammon would first learn the endgame, then the middle game, and finally the openings. This is in fact what happens in "tabular reinforcement learning," or "tabular RL," where there is a table of values for every state in the state space. But it's completely different with neural networks—they latch quickly onto simple and reliable signals in the input features, and more complex and unreliable input signals later. The first concept that TD-Gammon learns is "Bear off pieces," by attaching positive weight to the input feature that represents number of pieces borne off. The second concept is "Hit the opponent pieces"— a fairly good heuristic in all phases, learned by putting positive weight on the input unit encoding number of opponent pieces that were hit. The third concept, "Avoid being hit" is a natural reaction to the second concept, and is learned by putting negative weight on single pieces that can be hit. The fourth concept is "Build new points" to block the opponent's progress, learned by putting positive weights on made-point inputs. Getting these basic concepts requires a few thousand training games. By 10,000 games, TD-Gammon is learning intermediate concepts; by 100,000 games, it starts to learn advanced concepts, and by one million games, it has learned concepts that were either world class, or beyond the knowledge of humans in the early 1990s.

TD-Gammon surprised me and many others when Gerry Tesauro revealed it to the world in 1992.[5] The value function was a backprop network with eighty hidden units. After three hundred thousand games, the program was beating Gerry, so he contacted a famous world-champion backgammon player and author, Bill Robertie, and invited him to visit IBM at Yorktown Heights to play TD-Gammon. Robertie won most of the games but was surprised to lose several well-played ones and declared it the best backgammon program he had ever played. Some of TD-Gammon's unusual moves he had never seen before; on closer examination, these proved to be improvements on human play overall. Robertie returned when the program had reached 1.5 million self-played games and was astonished when TD-Gammon played him to a draw. It had gotten so much better that he felt it had achieved human-championship level. One backgammon expert, Kit Woolsey, found that TD-Gammon's positional judgment on whether to play "safe" (low risk/reward) or play "bold" (high risk/reward) was at that time better than that of any human he had seen. Although 1.5 million may seem like a lot of training games, it represented only an infinitesimal fraction of all 10^{20} possible backgammon board positions; this required TD-Gammon to generalize to new board positions on almost every move.

TD-Gammon did not get as much publicity as IBM's Deep Blue, which beat Gary Kasparov at chess in 1997. Chess is much more difficult than backgammon, and Kasparov was the world champion at the time. In some ways, though, TD-Gammon was a more impressive achievement. First, TD-Gammon taught itself how to play, using pattern recognition, a style similar to how humans play, whereas Deep Blue won by brute force, using custom hardware to look more moves into the future than any human could. And, second, TD-Gammon was creative and came up with subtle strategies and positional play never before seen by humans. In doing so, TD-Gammon raised the level of human play. This achievement was a watershed in the history of artificial intelligence because we learned something new from an AI program that taught itself how to master a complex strategy in a well-trodden domain, a strategy that is worthy of human interest and effort.

Reward Learning in Brains

The heart of TD-Gammon is the temporal difference learning algorithm, which was inspired by learning experiments with animals. Nearly all species that have been tested, from bees to humans, can be taught associatively, just like Pavlov's dog. In Pavlov's experiment, a sensory stimulus such as a bell was followed by the presentation of food, which elicited salivation. After several pairings, the bell by itself would lead to salivation. Different species have different preferred unconditioned stimuli in associative learning. Bees are very good at associating the smell, color, and shape of a flower with the reward of nectar and use this learned association to find similar flowers that are in season. Something about this universal form of learning must be important, and there was a period in the 1960s when psychologists intensively studied the conditions that gave rise to associative learning and developed models to explain it. Behaviorists like B. F. Skinner trained pigeons to recognize humans in photos, which calls to mind what can be accomplished with deep learning, but there is a big difference. Backprop learning requires detailed feedback to all the units on the output layer, but associative learning provides only a single reward signal, correct or incorrect. The brain has to figure out what features of the world were responsible for a successful decision.

Only the stimulus that occurs just before the reward gets associated with the reward. This makes sense because a stimulus is more likely to have caused the reward if it comes just before than if it comes just after the reward. Causality is an important principle in nature. The opposite occurs when the conditioned stimulus is followed by punishment, such as a shock to the foot, which teaches an animal to avoid the stimulus. In some cases, the gap between the conditioned stimulus and the punishment can be quite long. In the 1950s, John Garcia showed that if a rat was fed sweetened water and made nauseous hours later, the rat would avoid sweetened water days later. This is called "taste aversion learning," and it also occurs in humans.[6] Sometimes, the nausea will be associated with the wrong ingested food, like chocolate, which unfortunately happened to be consumed at the same time but did not cause the nausea; the resulting aversion can last many years even though there is a conscious awareness that chocolate was not the problem.

Dopamine, a neuromodulator carried by a set of diffusely projecting neurons in the brainstem (figure 10.4), had long been associated with reward learning, but it was not known what exactly they signaled to the cortex. Peter Dayan and Read Montague, postdoctoral fellows in my lab in the 1990s, realized that dopamine neurons could implement temporal difference learning.[7] In one of the most exciting scientific periods of my life, these models and their predictions were published and subsequently

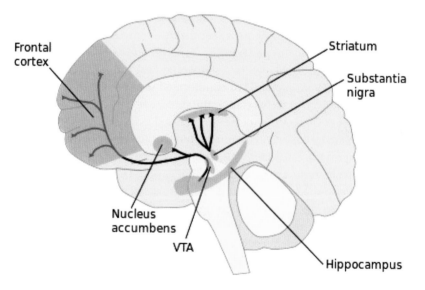

Figure 10.4
Dopamine neurons in the human brain. Several nuclei in the midbrain (VTA and substantia nigra) project axons into the cortex and the basal ganglia (striatum and nucleus accumbens). Transient bursts signify discrepancies between the reward predictions and received reward, which are used to choose actions and modify predictions.

confirmed by Wolfram Schultz and colleagues in monkeys with single-neuron recordings (figure 10.5)[8] and in humans with brain imaging.[9] It is now well established that transient changes in the activity of dopamine neurons signal reward prediction error.

We were making progress on reward prediction error in primates when I visited Randolph Menzel, who was studying fast learning in the bee brain, in Berlin in 1992. Bees are champion learners in the insect world. It only takes a few visits to a rewarding flower for a bee to remember the flower. The bee brain has around a million tiny neurons, and it is very difficult to record from them because they are so tiny. Menzel's group had discovered a unique neuron called "VUMmx1" that responded to sucrose but not to an odor. If delivery of the odor was shortly followed by the sucrose reward, however, VUMmx1 would now also respond to the odor.[10] The dopamine model of temporal difference learning might be implemented by a single neuron in the bee brain. VUMmx1 released octopamine, a neuromodulator closely related chemically to dopamine. This model of bee learning could explain some subtle aspects of bee psychology, such as risk aversion.[11] If a bee is given the choice between a constant reward and twice the reward, but only half the time, bees will stay with the constant reward even though the average is the same.[12] Dopamine neurons are also found in flies and have been shown to comprise several parallel reinforcement learning pathways for both short-term and long-term associative memories.[13]

Motivation and the Basal Ganglia

Dopamine neurons constitute a core system that controls motivation in the brain (figure 10.4). All addictive drugs act by increasing the level of dopamine activity. When enough dopamine neurons die, the symptoms of Parkinson's disease appear, which include motor tremor, difficulty in initiating actions, and, eventually, the complete loss of pleasure in any activity ("anhedonia"), ending in a complete lack of movement and responsiveness ("catatonia"). But normally behaving dopamine cells provide brief bursts of dopamine to the cortex and other brain areas when an unexpected reward occurs and diminished amounts of dopamine when a less than expected reward is experienced. This is precisely the signature of the temporal difference algorithm (figure 10.5).

Our dopamine neurons can be interrogated when we need to make a decision. What should we order from the menu? We imagine each item, and our dopamine cells provide an estimate of the expected reward. Should we marry this person? Our dopamine cells will give us a "gut" opinion that

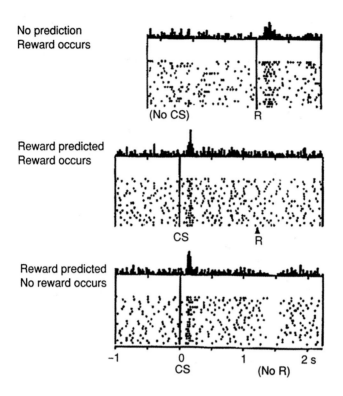

Figure 10.5

Response of a dopamine neuron in the monkey brain proving that it signals reward prediction error to the rest of the brain. Each dot is a spike in dopamine neurons. Each line is a single learning trial. The number of spikes in each time bin is shown at the top of each raster. (Top) At the beginning of learning, reward is unexpected and the dopamine consistently fires a burst of spikes shortly after the reward. (Middle) After many trials when a light (conditioned stimulus, CS) is consistently flashed before reward delivery, the dopamine cell responds to the CS but not the reward. According to temporal difference learning, the response after the reward is cancelled by the reward prediction. (Bottom) When the reward is withheld on catch trials, a dip in firing is revealed that represents the predicted reward. Adapted from Schultz, Dayan, and Montague, "A Neural Substrate of Prediction and Reward," 1594, figure 1.

is more trustworthy than reasoning. But here problems with many incommensurate dimensions are the most difficult to decide. How do we trade off a sense of humor against being messy or make hundreds of other trade-offs of positive against negative qualities when choosing a spouse? Our reward system reduces all these dimensions down to a common currency, the transient dopamine signal. Nature discovered the economic power of a universal currency long before we did.

There are two parameters in the temporal difference learning algorithm: the learning rate α and the discount factor γ in box 10.1. Whereas certain insects have a high learning rate, such as bees, which can learn to associate a flower with a reward after a single visit, learning rates are lower in mammals, which generally learn over many trials. The discount factor also varies over a wide range. When $\gamma = 0$, the learning algorithm is greedy, and decisions are made based only on immediate rewards; but when $\gamma = 1$, all future rewards are weighted equally. In a classic experiment, young children were given a choice between either eating a marshmallow immediately or waiting for fifteen minutes to get an additional marshmallow.[14] Age was a strong predictor, with younger children unable to delay gratification. Expecting a large reward in the distant future can lead us to make choices with negative rewards in the short term if we deem them necessary to achieve that expected reward.

Dopamine neurons receive inputs from a part of the brain called the "basal ganglia" (figure 10.4), which were known to be important for sequence learning and the formation of habitual behaviors. Neurons in the striatum of the basal ganglia receive input from the entire cerebral cortex. Inputs from the back half of the cortex are especially involved with learning sequences of motor actions to achieve a goal. Inputs to the basal ganglia from the prefrontal cortex are more concerned with planning sequences of actions. The loop from the cortex to the basal ganglia and back takes 100 milliseconds, which circulates information ten times a second. This allows sequences of fast decisions to be made toward achieving a goal. Neurons in the basal ganglia also evaluate cortical states and assign a value to them.

The basal ganglia perform a sophisticated version of the value function that Gerry Tesauro trained in TD-Gammon to predict the value of board positions. The surprising success of DeepMind's AlphaGo described in chapter 1 in achieving a world-championship level of play in Go is based on the same architecture as TD-Gammon, but on steroids. One layer of hidden units in the value network of TD-Gammon became a dozen layers in AlphaGo, which played many millions of games. But the basic algorithms were the same. This is a dramatic demonstration of how well learning algorithms for neural networks scale. How much better will performance be if we continue to increase the size of the network and training time?

Games are a much simpler environment than the real world. A stepping-stone toward more complex and uncertain environments comes from the world of video games. DeepMind had shown in 2015 that temporal difference learning could learn to play Atari arcade games such as *Pong* at superhuman levels, taking the pixels of the screen as input.[15] The next stepping-stone is video games in a three-dimensional environment. *Star-Craft* is among the best competitive video games of all time. DeepMind is using it to develop autonomous deep learning networks that can thrive in that world. Microsoft Research recently bought the rights to *Minecraft*, another popular video game, and has made it open source so others could customize its three-dimensional environment and speed up the progress of its artificial intelligence.

Playing backgammon and Go at championship levels is an impressive achievement, and playing video games is an important next step, but what about solving real-world problems? The perception-action cycle (figure 10.2) can be applied to solve any problem for which actions are planned based on sensory data. The result of the action can be compared with the predicted outcome and the difference then used to update the state of the system making the predictions; the memory of previous conditions can be used to optimize the use of resources and anticipate potential problems.

Simon Haykin at McMaster University in Hamilton, Ontario, used this framework to improve the performance of several important engineered software systems,[16] including cognitive radio, which dynamically allocates communications channels; cognitive radar, which dynamically shifts frequency bands to reduce interference; and the cognitive grid, which dynamically loads balances electrical power on the electrical grid. Risk control can also be managed within the same perception-action framework.[17] The improvements made by using the perception-action framework in each of these software systems and thus also the improvements in the areas they manage are substantial, significantly enhancing performance and reducing costs.

Learning How to Soar

In 2016, Massimo Vergassola, a physicist at UC, San Diego, and I wondered whether it was possible to use temporal difference learning to teach a glider how to soar and stay aloft for hours without expending much energy like many birds.[18] Thermal upwelling of air can carry birds to great heights, but, within a thermal, the air is turbulent and there are pockets of falling as well as rising air. The cues birds use to maintain their upward trajectory in the face of so much buffeting are not known. Our first step was to develop a physically realistic simulation of turbulent convective flow and a model of the aerodynamics of a glider. Our next step was then to simulate the trajectory taken by the glider in the turbulent flow.

At first, the glider was not able to take advantage of the rising columns of air and glided downward (figure 10.6). After being rewarded for going up, the glider began to learn a strategy, and, after a few hundred trials, the trajectories of the glider resembled the tight loops made by soaring birds (figure 10.6). The glider also learned different strategies for different degrees of turbulence. By analyzing these strategies, we could develop hypotheses, and we could ask whether soaring birds in fact used the strategies. We then instrumented a real glider with a six-foot wingspan and taught it to soar and stay aloft.[19]

Learning How to Sing

Another example of the power of reinforcement learning is the parallel between how birds learn to sing and how children learn to speak. In both cases, an initial period of auditory learning is followed by a later period of progressive motor learning. Zebra finches hear their father's song early in life but don't produce any sounds themselves until months later. Even when they are isolated from their father before the motor learning phase, they go through a period of scratchy-sounding subsong that continues to improve and eventually crystallizes into birdsong in their father's dialect. Zebra finches know what part of the forest a conspecific came from by its song, just as we know where a person is from by that person's accent. The hypothesis that has driven birdsong research is that, during the auditory learning phase, a template is learned that is then used to refine the sounds produced by the motor system in the motor learning phase. The pathways that are responsible for the motor learning phase in both humans and songbirds are in the basal ganglia, where we know that reinforcement learning takes place.

In 1995, Kenji Doya, a postdoctoral fellow in my lab, developed a reinforcement learning model for the motor refinement of birdsong (figure 10.7). The model improved its performance by tweaking synapses in the motor pathway to a model of the vocal organ in birds ("syrinx"), and then

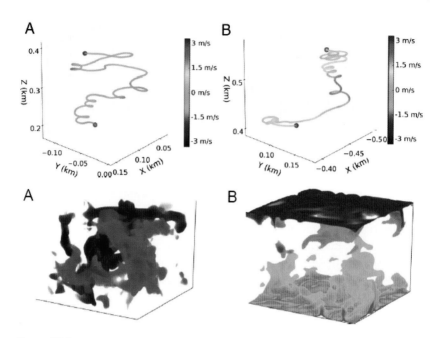

Figure 10.6

Simulations of a glider learning to soar in a thermal. (Upper panels) (A) Typical trajectories of an untrained glider (A) and a trained glider (B) flying within a Rayleigh-
Bénard turbulent flow. The colors indicate the vertical wind velocity experienced
by the glider. The green and red dots indicate the start and the end points of the
trajectory, respectively. The untrained glider takes random decisions and descends,
whereas the trained glider flies in characteristic spiraling patterns in regions of strong
ascending currents, as observed in the thermal soaring of birds and gliders. (Lower
panels) Snapshots of the vertical velocity (A) and the temperature fields (B) in our
numerical simulations of three-dimensional Rayleigh-Bénard convection. For the
vertical velocity field, the red and blue colors indicate regions of large upward and
downward flow, respectively. For the temperature field, the red and blue colors indicate regions of high and low temperature, respectively. From G. Reddy, A. Celani, T.
J. Sejnowski, and M. Vergassola, "Learning to Soar in Turbulent Environments," top:
figure 2; bottom: figure 11.

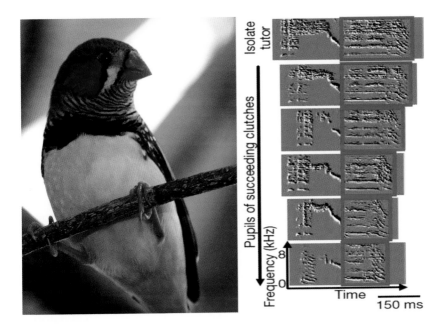

Figure 10.7
Zebra finch birdsong. In the spectrograms on right side of figure, the song of the father (tutor, top) teaches that of the son (pupil, second from top), and the dialect of the birdsong is passed on from generation to generation. Note the similarity of the motif (red outlined boxes) in the spectrograms (spectral power as a function of time). The motif grows shorter with each generation. Left: http://bird-photoo.blogspot. com/2012/11/zebra-finch-bird-pictures.html; right: Olga Feher, Haibin Wang, Sigal Saar, Partha P. Mitra, and Ofer Tchernichovski, "De novo Establishment of Wild-Type Song Culture in the Zebra Finch," figure 4.

testing to see if the new song was a better match to the template than the previous song. If so, the changes were kept, but if the new song was worse, the changes in the synapses were allowed to decay back to their original strengths.[20] We predicted that, at the top of the motor circuit that generates the sequence of syllables, there should be neurons that are only active on a single syllable of the song, in order to make it easier to adjust each syllable separately. Since then, findings from Michale Fee's lab at MIT and from other birdsong labs have confirmed this and other key predictions of the model.

Allison Doupe, who studied birdsong learning at UC, San Francisco, and Patricia Kuhl, who studied the development of speech in babies at the

University of Washington in Seattle, have drawn many parallels between songbird learning and the emergence of speech in toddlers.[21] Both syllables in birds and phonemes in babies are learned first as sounds (auditory learning), with motor learning coming only later, first as subsong in birds and as babbling in babies. There are many domain-specific learning and memory systems in brains that must work together toward the acquisition of new skills and the reinforcement learning algorithm for learning birdsongs in songbirds and temporal difference learning algorithm in the reward system for monkeys, humans, bees, and other animals are only two of many.

Other Forms of Learning

Despite the progress made in automating some cognitive functions like seeing and hearing, there are many other aspects of human intelligence where advances are needed in artificial intelligence. Representation learning in the cortex together with reinforcement learning in the basal ganglia powerfully complement each other. Can AI learning to play championship Go translate to solving other complex problems? Much of human learning is based on observation and mimicry, and we need far fewer examples than deep learning to learn to recognize a new object. Unlabeled sensory data are abundant, and powerful unsupervised learning algorithms might use these data to advantage before any supervision takes place. In chapter 7, an unsupervised version of the Boltzmann learning algorithm was used to initialize deep learning networks, and in chapter 6, independent component analysis (ICA), an unsupervised learning algorithm, extracted sparse population codes from natural images and in chapter 9, generative adversarial networks, an unsupervised learning system, can create novel photorealistic mages. Unsupervised learning is the next frontier in machine learning. We are just starting to understand brain-style computing.

The brain has many learning systems and many forms of plasticity that work together synergistically. Even within the cortex, there are several dozen forms of plasticity, including plasticity in neuronal excitability and gain. A particularly important form of synaptic plasticity is homeostatic, which ensures that neurons maintain activity levels within their optimal dynamic range. What happens when the synaptic strength decreases to zero or reaches a maximum limit? This could result in a neuron never receiving sufficient input to reach threshold, or in receiving too much input and staying always at a high level of activity. In the brain, a new form of synaptic plasticity was discovered by Gina Turrigiano that normalizes all the synapses on a neuron to maintain a balance of activity in the neuron.[22] If the average firing rate is too high, all the excitatory synaptic strengths are all scaled down; if too low, all strengths are scaled up. For inhibitory inputs, this is reversed, with synaptic strengths scaled up if the firing rate is too high and scaled down if the rate is too low. Similar forms of normalization have proven effective in modeling the development of neural maps in the brain.[23] Artificial neural networks that are driven by stochastic gradient descent could benefit from homeostatic scaling.

The brain has dozens of voltage-sensitive and ligand-gated ion channels in the membranes of its neurons that regulate excitability and signaling. There must be mechanisms based on local patterns of activity in the dendrites, somas and axons of neurons that dynamically regulate the locations and densities of these channels. Several algorithms have been suggested for how this could be accomplished.[24] This form of homeostasis is not as well understood as homeostatic synaptic plasticity.

What Is Missing?

Demis Hassabis and I participated in intense debates about the future of and next priority for artificial intelligence that took place during the Brains, Minds and Machines symposium at the 2015 NIPS Conference in Montreal and the Bits and Brains workshop at the NIPS 2016 Conference in Barcelona. There are still many open questions in AI that need to be addressed. Foremost is the question of causality, which informs the highest levels of human reasoning, and the intentionality of actions, both of which presuppose a theory of mind. I mentioned earlier that none of the deep learning systems we have created are able to survive on their own. The autonomy of these systems will only be possible if they include functions similar to those from many other parts of the brain hitherto ignored, such as the hypothalamus, which is essential for feeding, reproduction, the regulation of hormones, and the homeostasis of internal organs, and the cerebellum, which helps us refine movements based on movement prediction error. These are ancient structures found in all vertebrates and are important for survival.

Hava Siegelmann is a computer scientist at the University of Massachusetts at Amherst who has shown that analog computing is super-Turing; that is, capable of going beyond what can be computed with digital computers.[25] Recurrent neural networks that can adapt and learn based on the environment also have the super-Turing computational power, while networks that learn from a training set and are then frozen, and do not learn from their actual experience while they operate, are no more than Turing machines. However, our brains must continue to adapt to changing conditions, making us super-Turing. How this is done while maintaining previous knowledge and skills is an unsolved problem. Hava is the program manager for a DARPA project on Lifelong Learning. Her Lifelong Learning Program is funding advanced research aimed at creating a new integrated architecture for lifelong learning in autonomous systems.

11 Neural Information Processing Systems

Tracing the origins of ideas is difficult because science is a collective activity of many individuals often widely distributed over space and time. The Neural Information Processing Systems (NIPS; figure 11.1) conferences have been a thread throughout the narrative of this book, and, by now, it should be clear that these conferences have had an enormous influence not only on me but on the field as well.[1] My future wife, Beatrice Golomb, gave her SEXNET talk at an early NIPS conference (1990), and it was at another, shortly after we married, that we almost broke up. NIPS conferences are total immersion, with formal sessions during the day and poster sessions in the evening, going strong well past midnight. When I came back to our room from one such session at 3 a.m. and could not find Beatrice, I knew I was in trouble. We are still together after twenty-eight years.

Deep learning has a long bloodline that can be traced to the annual NIPS conferences and workshops and to earlier pioneers. In the 1980s, a diverse group of engineers, physicists, mathematicians, psychologists, and neuroscientists came together at the NIPS conferences to build a new approach to artificial intelligence. Rapid progress was spurred by advances made by physicists analyzing neural network models, psychologists modeling human cognition, neuroscientists modeling neural systems and analyzing neural recordings, statisticians exploring large data sets in high-dimensional spaces, and engineers building devices that could see and hear like humans.

There were 400 attendees at the first NIPS conference in 1987 at the Denver Tech Center. Academic conferences typically focus on narrow areas of research, which are comfortable because everybody speaks the same jargon, but the scientific diversity at early NIPS conferences was truly breathtaking. Biologists speak in code when they are giving a talk to other biologists.[2] It is even worse with mathematicians and physicists, who talk only in equations. Engineers are somewhat better because they build things that speak for themselves. But because of these cultural barriers, interdisciplinary research, though universally hoped for, is seldom achieved. At the early NIPS conferences, it was as if everyone was speaking in tongues.

After the main conference in 1987, the attendees convened to a workshop at Keystone, a nearby ski resort, and self-organized into smaller group meetings on the spot. This is where communication between disciplines really began, in a more informal setting. I vividly remember a neuroscientist suggesting we have a workshop on the sea slug *Aplysia* while in a hot tub at Keystone.[3] The gentleman next to me in the hot tub from the Department of Defense was probably wondering what *Aplysia* had to do with national security. Today, however, NIPS workshops are miniconferences with posters, some of which attract thousands of attendees.

What kept NIPS together year after year was, first, the excitement in the air that we were on the verge of solving difficult computational problems based on biologically inspired learning algorithms and, second, Ed Posner (figure 11.2), an information theorist at Caltech and the chief technologist at the Jet Propulsion Lab, who had a long-term vision for the field and founded the Neural Information Processing Systems Foundation to manage the conferences.

The culture of an organization is often a reflection of its founder; Ed gave NIPS a unique combination of wisdom, practical smarts, and sense of humor. He was an inspiring teacher and effective leader and was beloved at

Figure 11.1
Logo of the Neural Information Processing Systems conferences. Founded thirty years ago, NIPS conferences are the premier conferences on machine and deep learning. Courtesy of the NIPS Foundation.

Figure 11.2
Edward "Ed" Posner at Caltech, who founded the NIPS conferences, which are still going strong thirty years later in part because of his foresight. Courtesy of Caltech.

Caltech for his support of the Summer Undergraduate Research Fellowships (SURF) program, one of the "crown jewels of Caltech." Ed recruited Phil Sotel as pro bono legal counsel, who kept NIPS on track over the decades as it grew in size and complexity, when there were many ways that it could have derailed.

Ed knew Beatrice Golomb when she was a young girl and knew me separately through NIPS; so when, out of the blue, I told him at a NIPS conference that Beatrice and I were engaged, he replied, "Engaged in what?" When Ed died in a bicycle accident in 1993, I became president of the NIPS Foundation, which has continued to grow and prosper. We have an annual Ed Posner Lecture at NIPS to honor him. Invited speakers are generally working in areas outside the NIPS mainstream, but the Posner Lecture features someone from our own community who has made a major contribution to our field.

The general chairs of NIPS conferences are a distinguished group of scientists and engineers. To name just a few, Scott Kirkpatrick is a physicist who (as noted in chapter 7) invented a way for computers to solve difficult computational problems by "heating" them up and slowly "cooling" them down in a process called "simulated annealing"; Sebastian Thrun is a computer scientist who (as noted in chapter 1) won the 2005 DARPA Grand Challenge for an autonomous automobile, which opened the door to today's self-driving cars; and Daphne Koller is a computer scientist who cofounded Coursera (mentioned in chapter 12), which pioneered massive open online courses (MOOCs).

What made deep learning take off was big data. Not too long ago, a terabyte of data took up an entire rack of computers; it is now possible to store a terabyte (trillion bytes) of data on a single memory stick. Internet companies have data centers that store many petabytes, each a thousand terabytes (quadrillion or 10^{15} bytes). The amount of data in the world has doubled every three years since the 1980s. Thousands of petabytes of data are added every day to the Internet, whose total capacity has reached a zettabyte, which is a million petabytes (sextillion or 10^{21} bytes). The explosion of big data is having an influence not just on science and engineering but also on every area of society. It would have been impossible to train really big deep learning networks without the millions of images and other labeled data available on the Internet.

Universities throughout the world are setting up new centers, institutes, and departments for data science. In 2009, Alex Szalay founded the Institute for Data Intensive Engineering and Science (IDIES) at The Johns Hopkins University, building on his experience with the Sloan Digital Sky Survey (SDSS; http://www.sdss.org/), which began collecting astronomical data in 1998. It produced a thousandfold increase in the total amount of data that astronomers had ever collected and today is the most used astronomy facility in the world. But the terabyte-scale data sets collected by the Sloan Digital Sky Survey will themselves be outstripped a thousandfold by the petabyte-scale data sets to be collected by the Large Synoptic Sky Survey Telescope (https://www.lsst.org/) under construction. When Yann LeCun founded the Center for Data Science at New York University in 2013, faculty from every department came knocking on his door with data in hand. In 2018 UCSD dedicated a new Halıcıoğlu Data Science Institute. Master's in Data Science degrees (MDSs) are becoming as popular as MBAs.

Deep Learning at the Gaming Table

Deep learning came of age at the 2012 NIPS Conference at Lake Tahoe (figure 11.3). Geoffrey Hinton, an early pioneer in neural networks, and his students presented a paper reporting that neural networks with many layers were remarkably good at recognizing objects in images.[4] These networks weren't just better than the state-of-the-art computer vision at object recognition—they were in a different, higher league, much closer to human levels of performance. The *New York Times* ran an article on deep learning, and Facebook announced a new AI lab with Yann LeCun, another deep learning pioneer, as the founding director.

The participation of Mark Zuckerberg, the CEO of Facebook, at the NIPS deep learning workshop that year was a security headache but a huge draw, which required an overflow room with a video feed. At the reception afterward, I was introduced to Zuckerberg, who asked me questions about the brain. He had a particular interest in the theory of mind. In psychology, we have an implicit theory of how our minds work, and we use that as a guide

Figure 11.3
Held at a Lake Tahoe casino, the 2012 NIPS Conference was a turning point for the field and put the "Neural" back into "Neural Information Processing Systems." Courtesy of the NIPS Foundation.

to others' minds. When we text our friends, we are unaware of the many decisions our brains have made concerning what to type and how to type it. Zuckerberg asked a lot of questions. "How does my brain make a mental model of myself?" "How does my brain make mental models of other people based on experience?" "How does my brain predict the future behavior of others?" "Do other species have a theory of mind?" I had recently co-organized a symposium at the Salk Institute on the theory of mind, and Zuckerberg wanted all the symposium references.

In machine learning, whoever has the most data wins, and Facebook has more data about more people's likes, friends, and photos than anyone else. With all these data, Facebook could create a theory of our minds and use it to predict our preferences and political leanings. Facebook might someday know us better than we know ourselves. Will Facebook someday become the incarnation of Orwell's Big Brother?[5] Do you find this a chilling prospect, or would you find it convenient to have a digital butler to attend to your needs? We might well ask whether Facebook should have this power, but we may not have much say in the matter.

Although we held the 2012 and 2013 NIPS Conferences in Lake Tahoe casinos, attendees avoided the gaming tables. They knew the odds favored the house, and what they were working on was far more exciting. Gaming can be addictive because of the dopamine reward prediction error system that is a part of our brains (discussed in chapter 10). Casinos have optimized conditions that favor betting: the promise of a big payoff; the occasional smaller wins (rewards) randomly spaced, which studies have shown are the best way to keep laboratory rats pressing the bars for food; the noises and lights that are triggered when there is a win in a slot machine; dim lights night and day, which decouple your light-driven circadian from your normal day-night cycle, encouraging you to bet until you drop. But in the long run, of course, the house always wins.

At the 2015 NIPS Conference in Montreal, 3,800 international attendees overflowed the Palais des congrès. The deep learning tutorial at the beginning of the conference was so popular that we had to turn people away to stay within the fire code. Deep learning has been adopted by almost every company with big data in the high-tech sector and is spreading at an accelerating pace. The 2016 NIPS Conference in Barcelona had to be capped at 5,400 attendees two weeks before the conference. A walk-in who flew in from New York was disappointed to learn he could not register on site. Registration for NIPS in 2017 at Long Beach was capped twelve days after registration opened and reached 8,000. If the 50 percent increase in attendance per year since 2014 continues, everyone on the planet will eventually want to come to NIPS conferences. Of course, the bubble will eventually burst, but, as with most bubbles, no one knows when.

Researchers from the many tribes of science and engineering continue to gather at NIPS conferences, as they have done annually for thirty years, although, of the 5,400 attendees at the 2016 NIPS Conference in Barcelona, 40 percent were there for the first time. Up until 2016, the NIPS Foundation Board of Trustees wisely decided to keep the conferences single track, rare for large conferences. The idea was for everyone to sit in the same room to keep the field from fragmenting. But in 2016, the single track became two tracks because it was difficult to find a big enough room to fit everyone into. Still, this was far fewer than the ten tracks common at most other large conferences. The NIPS acceptance rate for submissions has been kept around 20 percent, which is below the acceptance rate for most journals. NIPS has hosted Women in Machine Learning (WiML),[6] which in 2016 brought nearly 600 women—10 percent of all conference attendees—to Barcelona and 1,000 women to Long Beach in 2017. Diversity continues to be a hallmark of NIPS conferences. No single field on its own could have brought together the diverse talent that created deep learning.

With its potential for affecting so many industries, it may be surprising that there are so few patents protecting the intellectual property for deep learning. In the 1980s, wanting to make learning algorithms the foundation for a new field of science, we felt that securing patents would not help. No doubt there are patents being filed by companies today for specific applications since companies won't make big investments in new technology without protection.

Preparing for the Future

Major breakthroughs in neural network learning have occurred every thirty years, starting with the introduction of perceptrons in the 1950s, learning algorithms for multilayer perceptrons in the 1980s, and deep learning in the 2010s. In each case, there was a period of exuberance, when much progress was made in a short time, followed by a longer period of slower, incremental advances. One difference, though, is that the impact of the exuberant periods has been increasing with each recurrence. The latest growth spurt has been fueled by the widespread availability of big data, and the story of NIPS has been one of preparing for this day to come.

III Technological and Scientific Impact

Timeline

1971—Noam Chomsky publishes "The Case against B. F. Skinner" in the *New York Review of Books*, an essay that steered a generation of cognitive scientists away from learning.

1982—Claude Shannon publishes the seminal book *A Mathematical Theory of Communication*, which laid the foundation for modern digital communication.

1989—Carver Mead publishes *Analog VLSI and Neural Systems*, founding the field of neuromorphic engineering, which builds computer chips inspired by biology.

2002—Stephen Wolfram publishes *A New Kind of Science*, which explored the computational capabilities of cellular automata, algorithms that are even simpler than neural networks but still capable of powerful computing.

2005—Sebastian Thrun's team wins the DARPA Grand Challenge for an autonomous vehicle.

2008—Tobias Delbrück develops a highly successful spiking retina chip called the "Dynamic Vision Sensor" (DVS) that uses asynchronous spikes rather than synchronous frames used in current digital cameras.

2013—U.S. BRAIN Initiative, to develop innovative neurotechnologies that accelerate our understanding of brain function, is announced in the White House.

The age of cognitive computing is dawning. Soon we will have self-driving cars that drive better than we do. Our homes will recognize us, anticipate our habits and alert us to visitors. Kaggle, a crowdsourcing website recently bought by Google, ran a $1 million contest for a program to detect lung cancer in CT scans and is running a $1.5 million contest for the Department of Homeland Security for a program to detect concealed items in body scans at airports.[1] With cognitive computing, doctor's assistants will be able to diagnose even rare diseases and raise the level of medical care. There are thousands of applications like these, and many more have yet to be imagined. Some jobs will be lost; others will be created. Although cognitive computing technologies are disruptive and will take time for our society to absorb and adjust to, they aren't existential threats. On the contrary, we are entering an era of discovery and enlightenment that will make us smarter, live longer, and prosper.

I was a speaker at an IBM-sponsored cognitive computing conference in San Francisco in 2015.[2] IBM was making a big investment in Watson, a program based on collections of large databases of facts about everything from history to popular culture that could be interrogated with a wide range of algorithms using a natural language interface. Ken Jennings had won 74 games in a row over 192 days on *Jeopardy!*, the longest winning streak in the history of the game show. When Watson nonetheless beat Jennings on *Jeopardy!* in 2011, the world took notice.

In the taxi from my hotel to the conference, I overheard two IBM executives in the back of the car talking shop. IBM was rolling out a platform around Watson that could be used to organize and answer questions from unstructured databases in specialized areas such as health and financial services. Watson can answer questions and make recommendations that are based on more data than any human could possibly know, although, of course, as with other machine learning programs, it still takes humans to ask the questions and choose among the recommendations made.

IBM had long since parted with its hardware division, and its computer services division was no longer competitive. By banking on Watson, IBM was counting on its software division to help replace a $70 billion revenue stream. The company has invested $200 million in a new global headquarters for its Watson Internet of Things business in Munich,[3] one of IBM's largest investments ever in Europe in response to growing demand from more than 6,000 customers who want to transform their operations with artificial intelligence—and only part of the company's global plan to invest $3 billion in cognitive computing. But many other companies are also making major investments into AI and it is too early to say which bets will be winners, and who will be the losers.

Life in the Twenty-First Century

In traditional medicine, the same treatment was typically made to fit all patients suffering from a given condition or illness, but now, thanks to cognitive computing, treatment has become personalized and precise. The progress of melanomas, which used to be death sentences, can now be halted and even reversed in many patients by sequencing a patient's cancer cells and designing a specific cancer immunotherapy treatment for that person's cancer. Although this treatment today costs $250,000, it will eventually be affordable for almost every melanoma patient since the base cost of sequencing a patient's cancer genome is only a few thousand dollars and the cost of the necessary monoclonal antibodies only a few hundred dollars. Medical decision making will get better and less expensive once sufficient data have been amassed from patients with a wide range of mutations and outcomes. Some lung cancers are also treatable with the same approach. Pharmaceutical companies are investing in cancer immunotherapy research, and many other cancers may soon be treatable. None of this would have been possible without machine learning methods for analyzing huge amounts of genetic data.

I served on the committee that advised the director of the National Institutes of Health (NIH) on recommendations for the U.S. Brain Research through Advancing Innovative Neurotechnologies (BRAIN) Initiative. Our report emphasized the importance of probabilistic and computational techniques for helping us interpret data being generated by the new neural recording techniques.[4] Machine learning algorithms are now used to analyze simultaneous recordings from thousands of neurons, to analyze complex behavioral data from freely moving animals and to automate reconstructions of 3D anatomical circuits from serial electron microscopic digital images. As we reverse engineer brains, we will uncover many new algorithms discovered by nature.

The NIH has funded basic research into neuroscience over the last fifty years, but the trend is to direct more and more of its grant support toward translational research with immediate health applications. Although we certainly want to translate what already has been discovered, if we do not also fund new discoveries now, there will be little or nothing to translate to the clinic fifty years from now. This also is why it is so important to start research programs like the BRAIN Initiative today in order to find future cures for debilitating brain disorders like schizophrenia and Alzheimer's disease.[5]

The Future of Identity

In 2006, the social security numbers and birth dates of 26.5 million veterans were stolen from the home of a Department of Veterans Affairs employee. Hackers wouldn't even have had to decrypt the database since the Veterans Administration was using social security numbers as the identifiers for veterans in their system. With a social security number and a birth date, a hacker could have stolen any of their identities.

In India, more than a billion citizens can be uniquely identified by their fingerprints, iris scans, photographs, and twelve-digit identity numbers (three digits more than social security numbers). India's Aadhaar is the world's largest biometric identity program. In the past, an Indian citizen who wanted a public document faced endless delays and numerous middlemen, each requiring tribute. Today, with a quick bioscan, a citizen can obtain subsidized food entitlements and other welfare benefits directly, and many poor citizens who lack birth certificates now have a portable ID that can be used to identify them anytime and anywhere in seconds. Identity theft that siphoned off welfare support has been stopped. A person's identity cannot be stolen, unless the thief is prepared to cut off the fingers and enucleates the eyes of that person.[6]

The Indian national registry was a seven-year project for Nandan Nilekani,[7] the billionaire and cofounder of Infosys, an outsourcing company. Nilekani's massive digital database has helped India to leapfrog ahead of many developed countries. According to Nilekani: "A small, incremental change multiplied by a billion is a huge leap. ... If a billion people can get their mobile phone in 15 minutes instead of one week that's a massive productivity injection into the economy. If a million people get money into their bank accounts automatically that's a massive productivity leap in the economy."[8]

The advantages of having a digital identity database are balanced by a loss of privacy, especially when the biometric ID is linked to other databases, such as bank accounts, medical records, and criminal records, and other public programs such as transportation. Privacy issues are already paramount in the United States and many other countries where databases are being linked, even when their data are anonymized.[9] Thus our cell phones already track our whereabouts, whether we want them to or not.

The Rise of Social Robots

Movies often depict artificial intelligence as a robot that walks and talks like a human. Don't expect an AI that looks like the German-accented Terminator in the 1984 science fiction/fantasy film *The Terminator*. But you will communicate with AI voices like Samantha's in the 2013 romance/science fiction film *Her* and interact with droids like R2-D2 and BB-8 in the 2017 science fiction/fantasy film *Star Wars: The Force Awakens*. AI is already a part of everyday life. Cognitive appliances like Alexa in the Amazon Echo speaker already talk to you, happy to help make your life easier and more rewarding, just like the clocks and tea setting in the 2017 fantasy/romance film *Beauty and the Beast*. What will it be like to live in a world that has such creatures in it? Let's take a look at our first steps toward social robots.

The current advances in artificial intelligence have primarily been on the sensory and cognitive sides of intelligence, with advances on motor and action intelligence yet to come. I sometimes begin a lecture by saying that the brain is the most complex device in the known universe, but my wife, Beatrice, who is a medical doctor, often reminds me that the brain is only a part of the body, which is even more complex than the brain, although the body's complexity is different, arising from the evolution of mobility.

Our muscles, tendons, skin, and bones actively adapt to the vicissitudes of the world, to gravity, and to other human beings. Internally, our bodies are marvels of chemical processing, transforming foodstuffs into exquisitely crafted body parts. They are the ultimate 3D printers, which work from the inside out. Our brains receive inputs from visceral sensors in every part of our bodies, which constantly monitor the internal activity, including at the highest levels of cortical representation, and make decisions on internal priorities and maintain a balance between all the competing demands. In a real sense, our bodies are integral parts of brains, which is a central tenet of embodied cognition.[10]

Rubi

Javier Movellan (figure 12.1) is from Spain and was a faculty member and co-director of the Machine Perception Laboratory at the Institute for Neural Computation at UC, San Diego. He believed that we would learn more about cognition by building robots that interact with humans than by conducting traditional laboratory experiments. He built a robot baby that smiled at you when you smile at it, which was remarkably popular with passersby. Among Javier's conclusions after studying babies interacting with their mothers was that babies maximize smiles from their moms while minimizing their own effort.[11]

Javier's most famous social robot, Rubi, looks like a Teletubby, with an expressive face, eyebrows that rise to show interest, camera eyes that move around, and arms that grasp (figure 12.2). In the Early Childhood Education Center at UCSD, 18-month-old toddlers interacted with Rubi using the tablet that serves as Rubi's tummy.

Toddlers are difficult to please. They have very short attention spans. They play with a toy for a few minutes, then lose interest and toss it away. How would they interact with Rubi? On the first day, the boys yanked off

Figure 12.1
Javier Movellan being interviewed by *The Science Network* in his robot workshop at UC, San Diego. Javier pioneered social robots in classrooms and programmed a social robot, Rubi, to hold the attention of 18-month-old toddlers. Courtesy of Roger Bingham.

Figure 12.2
Rubi interacting with toddlers in a classroom setting. Rubi's head can swivel, the eyes are cameras and the mouth and eyebrows are expressive. The bushy light fibers on the top of the head change colors with Rubi's moods. Courtesy of Javier Movellan.

Rubi's arms, which, for the sake of safety, were not industrial strength. After some repair and a software patch, Javier tried again. This time, the robot was programmed to cry out when its arms were yanked. This stopped the boys, and made the girls rush to hug Rubi. This was an important lesson in social engineering.

Toddlers would play with Rubi by pointing to an object in the room, such as a clock. If Rubi did not respond by looking at that object in a narrow window of 0.5 to 1.5 seconds, the toddlers would lose interest and drift away. Too fast and Rubi was too mechanical; too slow and Rubi was boring. Once a reciprocal relationship was formed, the children treated Rubi like a sentient being rather than a toy. When the toddlers became upset after Rubi was taken away (to the repair shop for an upgrade), they were told instead that Rubi was feeling sick and would stay home for the day. In one study, Rubi was programmed to teach toddlers Finnish words, which they picked up with as much alacrity as they had English words; a popular song was a powerful reinforcer.[12]

One of the concerns about introducing Rubi into a classroom setting was that teachers would feel threatened by a robot that might someday replace them. But quite the opposite occurred: teachers welcomed Rubi as an assistant that helped keep the class under control, especially when they had visitors in the classroom. An experiment that could have revolutionized early education was the "thousand Rubi project." The idea was to mass produce Rubis, place them in a thousand classrooms, and collect data over the Internet from thousands of experiments each day. One of the problems with educational studies is that what works in one school may not work in another because there are so many differences between schools, especially between teachers. A thousand Rubis could have tested many ideas for how to improve educational practice and could have probed the differences between schools serving different socioeconomic groups around the country. Although resources never materialized to run the project, it's still a great idea, which someone should pursue.

Two-legged robots are unstable and require a sophisticated control system to keep them from falling over. And, indeed, it takes about twelve months before a baby biped human starts walking without falling over. Rodney Brooks (figure 12.3), who made a brief appearance in chapter 2,

Figure 12.3
Rodney Brooks oversees Baxter, who is preparing to place a plug into a hole on the table. Brooks is a serial entrepreneur who previously founded iRobot, which makes Roombas, and now Rethink, which makes Baxters. Courtesy of Rod Brooks.

wanted to build six-legged robots that could walk like insects. He invented a new type of controller that could sequence the actions of the six legs to move his robo-cockroach forward and remain stable. His novel idea was to let the mechanical interactions of the legs with the environment take the place of abstract planning and computation. He argued that, for robots to accomplish everyday tasks, their higher cognitive abilities should be based on sensorimotor interaction with the environment, not on abstract reasoning. Elephants are highly social, have great memories, and are mechanical geniuses,[13] but they don't play chess.[14] In 1990, Brooks went on to found iRobot, which has sold more than 10 million Roombas to clean even more floors.

Industrial robots have stiff joints and powerful servomotors, which makes them look and feel mechanical. In 2008, Brooks started Rethink Robotics, a company that built a robot called "Baxter" with pliant joints, so its arms could be moved around (figure 12.3). Instead of having to write a program to move Baxter's arms, each arm could be moved through the desired motions, and it would program itself to repeat the sequence of motions.

Movellan went one step further than Brooks and developed a robot baby called "Diego San" (manufactured in Japan),[15] whose motors were pneumatic (driven by air pressure) and all of whose forty-four joints were compliant compared to the stiff torque motors used in most industrial robots (figure 12.4). The motivation for making them so is that when we pick something up, every muscle in our bodies is involved to some extent (when we move only one joint at a time, we look like robots). This makes us better able to adapt to changing conditions of load and interaction with the world. The brain can smoothly control all of the degrees of freedom in the body—all the joints and muscles—at the same time and the goal of the Diego San project was to figure out how. Diego San's face had twenty-seven moving parts and could express a wide range of human emotions.[16] The movements made by the robot baby were remarkably lifelike. Although Javier had several successful robot projects to his name, Diego San was not one of them, however. He simply didn't know how to make the robot baby perform as fluidly as a human baby.

Facial Expressions Are a Window into Your Soul

Imagine what it would be like to watch your iPhone as stock prices plummet and have it ask you why you're upset. Your facial expressions are a window into the emotional state of your brain and deep learning can now

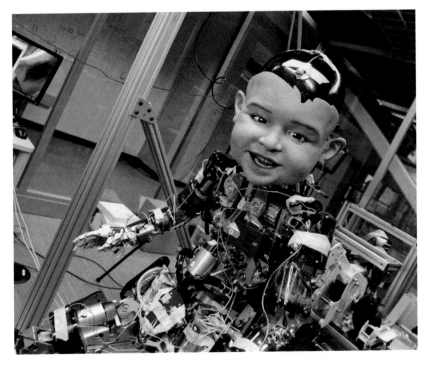

Figure 12.4
Diego San, a robot baby. Pneumatic actuators allowed all of the joints to move pliantly, so that you could shake the robot's hand. Face by David Hanson and Hanson Robotics. For facial animation, see "Diego Installed," Courtesy of Javier Movellan. https://www.youtube.com/watch?v=knRyDcnUc4U/.

see into that window. Cognition and emotion have traditionally been considered separate functions of the brain. It was generally thought that cognition was a cortical function and emotions were subcortical. In fact, there are subcortical structures that regulate emotional states, structures like the amygdala, which is engaged when the emotional levels are high, especially fear, but these structures interact strongly with the cerebral cortex. Engagement of the amygdala in social interaction, for example, will lead to a stronger memory of the event. Cognition and emotions are intertwined.

In the 1990s, I collaborated with Paul Ekman (figure 12.5), a psychologist at UC, San Francisco, who is the world's leading expert on facial expressions and the real-world inspiration for Dr. Cal Lightman in the TV drama series *Lie to Me*, though Paul is a lot nicer than Cal. Ekman went to Papua New Guinea to find out if preindustrial cultures responded emotionally

Figure 12.5
Paul Ekman with the Fore people of Papua New Guinea in 1967. He found evidence
for six universal facial expressions of emotions, happiness, sadness, anger, surprise,
fear and disgust. Paul consulted for the TV series *Lie to Me*, critiquing each episode
for scientific validity. The character Dr. Cal Lightman is based loosely on Ekman.
Courtesy of Paul Ekman.

with the same facial expressions that we do. He found six universal expressions of emotion in all the human societies he studied: happiness, sadness,
anger, surprise, fear, and disgust. Since then other universal facial expressions have been suggested, but there is no universal agreement, and some
expressions, like fear, are interpreted differently in a few isolated societies.

In 1992, Ekman and I organized a Planning Workshop on Facial Expression Understanding sponsored by the National Science Foundation.[17] At
the time, it was quite difficult to get support for research on facial expressions. Our workshop brought researchers from neuroscience, electrical engineering, and computer vision together with psychologists, which opened a

new chapter in analyzing faces. It was a revelation to me that, despite how important the analysis of facial expressions could be for so many areas of science, medicine, and the economy, it was being neglected by funding agencies.

Ekman developed the Facial Action Coding System (FACS) to monitor the status of each of the forty-four muscles in the face. FACS experts trained by Ekman take an hour to label a minute of videos, one frame at a time. Expressions are dynamic and can extend for many seconds, but Ekman discovered that there were some expressions that lasted for only a few frames. These "microexpressions" were emotional leaks of suppressed brains states and were often telling, sometimes revealing unconscious emotional reactions. Microexpressions of disgust during a marriage counseling session, for example, were a reliable sign that the marriage would fail.[18]

In the 1990s, we used video recordings from trained actors who could control every muscle on their face, as could Ekman, to train neural networks with backprop to automate the FACS. In 1999, a network trained with backprop by my graduate student Marian Stewart Bartlett (figure 12.6) had an accuracy of 96 percent in the lab, with perfect lighting, fully frontal faces, and manual temporal segmentation to video,[19] a performance good

Figure 12.6
Marian Stewart-Bartlett demonstrating facial expression analysis. The time lines are the output of deep learning networks that are recognizing facial expression for happiness, sadness, surprise, fear, anger, and disgust. Courtesy of Marian Stewart-Bartlett. Robert Wright/LDV Vision Summit 2015.

enough to merit an appearance by Marni and me on *Good Morning America* with Diane Sawyer on April 5, 1999. Marni continued to develop the Computer Expression Recognition Toolbox (CERT) as a faculty member in the Institute for Neural Computation at UC, San Diego,[20] and as computers became faster, CERT approached real-time analysis, so that it could label the changing facial expressions in a video stream of a person.

In 2012, Marni Bartlett and Javier Movellan started a company called "Emotient" to commercialize the automatic analysis of facial expressions. Paul Ekman and I served on its Scientific Advisory Board. Emotient developed deep learning networks that had an accuracy of 96 percent in real time and with natural behavior, under a broad range of lighting conditions, and with nonfrontal faces. In one of Emotient's demos, its networks detected within minutes that Donald Trump was having the highest emotional impact on a focus group in the first Republican primary debate. It took the pollsters days to reach the same conclusion and pundits months to recognize that emotional engagement was key to reaching voters. The strongest facial expressions in the focus group were joy followed by fear. Emotient's deep learning networks also predicted which TV series would become hits months before the Nielsen ratings were published. Emotient was bought by Apple in January 2016, and Marni and Javier now work for Apple.

In the not too distant future, your iPhone may not only be asking you why you're upset; it may also be helping you to calm down.

The Science of Learning

Twelve years ago, at the 2005 NIPS Conference in Vancouver, I sat down for breakfast with Gary Cottrell, a colleague in the Department of Computer Science and Engineering at UC, San Diego. Gary was a part of the original parallel distributed processing (PDP) group from the 1980s and is one of its last survivors at UCSD. He is also one of the last holdouts from the 1960s, with a ponytail and a beard gone gray. He had come across a National Science Foundation announcement requesting proposals for Science of Learning Centers. What caught his eye was the $5 million per year budget for five years, renewable for an additional five years. He wanted to submit a proposal and asked if I could help out. When he said that, if it was successful, he would never have to write another grant proposal, I told him that, if it was successful, this would be a career-ending grant. He chuckled and we started the ball rolling.

Ultimately, our proposal was successful and, as I had predicted, the reporting was bone crushing with 300-page annual reports, but the science was spectacular. Our Temporal Dynamics of Learning Center (TDLC) includes over 100 researchers at eighteen institutions around the world. Of the six Science of Learning Centers funded by the NSF, ours was the most neuroscience and engineering oriented and we incorporated the latest advances in machine learning into our projects (figure 12.7).[21] Rubi and CERT were two of the projects funded by the Temporal Dynamics of Learning Center. We also had a mobile EEG lab, where subjects were free to roam in a virtual environment while recording their brain waves. In most EEG labs, the subject is required to sit still and not to blink to avoid artifacts. We used Independent Component Analysis (ICA) to cancel movement artifacts, allowing us to look at brain activity while subjects actively explored the environment and interacted with other humans.

Here are a few of the many projects that have been undertaken by TDLC researchers:

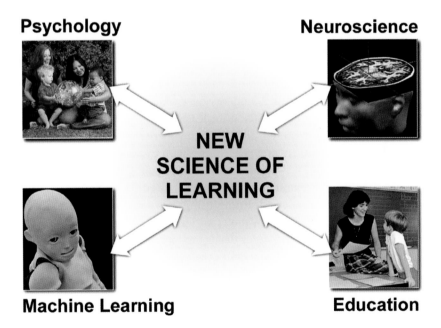

Figure 12.7
New Science of Learning includes machine learning and neuroscience along with insights from psychology and education. From Meltzoff, Kuhl, Movellan, and Sejnowski, "Foundations for a New Science of Learning," figure 1.

- April Benasich at the Center for Molecular and Behavioral Neuroscience at Rutgers developed a test that can predict whether a baby will have deficits in language acquisition and learning based on the baby's timing in auditory perception; she showed that these deficits could be corrected by adaptively manipulating the timing of sounds and reward feedback to allow the baby to develop normal hearing, speaking, and learning.[22] The experiments on which these results are based followed babies longitudinally from three months to five years of age. Even normally developing babies benefited from the interactive environment. April launched AAB Research LLC in 2006 to bring rapid auditory processing technology (RAPT) into the home to enhance an infant's ability to learn.
- Marian Stewart Bartlett and Javier Movellan used machine learning to register facial expressions of students automatically,[23] which could then alert the teacher when a student was looking frustrated and likely not comprehending what was being taught. With deep learning, this can be done automatically and accurately today for every child in a class at the same time. There are many other applications for facial expression analysis in marketing, psychiatry, and forensics that are untapped.
- Harold Pashler at UC, San Diego, and Michael Mozer at the University of Colorado at Boulder investigated improved long-term retention of learning through personalized review spaced out over time versus cramming by extending previous studies of college students over time frames of months to a study of K–12 students over time frames of years.[24] They showed that the optimal spacing for learning was longer when longer-term retention was required, and they implemented their optimal review schedule for students in language courses with excellent results.
- Beth Rogowsky, a TDLC postdoctoral fellow, Paula Tallal at Rutgers, and Barbara Calhoun at Vanderbilt University showed that there was no statistical difference between learning using spoken or written materials, and no relationship between preferred learning style and instructional method in either immediate or delayed comprehension.[25] That there is no benefit in adapting to a student's preferred learning style means that the large industry that promotes training and testing materials for individual learning styles is not adding value to the classroom.
- Paula Tallal was instrumental in the 2014 launch of the $15 million Global Learning X-Prize, which incentivizes innovation in education and whose goal is to develop open-source and scalable software that will enable children in developing countries to learn basic reading, writing, and arithmetic skills within eighteen months. The beneficial impact of research done for the Global Learning X-Prize will reverberate throughout the world for decades to come.

- TDLC Science Director Andrea Chiba presented research on how all learning changes the structure of the brain at the 2014 International Convention on the Science of Learning in Shanghai,[26] much to the surprise of many delegates who believed that children come into the world with a set potential and that education is wasted on those who are less capable or too old to learn. A vast reservoir of human potential exists around the world that is not being tapped.

We found that the biggest problems in education weren't scientific, but social and cultural. There are 13,500 school districts in the United States, each with its own school board that decides on the curriculum, teacher qualifications, and best practices; it would take decades to reach all of them and address each unique situation. Even before teachers can teach, they have to manage the classroom, which can be especially challenging for early grades and inner city schools. Parents making demands may fail to appreciate the high rate of teacher burnout due to a lack of resources, and the influence of teachers unions, which often block progressive efforts.

Teaching is fundamentally a labor-intensive activity. The best and most effective way to teach is through one-to-one interactions between skilled adult teachers and students.[27] We are saddled with an assembly-line system that was designed for mass education, in which students are segregated by age and are taught in large classes where teachers impart the same lessons year after year. This may be a good way to build an automobile and may have been adequate at a time when only a basic education was needed for the workforce, but this system is failing us today when jobs require a higher level of training and lifelong learning to renew job skills. Going back to school as an adult can be painful and impractical. The information revolution that we are living through has overtaken the generational time scale. Fortunately, new technologies are coming online that may change how we learn. The Internet is changing the learning landscape in ways we could never have anticipated when our Science of Learning Center was launched in 2006.

Learning How to Learn

Massively open online courses (MOOCs) burst on the scene in 2011 with a high-visibility article in the *New York Times* on the popularity of an online course on artificial intelligence at Stanford.[28] The large numbers of students who enrolled in MOOCs and their unprecedented reach through the Internet caught the attention of the world. Almost overnight, new companies were founded to develop and freely distribute lectures online by some of the best educators in the world. These are available on demand anytime and anyplace where there is an Internet connection. In addition to the lectures, the courses include quizzes, exams, forums where learners can ask questions, teaching assistants, and self-organized local "meet-ups" where students can discuss their course in an informal setting. The audience for MOOCs has greatly expanded—in 2015, the number of "MOOCers" doubled, from an estimated 17 million to more than 35 million. MOOCs bypass all the gatekeepers in the educational establishment.

I met Barbara Oakley at a meeting sponsored by the National Academy of Sciences at UC, Irvine, in January 2013. She is a professor of electrical engineering at the Oakland University in the cities of Auburn Hills and Rochester Hills, Michigan, even though she did poorly in mathematics and science in school. She was a humanities major, a captain in the U.S. Army, who worked as a Russian translator on Soviet trawlers in the Bering Sea before going back to school, where she overcame her mental block with math and received a doctorate in electrical engineering. Over dinner, I discovered that Barbara and I had similar views on learning and that she was writing a book, *A Mind for Numbers: How to Excel at Math and Science (Even If You Flunked Algebra)*. I invited her to UC, San Diego, to give a TDLC lecture for high school students and teachers.

Barbara was a great hit with the students, and it was clear that she was a gifted teacher. Her approach and practical insights had roots in what we know about the brain, so we teamed up to develop a MOOC for Coursera called "Learning How To Learn: Powerful Mental Tools to Help You Master Tough Subjects" (figure 12.8; https://www.coursera.org/learn/learning-how-to-learn/) that debuted in August 2014. It is currently the world's most popular MOOC, with over 3 million registered learners in its first four years, and it continues to attract 1,000 new learners a day from over 200 countries. "Learning How to Learn" gives you the tools you need to become a better learner based on our knowledge of how the brain learns. Feedback from our learners has been overwhelmingly positive, and we developed a second MOOC called "Mindshift" to help those who want to shift to new jobs or change their lifestyles. Both of these MOOCs are freely available.

"Learning How to Learn" gives practical advice on how to become a better learner, how to handle test anxiety, how to avoid procrastination, and what we know about how the brain learns. It is a free, month-long course with 5- to 10-minute video clips, quizzes, and tests that have been translated into more than twenty languages. One of the cornerstones of the course is what your unconscious brain can do for you while you are doing something else. Henri Poincaré was an eminent nineteenth-century

Figure 12.8
Barbara Oakley introducing "Learning How to Learn" MOOC. Over 3 million learners have taken the course, making it the most popular Internet course in the world. Courtesy of Barbara Oakley.

mathematician who once described how he finally solved a difficult mathematical problem he had been working on intensively for weeks without success. He took a vacation. As he was stepping onto a bus in the south of France, the solution to the problem suddenly came to him, unbidden, from a part of his brain that had continued to work on the problem while he was enjoying his vacation. He knew he had the right path to a proof and completed it when he returned to Paris. His intensive work on the problem before had prepared his brain so that his unconscious could work on it while he was relaxing. Both phases are equally important for creativity.

Surprisingly, your brain can work on a problem even while you're sleeping and not aware of anything. But it does this only if you concentrate on trying to solve the problem before falling asleep. In the morning, as often as not, a fresh insight will pop into your mind that can help you solve the problem. The intense effort before a vacation or falling asleep is important for priming your brain; otherwise, it's just as likely to work on some other problem. There is nothing special about math or science in this regard—your brain will work just as hard solving social problems as on math and science problems if that is what has been on your mind recently.

One of the most satisfying outcomes from "Learning How to Learn" was receiving letters from happy learners thanking us for the best course they took or how it influenced their career choices.[29] Teachers also wrote us that they were incorporating lessons from "Learning How to Learn" into their classes.

We had originally aimed "Learning How to Learn" at high school and college students, but they turned out to be less than 1 percent of all the learners who took the course. Because schools are being driven to teach to "Common Core" tests, they have no time for teaching their students how to learn, which would be far more helpful. And asking school districts to adopt "Learning How to Learn" would be an uphill battle since operating budgets at schools are limited. School districts are not open to revamping their curricula to incorporate the teachings in "Learning How to Learn" on a large scale as any effort at scale requires an expensive reworking of schedules, retraining of teachers, and development of new teaching materials. But somehow we need to reach twelve-year-olds before they enter high school. Barbara and I have written a book aimed at this audience in hopes it will reach these younger students before they hit roadblocks in their math courses, which often occurs in middle school.[30]

A different learning model from classroom courses that are taken "all-or-none," MOOCs are more like books you can pick up and read anytime, selectively: learners have a tendency to "graze" and selectively choose lectures that meet their immediate needs. Originally thought to be an alternative to the traditional classroom, MOOCs are finding a complementary place in the educational firmament that is different from other teaching venues, one that fulfills learners' needs in a way more conventional educational approaches do not. Thus, for example, MOOCs have been adopted in flipped classes, in which students watch selected lectures on their own time and the teacher leads a discussion of the material in the class. Our educational system was designed for the industrial age, and the knowledge imparted in schools was all you needed to hold a job and be a productive citizen for the rest of your life. Today, the knowledge imparted by schools is already obsolete by the time students graduate. MOOCs are an end run around the educational system by going directly into homes. At Coursera, the peak in the demographics of those enrolling online is in the 25–35 age bracket, and more than half of enrollees have a college education. These are young adults in the workforce who need new skills and are learning them online. More fundamental changes will be needed in our educational system to adapt our brains to rapidly expanding jobs in the information sector of the economy. For example, gathering information through the Internet requires judgment and basic skills in formulating search terms and sorting through false trails. Alas, there seems to be no time to teach basic

Internet skills in the school day, even though students would benefit from learning how to actively seek information rather than passively receiving lessons.

Founded by Sebastian Thrun of self-driving-car fame, Udacity is another educational organization that makes MOOCs. In addition to free access to its courses, Udacity also partners with companies that want to upgrade the skills of their workers. Udacity creates MOOCs tailored to the company's needs, and employees are motivated to take them. This is a win-win-win for employers, employees, and Udacity. Udacity also has clusters of courses that lead to nanodegrees in topics such as self-driving car technology (for $800), which come with a money-back guarantee of finding a job in 6 months.[31] The educational sector outside traditional schools is evolving rapidly, and MOOCS can generate a variety of solutions for lifelong learning.

Our follow-up MOOC "Mindshift: Break through Obstacles to Learning and Discover Your Hidden Potential" (https://www.coursera.org/learn/mindshift/) was launched in April 2017. It is accompanied by a new book by Barbara Oakley,[32] which uses case histories (mine included) to illustrate the issues that arise when you want to change your life in some way, based on experiences that others have had. In my case, I switched from physics to neurobiology, but in another case, a successful concert soloist gave up his career to become a medical doctor. Job shifts are becoming more common, and "Mindshift" was designed to make the process easier. Mindshift is now the no. 3 most popular MOOC in the world.

Another way to become better learners is through interactive computer games. Companies like Lumosity offer games you can play online that claim to improve memory and attention. The problem is that the research to back such claims is often lacking or of poor quality, especially with respect to the transfer of training to real-world tasks. But these are early days and better research is beginning to help us sort out what works from what doesn't. The results are often surprising and counterintuitive.

Brain Training

The video games that are the most effective in improving cognitive function broadly are those where you have to chase zombies, war games where you have to kill the bad guys, and race car driving games. Daphne Bavelier at the University of Geneva has shown that playing first-person shooter games like *Medal of Honor: Allied Assault* improved perception, attention, and cognition—in particular, vision, multitasking, and task switching—and that they led to faster decision making as well.[33] She concluded that play-ing some of these shooter games could make older brains react as quickly as younger brains (good news for anyone who's growing older). But some shooter games may also reduce long-term retention.[34] Each game has vari-ous benefits and liabilities that need to be examined individually.

Adam Gazzaley at UC, San Francisco, has custom-designed a three-dimensional video game called *NeuroRacer* that improves your ability to multitask, based on research showing that the activity of neuromodulators in brains is important for attention, learning, and memory.[35] *NeuroRacer* players steer a car along a winding, hilly road while keeping an eye out for some signs that randomly pop up while ignoring others. This requires players to multitask using several cognitive skills such as attention and task switching. In testing *NeuroRacer*, Adam and his colleagues found that, after training, subjects significantly improved these skills and achieved higher scores on working memory and sustained attention tasks that were not part of the training. Furthermore, their performances were better than those of untrained twenty-year-olds, and their improved skills were retained six months later without practice.[36] *NeuroRacer* is now in clinical trials as a ther-apy for patients with attention and memory deficits.

Paula Tallal, then at Rutgers, and Michael Merzenich, then at UCSF, started a company in 1997 called "Scientific Learning" for children with language and reading disorders (such as dyslexia). Speech understanding depends on hearing fast acoustic transitions. For example, the difference between hearing "ba," "ga," or "da" depends on timing differences in the millisecond range at the beginning of the syllable. Children who cannot detect these timing differences are at a learning disadvantage since they confuse words that have these sounds. In order to learn to read, a child must be able to recognize and distinguish the brief sounds that the letters in words represent. Tallal and Merzenich developed what is now a large series of computer games, called "Fast ForWord," that improve auditory discrimination, language, and reading comprehension by first exaggerat-ing acoustic time differences within syllables, words, and sentences, then gradually reducing these differences as the child gets better at each level of language and reading.[37] Top rated among educational games, Fast For-Word computer games have been used in 6,000 schools and by more than 2.5 million children. They are also being used to help children learn Eng-lish as a second language in more than fifty-five countries. Merzenich has gone on to develop *BrainHQ* (https://www.brainhq.com), a game based on similar scientific principles, aimed at reducing cognitive decline in aging adults.

You can also improve your motor skills with brain exercises. Aaron Seitz at UC, Riverside, developed a computer program that sharpens visual perception and reaction times. After using this program, the baseball team reported having better vision, fewer strikeouts, and more runs created, and they ultimately won 4–5 more games out of a 54-game season.[38] Seitz developed an inexpensive app called "UltimEyes" that made his research available to the public, although the Federal Trade Commission has stopped its dissemination until more studies can confirm his claims.[39]

Improvement in certain cognitive skills tends to transfer to other cognitive skills when you play reaction time games, but not when you play many other, domain-specific games, such as memory games. Although we're getting better at designing interactive video games that improve our brains, are fun to play, and can be delivered in an app, more research is needed to understand the conditions when transfer occurs. The potential for cognitive improvement worldwide is enormous.

The AI Business

At the opening session of the 2015 NIPS Conference, I welcomed the participants while wearing a NASCAR-style jacket with logos from all forty-two of our sponsors (figure 12.9). At the 2016 NIPS Conference in Barcelona, there were sixty-five sponsors, too many patches to fit on a jacket, and ninety-three sponsors supported the 2017 NIPS conference in Long Beach. This explosive growth will eventually end, but its reverberations through society could last for decades. These sponsoring companies send recruiters to NIPS conferences, eager to hire talented researchers who are in short supply. Many of my colleagues have taken jobs with Google, Microsoft, Amazon, Apple, Facebook, Baidu, and many start-up companies. This has stripped talent from universities. Sebastian Thrun has estimated that when a start-up self-driving company like Otto or Cruise is bought by a larger company, the cost is $10 million per machine learning expert.[40]

Geoffrey Hinton became an employee of Google in 2013 when it bought his company, DNNresearch, which consisted of Geoffrey and two of his graduate students at the University of Toronto. He now has access to more computer power than he could ever dream of having in Toronto, but even more important is the massive amount of data that Google has available. Google Brain is an extraordinary collection of highly talented engineers and scientists assembled by Jeff Dean, who designed MapReduce, Google's file system upon which all their services depend. When you get Google to translate for you, it now uses deep learning designed by Dean's Google

Figure 12.9
NASCAR jacket Terry Sejnowski wore to open the 2015 NIPS Conference in Montreal. Sponsors ranged from top-tier Internet companies to financial and media companies. They all have a stake in deep learning. Courtesy of the NIPS Foundation.

Brain team. When you google a search term, deep learning helps to rank the results. When you talk to the Google assistant, it uses deep learning to recognize the words you are saying, and as it gets better at holding a conversation with you, it will be using deep learning to serve you better. Google has gone all out for deep learning and so has the rest of the high-tech industry, but this is just the beginning.

The United States is losing its lead in artificial intelligence, and, by the time you read this, other countries may have already raced past us. The Vector Institute in Toronto was launched in March 2017, with C$175 million dollars of support from the Canadian and Ontario governments, the University of Toronto, and private industry.[41] Vector's goal is to be a world-leading center for AI research; to graduate the greatest number of doctoral and master's students in machine learning; and to become the engine for an AI supercluster that drives the economy of Toronto, Ontario, and, indeed, all of Canada. But Canada will have steep competition from China, which is training thousands of machine learning engineers, and where neuromorphic computing is one of the two wings of its Brain Project. Spurred by AlphaGo's defeat of Ke Jie in 2017, which had much the same impact on China that Sputnik did on the United States in 1957, Beijing has launched a new multibillion-dollar AI initiative of ambitious projects, start-ups, and academic research, with the aim of achieving world domination by 2030.[42] With its vast amounts of medical and personal data and far less concern for privacy than in Western democracies, China can leap ahead of other countries that keep personal data in proprietary silos. China has also targeted agriculture and manufacturing for data collection. Whoever has the most data wins, which stacks the deck for China.

More ominously, China also wants "to integrate A.I. into guided missiles, use it to track people on closed-circuit cameras, censor the internet and even predict crimes."[43] Meanwhile, political leaders in the United States are planning to cut back funding for science and technology. In the 1960s, the United States made a $100 billion investment in the space race (adjusted for inflation),[44] which created a satellite industry, gave the United States the lead in microelectronics and materials, and made a political statement on the strengths of the nation in science and technology. This investment is still paying off today since microelectronics and advanced materials are the among the few industries where the United States is still competitive. Thus, China's big investment in the AI race could give it the lead in several key industries well into the twenty-first century. This is our wakeup call.

AI is accelerating the "intangible" information economy. The output of an economy is measured by its Gross Domestic Product (GDP), the total value of all goods and services in dollars. This measure was designed for an industrial economy whose primary products and services were tangible, such as food, automobiles and medical care. However, more and more of the value of an information company is not measured by such products. The buildings and equipment owned by Microsoft, for example, are only worth $1 billion, which is 1 percent of its market value.[45] The rest of its value is based on software and the expertise of Microsoft's programmers. What value would you put on the information you download with your smart phone? We need a new measure that takes into account the value of information in all its forms: Gross Domestic Intangibles (GDI), to augment GDP as a measure of productivity.[46]

Present applications of artificial intelligence are based on basic research that was done thirty years ago. Applications thirty years from now will depend on the basic research being done today, but the best and brightest researchers are working for industry and focused on near-term products and services. This is being balanced by the best and brightest students who are streaming into machine learning, who a generation ago would have gone into investment banking.

In thinking about the future of AI, we need to take the long view, since we are far short of the computing power needed to achieve human levels of intelligence. Deep learning networks now have millions of units and billions of weights. This is a factor of 10,000 fewer than the numbers of neurons and synapses in the human cerebral cortex, where there are a billion synapses in a cubic millimeter of tissue. If all the sensors in the world were connected to the Internet and interconnected by deep learning networks, it might wake up one day and say:

"Hello, world!"[47]

13　The Age of Algorithms

I was in Singapore in June 2016 for a week of discussions at the Grand Challenges for Science in the 21st Century conference held by the Nanyang Technological University. The discussions were wide ranging, from cosmology and evolution to science policy.[1] W. Brian Arthur, an economist with an abiding interest in technology,[2] pointed out that, in the past, technology was driven by the laws of physics: in the twentieth century, we sought to understand the physical world using differential equations and the mathematics of continuous variables, which vary smoothly across time and space. In contrast, today's technology is driven by algorithms: in the twenty-first century, we seek to understand the nature of complexity in computer science and biology using discrete mathematics and algorithms. Arthur is on the faculty of the Santa Fe Institute in New Mexico, which is one of many centers that sprung up in the twentieth century to investigate complex systems.[3]

Algorithms are ubiquitous. We are using algorithms every time we google a query.[4] The news we read on the Facebook newsfeed is chosen by algorithms based on our respective histories of newsfeed clicks, and this affects our emotional reactions.[5] The intrusion of algorithms into our lives is accelerating as deep learning delivers speech recognition and natural language capabilities to our cell phones.

An algorithm is a process with a set of discrete steps or rules to be followed in performing a calculation or solving a problem. The word "algorithm" is derived from the Latin *algorismus*, named after the ninth-century Persian mathematician al-Khwarizmi and refashioned from "algorism" into "algorithm" in the seventeenth century under the influence of the Greek *arithmos*, "number." Although the origin of algorithms is ancient, digital computers have more recently elevated them to the forefront of science and engineering.

Complex Systems

There was a flowering of new approaches to complexity in the 1980s. The goal was to develop new ways to understand systems like those found in living things, systems more complex than those of physics and chemistry. Unlike the simplicity of how rockets move, which follows Isaac Newton's laws of motion, there was no simple way to describe how a tree grows. Computer algorithms were used by a colorful group of pioneers to explore these age-old questions about living things.

Stuart Kauffman was trained as a physician and became intrigued with gene networks in which proteins called "transcription factors" target genes and influence whether or not they are activated.[6] His models were self-organizing and based on networks of binary units that were similar in some respects to neural networks but on much slower timescales. Christopher Langton coined the term "artificial life" in the late 1980s,[7] which led to a flurry of attempts to understand the principles that underlie the complexity of living cells and the development of complex behaviors. Despite the progress we have made in cell biology and molecular genetics to shed light on the highly evolved complexity of the molecular mechanisms inside cells, the mysteries of life continue to elude us.

Algorithms offer new opportunities to create worlds with complexities that we can compare to our own. Indeed, algorithms discovered in the twentieth century have made us rethink the nature of complexity. The neural network revolution in the 1980s was driven by similar attempts to understand the complexity of the brain, and although our neural network models were vastly simpler than the brain's neural circuits, the learning algorithms we developed made it possible to explore general principles such as the distribution of information across large populations of neurons. But how does the complexity of network function arise from relatively simple learning rules? Is there an even simpler system that exhibits a complexity that is easier to analyze?

Cellular Automata

Another colorful character with a scientifically serious approach to complexity, Stephen Wolfram (figure 13.1) was a wunderkind, the youngest person ever to earn a doctorate in physics from Caltech at the age of 20, and the founder of the Center for Complex Systems Research at the University of Illinois in 1986. Wolfram thought that neural networks were too complex and decided instead to explore cellular automata.

Figure 13.1
Stephen Wolfram at his home in Concord, Massachusetts, standing on an algorithmically generated floor. Wolfram was a pioneer in complexity theory and showed that even simple programs can give rise to the complexities of the kind we encounter in the world. Courtesy of Stephen Wolfram.

Cellular automata typically have only a few discrete values that evolve in time, depending on the states of the other cells. One of the simplest cellular automata is a one-dimensional array of cells, each with value of 0 or 1 (box 13.1). Perhaps the most famous cellular automaton is called the "Game of Life," which was invented by John Conway, the John von Neumann professor of mathematics at Princeton, in 1968, popularized by Martin Gardner in his "Mathematical Games" column in *Scientific American*, and is illustrated in figure 13.2. The board is a two-dimensional array of cells that can only be "on" or "off" and the update rule only depends on the four nearest neighbors. On each time step, all the states are updated. Complex patterns are generated in the array, some of which have names, like "gliders," which flit across the array and collide with other patterns. The initial conditions

Box 13.1
Cellular Automaton

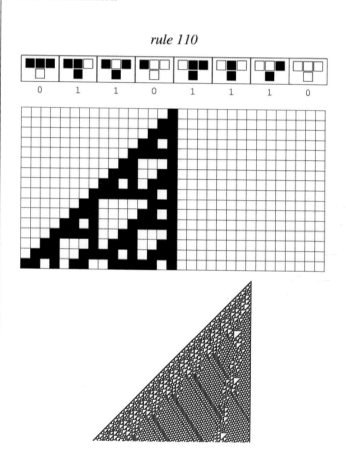

Rule 110. A cellular automata rule specifies the color of a cell, depending on its color and the color of its immediate neighbors. For example, for the eight possible combinations of black and white for three cells shown at the top, rule 110 above specifies the next color under that box. The evolution of this rule applied one line at a time, starting from a single black cell, is shown below for fifteen time steps, and for 250 time steps below that. The simple initial condition evolves into a highly complex pattern that continues indefinitely. Where is the complexity coming from? For more details, see http://mathworld.wolfram.com/Rule110.html.

Figure 13.2
Game of life. Snapshot of a Gosper's Glider Gun (above) that emits a sequence of gliders that travel diagonally, from the "mother ship" (above) to bottom right. From Wikipedia: Gun (cellular automaton), which has an animated gif of the glider gun in action.

are critically important for finding a configuration that displays complex patterns.

How common are rules that generate complexity? Wolfram wanted to know the simplest cellular automata rule that could lead to complex behaviors and so he set out to search through all of them. Rules 0 to 29 produced patterns that would always revert to boring behaviors: all the cells would end up in a repeating pattern or some nested fractal pattern. But rule 30 produced unfolding patterns and rule 110 dazzled with continually evolving complex patterns (box 13.1).[8] It was eventually proved that rule 110 was capable of universal computation; that is, some of the simplest of all possible cellular automata have the power of a Turing machine that can compute any computable function, so it is in principle as powerful as any computer.

One of the implications of this discovery is that the remarkable complexity we find in living things could have evolved by sampling the simplest space of chemical interactions between molecules. That complex combinations of molecules have emerged from evolution should be expected and not considered a miracle. But cellular automata may not be good models for early life, and which simple chemical systems are capable of creating complex molecules remains an open question.[9] It might be that only special biochemical systems have this property, which could help narrow the possible set of interactions from which life could have originated.

An essential property of life is a cell's ability to replicate itself, an ability explored by the Hungarian-born American mathematician John von

Neumann at the Institute for Advanced Study in Princeton in the 1940s using cellular automata. Von Neumann's works had a major impact on many areas of mathematics, especially his seminal work on game theory (mentioned in chapter 1). Looking for the simplest cellular automaton that could replicate itself exactly, von Neumann found a complex cellular automaton with twenty-nine internal states and a large memory that self-replicated.[10] This was of considerable biological interest because cells that are able to self-replicate also have many internal states and memory in the form of DNA. Since then, much simpler cellular automata have been found that also can self-replicate.

Is the Brain a Computer?

In 1943, Warren McCulloch and Walter Pitts showed that it was possible to build a digital computer out of simple binary threshold units like the perceptron, which could be wired up to make the elementary logical gates in a computer.[11] We now know that brains have mixed analog and digital properties and that their neural circuits generally do not compute logical functions. But McCulloch and Pitts's 1943 paper received a lot of attention at the time and, in particular, inspired John von Neumann to think about computers. He built one of the first digital computers that had stored programs, an unusual project for a mathematician at that time, although when von Neumann died in 1957, the Institute for Advanced Study did not continue his line of research and scrapped his computer.[12]

Von Neumann also was interested in the brain. In his 1956 Silliman lectures at Yale,[13] he pondered the question of how the brain could function reliably with such unreliable components. When a transistor in a digital computer makes a mistake, the whole computer can crash, but when a neuron in the brain misfires, the rest of the brain adapts to the misfire and carries on. Von Neumann thought that redundancy might be the reason for the robustness of brains since many neurons are involved in every operation. Redundancy is traditionally based on having a backup, in case the primary system fails. But we now know that redundancy in the brain is based on diversity rather than duplication. Von Neumann also was concerned about logical depth: how many logical steps can a brain make before accumulated errors corrupt the results? Unlike a computer, which can perform each logical step perfectly, brains have many sources of noise. A brain may not achieve perfection, but because so many of its neurons are working together in parallel, it accomplishes much more with each step than a computer can in a single step, and it needs less logical depth.

The Space of Algorithms

Imagine the space of all possible algorithms. Every point in this space is an algorithm that does something, and some algorithms are amazingly useful and productive. In the past, such algorithms were handcrafted by mathematicians and computer scientists working like artisans in guilds. Stephen Wolfram automated the finding of algorithms for cellular automata by exhaustive search, starting with the simplest automata, some of which produced highly complex patterns. This insight can be summarized by Wolfram's law, which states that you don't have to travel far in the space of algorithms to find one that solves an interesting class of problems. This is like sending bots to play games like *StarCraft* on the Internet to try all possible strategies. According to Wolfram's law, there should be a galaxy of algorithms somewhere in the universe of algorithms that can win the game.

Wolfram focused on the space of cellular automata, a small subspace in the space of all possible algorithms. But what if cellular automata are atypical algorithms that exhibits more universality than other classes of algorithms? We now have confirmation of Wolfram's law in the space of neural networks. Each deep learning network was found using a learning algorithm, which is a meta-algorithm that finds new algorithms. For a large network and a large set of data, learning from different starting states can generate a galaxy of networks roughly as good as one another at solving a problem. This raises the question of whether there might be a faster way to find the region of algorithm space than by gradient descent, which is slow and requires a lot of data. A hint that this might be possible is that each species of living organisms is a cloud of individuals created by variant DNA sequences around a point in the space of living algorithms, and nature has managed to jump from cloud to cloud by natural selection, in a saltatory process called "punctuated equilibria,"[14] together with local search by random mutations. Genetic algorithms were designed to make such jumps, based loosely on how nature evolves new organisms.[15] We need a mathematics to describe these clouds of algorithms. Who knows what the universe of algorithms looks like? There are many more galaxies of algorithms that we have not yet discovered, but these can be found by automated discovery—the final frontier.

A simple example of this process was followed by Klaus Stiefel, a postdoctoral fellow in my lab, who, in 2007, used an algorithm that grew model neurons with complex dendritic trees in a computer.[16] Dendrites are like antennas that collect inputs from other neurons. The space of possible dendritic trees is vast, and the goal was to specify the desired function and search the space of dendritic trees for a model neuron that could compute the function. One useful function is to decide on the order of arrival of input spikes: When a particular input arrives before another input, the neuron should output a spike, but if it arrives later, the neuron should remain silent. Such a model neuron was discovered by searching through all possible dendritic trees using a genetic algorithm and the solution looked just like a cortical pyramidal neuron, with a synapse on a thin dendrite coming out the bottom (a basal dendrite) and another synapse on the thick dendrite coming out from the top of the neuron (an apical dendrite; figure 14.6). This is a possible explanation for why pyramidal cells have apical and basal dendrites, a function that might not have been imagined without the help of a deep search through the space of all possible dendrites. By repeating this search starting with other functions, a directory of functions listed by their dendritic shapes could be compiled automatically, and when a new neuron is discovered, its shape could be looked up in the directory to find its possible functions.

Stephen Wolfram left academia to run Wolfram Research, which created Mathematica, a program that supports a wide range of mathematical structures and is widely used for practical applications. Mathematica is written in the Wolfram language, a general multiparadigm programming language that also powers Wolfram Alpha, the first working question-and-answer system for facts about the world based on a symbolic approach.[17] In academia, the coin of the realm is the published paper, but, when you are a self-supporting gentleman scientist, you can afford to bypass bite-sized papers and publish books that allow enough room to thoroughly explore a new area. This was the norm for many centuries when only the wealthy or those with wealthy patrons could afford to be scientists.

Wolfram wrote *A New Kind of Science* in 2002.[18] Weighing in at 5.6 pounds, it was 1,280 pages long, of which 348 pages were notes that contained the equivalent of a hundred new scientific papers. The book appeared with great fanfare in the press but elicited a mixed response from the complex systems community, some of whom thought it failed to fully acknowledge their own work. This objection missed the point of the book, which was to put previous work into a new context. Carolus Linnaeus had developed a modern taxonomy for classifying plants and animals ("binomial nomenclature," e.g., *E. coli*), which was an important precursor to Charles Darwin's theory of evolution and provided a context for previous taxonomies. The trail that Wolfram blazed is now being followed by a new generation of researchers.

In the 1980s, Wolfram was skeptical that much would come from neural networks in the real world, and, indeed, they did not have much impact for the next thirty years. Progress in last five years, however, has changed that: Wolfram and many other researchers have admitted they underestimated what the networks could accomplish.[19] But who could have predicted how well neural networks would scale in their performance? The Wolfram language that supports Mathematica now also supports deep learning applications, one of which was the first to provide online object recognition in images.[20]

Stephen introduced me to Beatrice Golomb, who was working on her doctorate at UCSD when I visited San Diego in 1987. He called me to say that his friend Beatrice would be at my PDP talk (and then called us each afterward to ask how it went). Several years later, I would move to San Diego, and Beatrice and I would become engaged. After our marriage at the Caltech Athenaeum in 1990, we went to the Beckman Auditorium for a marriage symposium, where Beatrice gave a talk ("Marriage: Theory and Practice.") in her wedding gown. Stephen spoke with conviction and pride about how he had introduced us, but when Beatrice pointed out that if he was going to take credit, he also had to take responsibility, he cautiously demurred.

14 Hello, Mr. Chips

We are seeing the birth of a new architecture for the computer chip industry. The race is on to design and build a new generation of chips to run learning algorithms, whether deep, reinforcement, or other, thousands of times faster and more efficiently than the way they are now simulated on general-purpose computers. The new very large-scale integration (VLSI) chips have parallel processing architectures, with memory onboard to alleviate the bottleneck between memory and the central processing unit (CPU) in the sequential von Neumann architectures that have dominated computing for the last fifty years. We are still in an exploratory phase with regard to hardware, and each type of special-purpose VLSI chip has different strengths and limitations. Massive amounts of computer power will be needed to run the large-scale networks that are being developed for AI applications, and there is tremendous potential for profit in building efficient hardware.

Major computer chip companies and startups alike are making substantial investments in developing chips for deep learning. In 2016, for example, Intel purchased Nervana, a small start-up company in San Diego that has designed special-purpose VLSI chips for deep learning, for $400 million; former Nervana CEO Naveen Rao is now heading Intel's new AI Products Group, which reports directly to the CEO of Intel. In 2017, Intel purchased Mobileye, a company that specializes in sensors and computer vision for self-driving cars, for $15.3 billion dollars. Nvidia, which developed special-purpose digital chips optimized for graphics applications and gaming, called "graphics processing units" (GPUs), is now selling more special-purpose chips for deep learning and cloud computing. And Google has designed a far more efficient special-purpose chip, the tensor processing unit (TPU), to power deep learning for its Internet services.

But specialized software is equally important for developing deep learning applications. Google has made its TensorFlow program for running deep learning networks openly available, though this may not be as altruistic as it seems. Making Android freely available, for example, gave Google control of the operating system now used on most smartphones around the world. But now there are openly available alternatives to TensorFlow: CNTK from Microsoft, MVNet, backed by Amazon and other major Internet companies, and other viable deep learning programs, such as Caffe, Theano, and PyTorch.

Hot Chips

In 2011, I organized "Growing High Performance Computing in a Green Environment," a symposium sponsored by the Kavli Foundation and held in Tromsø, Norway.[1] We estimated that, with current microprocessor technology, exascale computing (a thousand times more powerful than petascale computing) would require 50 megawatts—more power than needed to run the New York City subways. The next generation of supercomputers may therefore have to run on low-power chips like the ones developed and optimized for cell phones by the UK-based multinational semiconductor company Arm Holdings (ARM). Soon it will no longer be practical to use general-purpose digital computers for the most compute-intensive applications, and special-purpose chips will dominate, as they already have in cell phones.

There are around 100 billion neurons in a human brain, each connected to around several thousand others, adding up to a thousand trillion (10^{15}) synaptic connections. The power needed to run the brain is around 20 watts, or 20 percent of the power needed to run the entire body, even though the brain accounts for only 3 percent of the body's mass. In contrast, a petascale supercomputer, which is not nearly as powerful as the brain, consumes 5 megawatts, or 250,000 times as much power. Nature accomplished this marvel of efficiency by miniaturizing the components of neurons needed for signaling and communicating down to the molecular level and by interconnecting the neurons in three dimensions (transistors on the surface of microchips are interconnected in only two), making it possible to minimize the volume needed. And because nature evolved these technologies long ago, we have plenty of catching up to do.

Deep learning is highly compute intensive and is now done on centralized servers, with the results delivered to edge devices like cell phones. Ultimately, the edge devices should be autonomous, which will require radically different hardware—hardware that is much lighter and much less power hungry than cloud computing is. But, fortunately, such hardware already exists—neuromorphic chips, whose design was inspired by the brain.

Cool Chips

I first met Carver Mead (figure 14.1) at a workshop held at a resort outside Pittsburgh in 1983. Geoffrey Hinton had assembled a small group to explore where neural networks were heading. Mead was famous for his major contributions in computer science. He was the first to realize that, as the transistors on very large-scale integration chips became smaller and smaller, the chips would become more and more efficient, and therefore computational power should continue to increase for a long time. He coined the term "Moore's law," based on Gordon Moore's observation that the number of transistors on chips was doubling every eighteen months. He was already legendary for inventing, in 1981. the silicon compiler, a program that automatically laid out the pattern of wires and system-level functional modules on a chip.[2] Before the silicon compiler, each chip was handcrafted by engineers based on experience and intuition. In essence, Mead's solution was to program computers to design their own chips. These were our first steps toward nanoscale engineering.

Mead is a visionary. Even as we were huddling around a table in a small room at the workshop outside Pittsburgh, a supercomputer convention was

Figure 14.1
Carver Mead in 1976, around the time he created the first silicon compiler at Caltech. Carver was a visionary whose insights and technological advances have had a major impact on both digital and analog computing. The phone dates the photo. Caltech archives. Courtesy of Caltech.

taking place upstairs. Major supercomputer companies like Cray Inc. and Control Data Corporation were designing special-purpose hardware with $100 million price tags that was hundreds of times faster than the computers in our labs. Cray supercomputers were so fast they had to be liquid cooled with Freon. Mead told me that supercomputer companies didn't know it yet, but microprocessors would eat their lunch and they would soon be extinct. Although much slower than the special-purpose chips in supercomputers, the microprocessors in personal computers evolved faster than the supercomputers because of the ever greater cost reductions and performance improvements brought about by scaling down the basic device dimensions. The microprocessor in a cell phone now has ten times the computational power of a Cray XMP supercomputer from the 1980s, and high-performance supercomputers with hundreds of thousands of microprocessor cores have now reached petascale, a million times faster than the extinct Cray supercomputers, for about the same cost, adjusted for inflation.

At that 1983 workshop, Mead showed us a silicon retina, which was built with the same technology as VLSI chips but used analog rather digital circuits. In an analog circuit, the voltages on the transistors can vary continuously, whereas the transistors in a digital circuit take only one of two binary values, "on" or "off." The human retina has an array of one hundred million photoreceptors, but, unlike a camera that just transmits the photon buckets to memory, the retina has several layers of neural processing that transform the visual input into efficient neural codes. All of the retina's processing is analog until its encoded signals reach the ganglion cells, which carry these signals to the brain in the form of all-or-none spikes along a million axons. The all-or-none character of spikes is like digital logic, but the timing of the spikes is an analog variable, and there is no clock, making spike trains a hybrid code.

In Mead's retina chip, the graded part of the processing was accomplished by using voltages below the knee of the threshold from "off" to the near "off" state. In contrast, running in digital mode, a transistor rapidly jumps to the fully "on" state, which takes much more power. As a consequence, an analog VLSI chip consumes only a tiny fraction of the power of a digital chip, ranging from nanowatts to microwatts rather than from milliwatts to watts, and making it millions of times more energy efficient. The founder of neuromorphic engineering, whose goal is to build chips based on brain-style algorithms, in 1989, Mead showed that neural algorithms embedded in the neural circuits of insect and mammal eyes could be efficiently replicated in silicon.[3]

The retina chip was a 1988 tour de force invention by Mead's star graduate student, Misha Mahowald (figure 14.2).[4] Her insights combined her experience as an undergraduate biology major at Caltech with her graduate work in electrical engineering, which led to four patents. In 1992, she received the Milton and Francis Clauser Prize for her doctoral dissertation on a microchip that did real-time binocular matching, the first chip to use real collective behavior for a demanding task. And, in 1996, she was inducted into the Women in Technology International (WITI) Hall of Fame.

There is a close correspondence between the physics of transistors near threshold and the biophysics of ion channels in biological membranes. Mahowald worked with neuroscientists Kevan Martin and Rodney Douglas at the University of Oxford to develop silicon neurons[5] and moved with them to Zurich to help found the Institute of Neuroinformatics at the University of Zurich and the Swiss Federal Institute of Technology in Zurich (figure 14.3). After suffering from depression, however, Misha took her life in 1996 at the age of 33, a brilliant falling star.

Figure 14.2
Misha Mahowald at Caltech in 1982, at the time she created the first silicon retina as a student of Carver Mead. Her contributions to neuromorphic engineering were seminal. Courtesy of Tobias Delbrück.

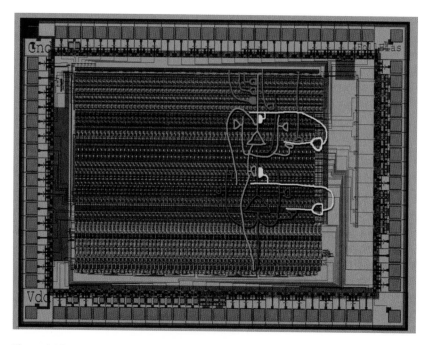

Figure 14.3
Silicon neuron. This analog VLSI chip has circuits that behave like ion channels
in neurons and are able to emulate neural circuits in real time, shown as a cartoon
drawn by Misha Mahowald over the chip. Courtesy of Rodney Douglas.

Carver Mead retired from Caltech in 1999 and moved to Seattle, where I
visited him in 2010. From his backyard, you can see jets over the water vec-
toring in on the final approach to Sea-Tac Airport. His father was an engineer who worked in a power plant at the Big Creek Hydroelectric Project, an
extensive hydroelectric power scheme on the upper San Joaquin River system in the Sierra Nevada of Central California. The technological leap from
early hydroelectrics to microelectronics in a generation is breathtaking.
Carver's hobby is collecting antique glass and ceramic insulators used to
suspend power lines. These can be found scattered like Indian arrowheads
if you know where to look. Carver is a visionary (he has a laser gyroscope
he used to test a new approach to quantum physics),[6] but what made him
so effective was his commitment to building things that not only work but
that you can hold in your hand.

Neuromorphic Engineering

In 1990, as a Fairchild distinguished scholar on sabbatical at Caltech, I enjoyed sitting in on lab meetings, especially those of Christof Koch, a computational neuroscientist with shared interests, and his colleagues, and of Carverland—Carver Mead's research group—one of whose amazing projects was a silicon cochlea, which had frequency-tuned circuits similar to those of the cochleas in our ears. Other researchers were working on silicon synapses, including silicon mechanisms for synaptic plasticity, so that long-term changes in weights could be implemented on silicon chips. Students from Carverland have since gone forth and populated engineering departments around the world.

In 1993, Christof Koch, Rodney Douglas, and I founded the Workshop on Neuromorphic Engineering, sponsored by the NSF, which continues to meet every July for three weeks in Telluride, Colorado. The workshop is international, with students and instructors coming from many different backgrounds and countries. Unlike most workshops, which are more talk than work, the Telluride workshop has rooms filled with students working on microchips and using them to build robots. There was a problem, though, with connecting a retina chip to a visual cortex chip, and cortex chips to motor output chips—too many wires were needed to connect them.

A far better alternative to connecting up analog VLSI chips is to use spikes, which is what our brains do through the long-distance axons of the white matter that makes up half of the cerebral cortex. But it would not be feasible to connect up a retina chip and a cortex chip with a million wires. Fortunately, fast digital logic can be used to multiplex each wire, allowing many retinal cells to communicate with many cortical cells on the same wire. This is done by transmitting to the receiving chip the address from each originating spike in the sending chip, which is then decoded and routed to the units it connects to in what is called "address event representation."

Now at the University of Zurich's Institute of Neuroinformatics, Tobias Delbrück (figure 14.4, top) was one of Carver Mead's graduate students.[7] In 2008, he developed a highly successful spiking retina chip called the "Dynamic Vision Sensor" (DVS) that greatly simplified tasks such as tracking moving objects and locating objects in depth with two cameras (figure 14.4, bottom).[8] Conventional digital cameras are frame based, storing a sequence of 26-millisecond snapshots. Information is lost within each frame: Imagine a spinning disc with a spot on it rotating at 200 revolutions

Figure 14.4

Dynamic Vision Sensor (DVS). (Top) Tobias Delbrück holding a DVS camera that he invented at the Institute for Neuroinformatics at the University of Zurich. The camera is a special-purpose chip that emits spikes asynchronously rather than frames like a digital camera. (Bottom) the camera has a lens that focuses images on an analog VLSI chip that detects incremental increases and decreases in light intensity at each pixel. Spikes are emitted along an "on" wire for positive increments and along an "off" wire for negative increments. The output spikes are processed by the circuit board, which displays the spike patterns seen in box 14.1. Your retina is a highly advanced DVS camera. The pattern of spikes from a retina is transformed in the brain but remains a pattern of spikes—there is no image anywhere in your brain even though you perceive the world that way. Top: Courtesy of Tobias Delbrück. Bottom: Courtesy of Samsung.

per second; the spot will rotate five times in each frame, and the playback of a digital camera will look like a static ring (box 14.1). Tobias's spiking camera, in contrast, can track the moving spot with microsecond precision with very few spikes, which makes it both fast and efficient. The first of a new class of sensors based on spikes and spike timing, the DVS camera has great potential for improving the performance of many applications, including self-driving cars. One of the projects at the 2013 Telluride workshop was to use it to defend a goal from incoming shots (figure 14.5).

Spiking neurons open up new computational opportunities. For example, the timing of the spikes in a population of neurons can be used to regulate what kind of information is stored. In 1997, Henry Markram and Bert Sakmann in Germany reported that they could both increase and decrease synaptic strengths by repeated pairing of an input spike to a synapse with an output spike in the postsynaptic neuron.[9] If the input occurred within a 20-millisecond window before the output spike, there was long-term potentiation, but if the repeated pairing of the input spike occurred within a 20-millisecond window after the output spike, there was long-term depression (figure 14.6). "Spike-timing-dependent plasticity" (STDP), which has been reported in many parts of the brain of many species, is probably important for forming long-term memories of sequences of events—but, perhaps just as important, it offers a better interpretation of Hebb's postulate (discussed in chapter 7).[10]

The general view of Hebbian plasticity was that the strength of a synapse should increase when there was a simultaneous spike on the input and output of a neuron, a form of coincidence detection. But what Hebb actually said was "When an axon of cell *A* is near enough to excite a cell *B* and repeatedly or persistently takes part in firing it, some growth process or metabolic change takes place in one or both cells such that *A*'s efficiency, as one of the cells firing *B*, is increased."[11] For cell A to contribute to firing cell B, cell A has to fire a spike before the spike in cell B. As described by Hebb, this condition suggests causation, not just correlation. Although Hebb was silent on the conditions for decreasing the strength of a synapse, when an input spike occurs after the output spike, it is less likely to be causally connected to the output neuron, and disconnecting the synapse would make sense if increases and decreases in strength have to be balanced in the long run.

There is a running debate at the Telluride Neuromorphic Workshop between the analog VLSI advocates and the digital designers. Analog VLSI chips have many advantages, such as consuming very little power with all circuits working in parallel, but they also have shortcomings, such as

Box 14.1

How a Dynamic Vision Sensor Camera Works

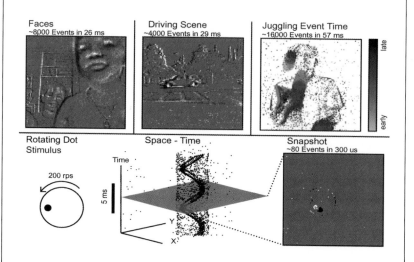

In the frames from a DVS camera shown in the figure above, the white spots are spikes from the "on" channels and the black spots are spikes from the "off" channels. Gray indicates no spikes. In the upper left frame, two faces can be detected because they moved slightly during the 26-millisecond frame. In the upper right (juggling) frame, the spots have their arrival time indicated by gray level so you can see the trajectory. The spinning disk in the bottom left panel is rotating at 200 revolutions per second (rps). In the bottom middle panel, the trajectory is a spiral moving upward. In a brief 300-microsecond slice of the spiral shown in the bottom right panel, there are only 80 spikes and it is easy to calculate the speed by measuring the displacement of the black and white spikes divided by the time interval. Note that a digital camera with a 26-millisecond frame duration will not be able to follow the spot rotating at 200 Hertz because the rotation period is 5 milliseconds, and every frame will be an annulus. The only output from the camera is a stream of spikes, just like a retina. This is an efficient way to represent the scene since most pixels are silent most of the time, and each spike carries useful information. From P. Lichtsteiner, C. Posch, and T. Delbrück, "A 128×128 120 dB 15 µs Latency Asynchronous Temporal Contrast Vision Sensor," *IEEE Journal of Solid-State Circuits* 43, no. 2 (2008): figure 11. Courtesy of Tobias Delbrück.

Figure 14.5
Neuromorphic goalkeeper at the 2013 Workshop on Neuromorphic Engineering in Telluride. (Top) Fopefolu Folowosele (left) tests the neuromorphic goalkeeper (right). Other students and their projects can be seen in the background. (Bottom) Delbrück's DVS camera directs a paddle at the end of a paint mixing stick. The goalkeeper is much faster than the students and saves every shot on goal. I also tried and failed to make a goal. Courtesy of Tobias Delbrück.

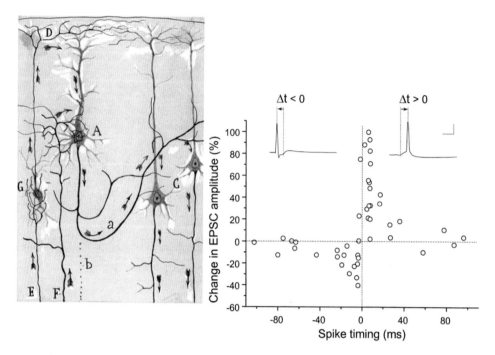

Figure 14.6

Spike-timing-dependent plasticity (STDP). (Left) Drawing of pyramidal neurons from the cortex by the great Spanish neuroanatomist Santiago Ramón y Cajal. The output axon from neuron A makes synaptic contacts onto the dendrite of neuron C (arrows). (Right) Two neurons like those on the left were impaled with an electrode and stimulated to produce spikes with a time delay between the spikes in the two neurons. When an input spike to a neuron is repeatedly paired with an output spike, the change in the strength of a synapse (vertical axis) can either increase if the presynaptic input arrives before the postsynaptic spike within a window of 20 milliseconds (horizontal axis), or decrease in strength in the opposite order. From Left: Ramón y Cajal, S. *Estudios Sobre la Degeneración y Regeneración del Sistema Nervioso* (Moya, Madrid, 1913–1914), figure 281. Right: G. Q. Bi and M. M. Poo, "Synaptic Modifications in Cultured Hippocampal Neurons: Dependence on Spike Timing, Synaptic Strength, and Postsynaptic Cell Type," *Journal of Neuroscience* 18 (1998): 10464–10472, figure 7. Courtesy of Mu-ming Poo.

transistor variability, which results in identically drawn transistors producing currents that can differ by ±50 percent. Digital VLSI, in comparison, though more accurate, faster, and easier to design, requires a lot more power. Dharmendra Modha's team at IBM Research in Almaden, California, developed a digital chip with 4,096 processing cores and 5.4 billion transistors called "True North."[12] Though the chip can be configured to simulate a million spiking neurons connected by 268 million synapses, it consumes only 70 milliwatts. But the strengths of these synapses are fixed, and this inflexibility limits the implementation of many important features, such as weakening or strengthening.

Another shortcoming of networks with spiking neurons is that gradient descent, which has propelled learning in networks of continuously valued neurons, is not possible because of the discontinuities at the spike times. This limits the complexity of what a spiking network can be taught. Gradient descent has been hugely successful in training deep networks with model neurons that have continuously varying output rates, so that the output function is differentiable, an essential feature for the backprop learning algorithm. Although nondifferentiable spiking networks have discontinuities when a spike occurs, this drawback was recently overcome by Ben Huh, a postdoctoral fellow in my lab, who found a way to make recurrent network models of spiking neurons perform complex tasks over long temporal sequences using gradient descent.[13] This opens the door to training deep spiking networks.

No More Moore's Law?

As predicted by Moore's law, computer power has increased more than a trillionfold since digital computers were invented in the 1950s. Never before has any technology been able to grow exponentially through so many orders of magnitude, which has resulted in the embedding of computers into almost every manufactured device, from toys to automobiles. Computers can automatically adjust the adaptive optics of modern telescopes to maximize their resolution; they can analyze the photons captured by modern microscopes to localize molecules with super-resolution. Every area of science and technology is now dependent on VLSI chips.

Carver Mead predicted the rise of these chips based on the potential for shrinking the line width on them, but the width has now reached a physical limit: there are too few electrons in the wires, and they tend to leak out or be blocked by random charges, making even digital circuits unreliable.[14] Is Moore's law no more? A radically different architecture is needed to continue increasing processing power, one that does not depend on the perfect accuracy of digital designs. Just as hybrid automobiles married the efficiency of electric motors with the range of gasoline engines, a hybrid digital and neuromorphic design is emerging that takes advantage of the low power needs of neuromorphic chips for computing and the high bandwidth of digital chips for communicating.

Moore's law is based only on the processing power of chips. As parallel architectures continue to evolve over the next fifty years, Moore's law should be replaced with a law that takes into account energy as well as throughput. At the 2018 NICE Conference hosted by Intel in Portland, Oregon, researchers from the United States and Europe presented three new neuromorphic chips, the Loihi research chip from Intel, and two second generation chips supported by the European Human Brain Project. With the development of massively parallel architectures, new algorithms are being created to run on these architectures. But the chips within these architectures need to communicate information, which is the focus of chapter 15.

15 Inside Information

It never occurred to me that I would someday become omniscient, which for all practical purposes I and indeed anyone else with access to the Internet now is. Information flows through the Internet at the speed of light. It is easier to get a fact from the Internet than from a book on my shelf. We are living through an explosion of information in its many forms. Scientific instruments, from telescopes to microscopes, are collecting larger and larger data sets that are being analyzed with machine learning. The National Security Agency uses machine learning to sift through all of the data it has been collecting everywhere. The economy is going digital, and programming skills are in great demand at many companies. As the world shifts from an industrial to an information economy, education and job training will have to adapt. This already is having a profound impact on the world.

Information Theory

In 1948, Claude Shannon (figure 15.1) at the AT&T Bell Laboratories in Murray Hill, New Jersey, proposed a remarkably simple but subtle theory for information to understand signal transmission through noisy phone lines.[1] Shannon's theory drove the digital communications revolution that gave rise to cell phones, digital television, and the Internet. When you make a cell phone call, your voice is encoded into bits and transmitted over radio waves and digital transmission lines to a receiver, where the digital signals are decoded and converted to sounds. Information theory puts bounds on the capacity of the communications channel (figure 15.2), and codes have been devised that approach the Shannon limit.

Despite the many forms of information in the world, there is a way to measure precisely how much of it is in a data set. The unit of information is a "binary bit," which can take on a value of 1 or 0. A "byte" is eight bits.

Figure 15.1

Claude Shannon around 1963 in front of a telephone switching network. He worked at AT&T Bell Laboratories when he invented information theory. From Alfred Eisenstaedt/The LIFE Picture Collection/Getty Images.

The information content of a high-quality photo is measured in megabytes, or millions of bytes. The amount of information stored in your cell phone is measured in gigabytes, or billions of bytes. Data on the Internet are measured in petabytes, or quadrillions (millions of billions) of bytes.

Number Theory

At its annual international symposium, the IEEE Information Theory Society (ITS) confers the Claude E. Shannon Award, a high honor, in recognition of distinguished research in the field. At the society's 1985 symposium in Brighton, England, the Shannon Award was given to Solomon

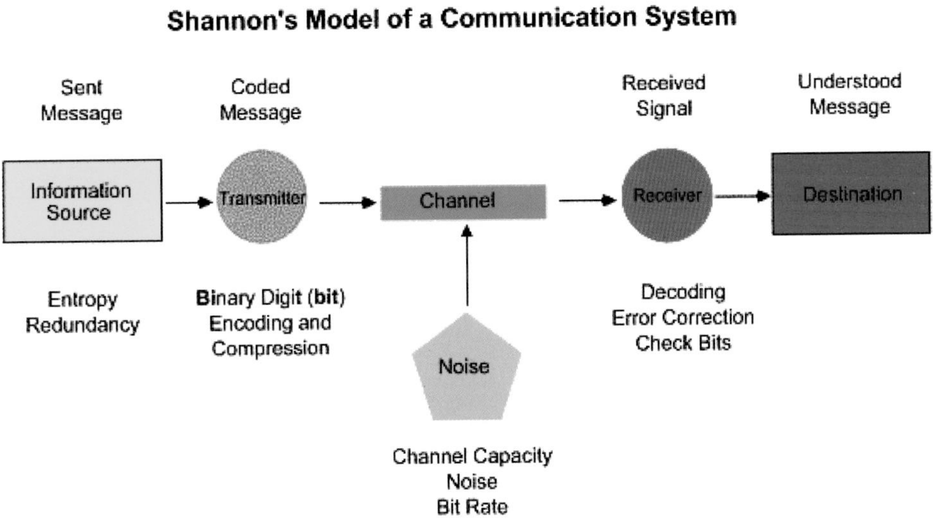

Shannon's Model of a Communication System

Figure 15.2

Shannon's model of a communication system. The message is coded into binary bits and transmitted down a channel, which could be a phone line or radio wave, where it is received and decoded. The channel capacity in bits per second depends on the amount of noise in the system. From https://dennisdjones.wordpress.com. Courtesy of Dennis Jones.

Golomb (figure 15.3) of the University of Southern California, whose work on shift register sequences was fundamental to modern digital communication.[2] A shift register sequence is an algorithm that generates long pseudorandom sequences of 0s and 1s. Every time you make a call on your cell phone you are using a shift register sequence. Golomb showed how to use a shift register sequence to efficiently encode signals, which could then be transmitted and decoded at the receiver. If you were to add up all the times that cell phones and other communications systems have generated a shift register sequence, the number would be staggering: more than an octillion times, which is 10^{27}, a billion billion billion (1,000,000,000,000,000,000,000,000,000).[3]

I once asked Solomon Golomb (who was my father-in-law) how he hit upon such an elegant solution to the communication problem. He said that it came from his training in number theory, one of the most abstract parts of mathematics. He had been introduced to shift register sequences when he was a summer intern at the Glenn L. Martin Company in Baltimore. In 1956, after receiving a doctorate from Harvard in number theory, a highly

Figure 15.3
Solomon Golomb in 2013 upon receiving the National Medal of Science. His mathematical analysis of shift register sequences made it possible to communicate with deep space probes when he was at the Jet Propulsion Laboratory at Caltech in Pasadena; the shift register sequences later became embedded in cell phone communication systems. Every time you use your cell phone you are using his mathematical codes. Courtesy of the University of Southern California.

abstract area of mathematics, he took a job at Caltech's Jet Propulsion Laboratory (JPL), where he was head of the communications group and worked on space communications. Deep space probes were being sent out to the far reaches of the solar system, but the signals coming back were weak and noisy. Shift register sequences and error-correcting codes greatly improved communication with space probes, and the same mathematics laid the foundation for modern digital communications.

Golomb hired Andrew Viterbi at JPL, another distinguished information theorist, and introduced him to Irwin Jacobs, whom he had invited to visit JPL on a sabbatical from MIT. Decades later, in 1985, Viterbi and Jacobs would cofound Qualcomm, which revolutionized the technology in cell phones by using shift register sequences that spread the information across a broad frequency band rather than using a single frequency as a more

Figure 15.4
Hedy Lamarr in a 1940 MGM publicity photo. Star of stage and screen during the Second World War, she coinvented frequency hopping, which is related to spread spectrum communication used by the military and in many cell phones.

efficient way to communicate. A simpler version of this idea goes back to Hedy Lamarr (figure 15.4), a movie actress and inventor who, in 1941, shared the patent on frequency hopping, which she developed as a secure communication system for the military during World War II.[4] When Sol Golomb left JPL to join the faculty at the University of Southern California, Ed Posner took over his group, the same Ed Posner who founded NIPS, but Golomb continued to support his former JPL group with advice.

The mathematics behind shift register sequences is a deep part of number theory. When Golomb received his doctorate from Harvard, his doctoral advisor, and most mathematicians at that time, were proud to believe that pure mathematics would never have any practical applications. This view was shared by G. H. Hardy, a Cambridge don whose influential book *A Mathematician's Apology*[5] declared that "good" mathematics had to be pure and that applied mathematics was "uninteresting." But mathematics is what it is, neither pure nor applied. Some mathematicians may want their mathematics to be pure, but they can't stop it from solving practical problems in the real world. Indeed, Golomb's career was largely defined by finding important practical problems he could solve using the right tools from "pure mathematics."

Golomb also invented mathematical games. His book *Polyominoes*[6] introduced the world to games that involved shapes composed of many squares, generalizing dominoes, which have only two. Martin Gardner popularized Polyominos in his "Mathematical Games" column in *Scientific American.* Tetrominoes, shapes made from four squares, were the inspiration for *Tetris,* an addictive game in which Tetrominoes rain from above and have to be guided into slots below. Polyominos remains a popular board game and has led to a wide range of interesting combinatorial problems in a subfield of mathematics.

Golomb was also a biblical scholar and could speak dozens of languages, including Japanese and Mandarin Chinese. Beatrice once brought him a first edition of *Gödel, Escher, Bach: An Eternal Golden Braid* by Douglas R. Hofstadter. Sol opened to the frontispiece, which the caption said was the first twenty lines of the Book of Genesis in ancient Hebrew. "First of all, it's upside down," he said and then turned it around. "Second, this is in ancient Samaritan, not ancient Hebrew. Third of all, this isn't the first twenty lines of Genesis, but only the first seven words of each of the first twenty lines of Genesis." He proceeded to read and then translate the text.

Claude Shannon attended the 1985 IST symposium in Br Golomb gave the Shannon Lecture, the only Shannon Lec attended other than his own in 1972.

Predictive Coding

In a communication system, change has high information v the change is across space or over time. An image with uniform intensity carries little information, and neither does a signal that is not changing. Sensors that send signals to the brain mainly detect change, and we have already seen examples in the retina in chapter 5 and Tobias Delbrück's DVS camera in chapter 14. Once stabilized on the retina, images fade away after a few seconds.[7] Though we are unaware of it, our eyes make tiny jumps called "microsaccades" several times a second, each jump refreshing our internal model of the world. When something moves in the world, retinas duly report that upstream, and their reports update the brain's world model, an operation diagrammed in figure 15.5. The brain's model is a hierarchical one, and comparison between the incoming sensory information and the expectations of the model take place at multiple levels.[8] A bright flash or loud noise gets your immediate attention by bottom-up saliency.

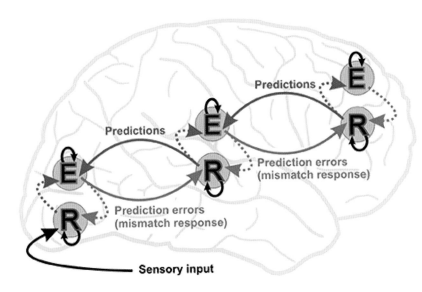

Figure 15.5

A hierarchical predictive coding framework. Perception depends on prior expectations based on regularities extracted from earlier sensory events. In this framework, predictions about current sensory signals made by higher levels of the cortex arise from the interaction between the E and R populations and are fed back to the earlier level. Only the prediction errors are propagated forward. This is an implementation of Helmholtz's unconscious inference. From Gábor Stefanics, Jan Kremláček, and István Czigler, "Visual Mismatch Negativity: A Predictive Coding View," *Frontiers in Human Neuroscience* 8 (2014): 666, figure 1. doi:10.3389/fnhum.2014.00666.

But you notice that something on your desk has changed at a much higher level, by making top-down comparisons from memory. That all of this is happening in real time in the brain leads us to the Carver Mead mantra that "time is its own representation."[9]

Predictive coding goes back to Hermann von Helmholtz, who explained vision as unconscious inference, or top-down generation of visual information to cancel noise, fill in incomplete information, and interpret the visual scene.[10] For example, the size of a known person's image on one of our retinas is a monocular cue for depth since we are familiar with that person's actual size and have experience with how retinal size varies with distance. At a higher cognitive level, James McClelland and David Rumelhart found that when letters were situated in the context of a word, subjects were able to identify them faster than when they were in a nonword without semantic context.[11] Their parallel processing model exhibited similar behavior, which gave the two researchers confidence they were on the right track to understanding how information is represented in our brains.

The Global Brain

Launched by the White House on April 2, 2013 (figure 15.6), the U.S. BRAIN Initiative is creating new neurotechnologies to accelerate the rate at which we can improve our understanding of function and dysfunction in the ultimate information machine—the brain. Just as the NIPS conferences brought together researchers from many disciplines to create learning machines, the BRAIN Initiative is drawing engineers, mathematicians, and

Figure 15.6
Representatives from the agencies and institutions involved, shortly before the announcement of the BRAIN Initiative at the White House on April 2, 2013. (Right to left) Miyoung Chun, chief science officer at the Kavli Foundation, who spearheaded the white paper for the BRIAN Initiative; William Newsome, the cochair of the NIH Advisory Committee on the BRAIN Initiative; Francis Collins, NIH director; Gerald Rubin, director of the Janelia Research Campus of the Howard Hughes Medical Institute; Cora Marrett, NSF director, President Barack Obama, Amy Gutmann, chair of the presidential Bioethics Committee; Robert Conn, president of the Kavli Foundation, Arati Prabhakar, DARPA director; Alan Jones, director of the Allen Institute for Brain Science; Terry Sejnowski, Salk Institute. Courtesy of Thomas Kalil.

physicists into neuroscience to improve tools to probe the brain. As we learn more about the brain, and especially about the mechanisms underlying learning and memory, we will have a much better understanding of the principles of brain function.

Although much about the brain is known at the molecular and cellular levels, we have not yet achieved a comparable understanding of how the brain is organized at higher levels. We know that different types of information are stored in widely distributed parts of the cortex, but we don't know how all the disparate pieces of information can be retrieved so quickly to solve a complex problem like recognizing the name of a person from the image of that person's face, which is stored in different parts of the cortex. This question is closely tied to the origin of consciousness in brains.

My lab recently discovered global patterns of activity in sleeping human brains that may give us insight into how pieces of information distributed broadly in the cerebral cortex are linked together. In a stage of sleep intermediate between restorative slow-wave sleep and rapid eye movement (REM) dream sleep, highly synchronized spatiotemporal oscillations called "sleep spindles" dominate cortical activity. These 10–14-Hertz oscillations last for a few seconds and recur thousands of times during the night. There is experimental evidence that sleep spindles participate in memory consolidation while we are sleeping. In recordings from the human cortex, Lyle Muller, Sydney Cash, Giovanni Piantoni, Dominik Koller, Eric Halgren, and I discovered that sleep spindles are global, circular traveling waves of electrical activity that sweep through all sectors of the cortex (figure 15.7).[12] We call them "Princess Leia waves" because they look like her hairstyle (figure 15.8). We speculated that sleep spindles may be a way for the cortex to integrate new information acquired during the day with previous memories, distributed widely in the cortex, by strengthening the long-distance connections between them. This is one of many research projects at the level of systems neuroscience spurred on by the BRAIN Initiative.

Operating Systems

The architecture of digital computers is different from that of neural networks. In digital computers, the memory and the central processing unit (CPU) are spatially separated, and data in memory must be moved to the CPU sequentially. In neural networks, the processing takes place in the memory in parallel, which eliminates the digital bottleneck between memory and processing, and which allows massively parallel processing since all

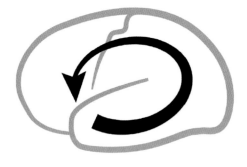 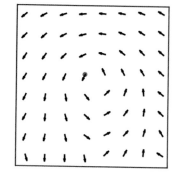

Figure 15.7

Rotating electrical traveling waves in human cerebral cortex. Recordings from an 8×8 grid of electrodes on the cortical surface during sleep spindles, which are involved in memory consolidation. (Left) Spindles are circular waves that travel across the side view of the cortex in the direction shown by the arrow, making a loop every 80 milliseconds. This is repeated thousands of times during the night. (Right) The small arrows show the direction of maximum increase in the phase of the traveling wave at the sixty-four recording sites on the surface of the cortex. From: L. Muller, G. Piantoni, D. Koller, S. S. Cash, E. Halgren, and T. J. Sejnowski, "Rotating Waves during Human Sleep Spindles Organize Global Patterns of Activity during the Night" supplement 7, subject 3, TPF. Left: figure 2B, right: figure 1.

Figure 15.8

Carrie Fisher playing Princess Leia consolidating a memory in the epic 1977 science fiction/fantasy film *Star Wars*. Her hair buns resemble the circular flow fields that course across the cortex during sleep spindles. (Compare with figure 15.7.) Photo courtesy of Sunset Boulevard/Corbis/Getty Images.

the units in the network are all working at the same time. There is also no distinction between software and hardware in neural networks. Learning takes place by making changes to the hardware.

Starting in the 1980s, when clusters of computers were assembled in one rack, digital computers have become massively parallel. One of the earliest parallel computers was the Connection Machine, designed by Danny Hillis in 1985 and sold by Thinking Machines, Inc. An engineer and inventor, Hillis trained at MIT when it was becoming clear that much more computational power would be needed to make artificial intelligence achieve solutions to immensely complex real-world problems. As the number of transistors on a computer chip continued to increase according to Moore's law in the 1990s, it became possible to put many processing units on the same chip, many chips on the same board, many boards in the same cabinet, and many cabinets in the same room—with the result that today the fastest computers on the planet have millions of cores and can achieve many millions of billions of operations per second. Exascale computing is on the horizon with billions of billions of operations per second.

Simulations of neural networks can take maximum advantage of this massively parallel hardware. Multiple cores can be programmed to work in parallel on the same network model, which greatly speeds up processing, but this also results in delays in communicating between the processors. To reduce these delays, companies are building special-purpose digital coprocessors that will vastly speed up network simulations, so that cognitive tasks like speech and seeing will become single powerful instructions. Our smartphones will become a lot smarter when they're built with deep learning network chips.

Digital computers have operating systems that separate us from the hardware (box 15.1). When we run word processing programs on our laptops or apps on our cell phones, the operating systems take care of all the details about where to put our keystrokes into memory, and how to display the output on a screen. Our minds run the equivalent of apps on our brains' operating systems, which isolate us from what, where, and how information is stored. We are unaware of how our brains store the vast databases of experience we have accumulated during our lifetimes, or how our behavior is shaped by these experiences. It is possible to make some of the experiences explicit, but we are consciously aware of only the very tip of an iceberg. It is a mystery how our brains manage this. If we could figure out how the operating systems of our brains work, we could organize big data based on the same general principles. Consciousness could then be explained as an app running on the brain's operating system.

Box 15.1
Operating System of a Digital Computer

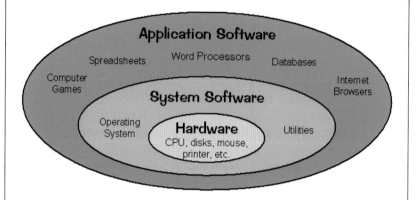

An operating system controls the programs that run on the hardware of a computer. If you are using a PC, the operating system is most often Windows; if you are using an iPhone, it is iOS; most servers are running some version of UNIX. The operating system allocates memory when needed by the programs; it also works behind the scenes to keep track of programs, using processes called "daemons," which run in the background and keep track of utilities like printers and displays. The operating system is designed to work on any hardware, making your applications portable between computers.

It's Information, All the Way Down

The information explosion has transformed biology into a quantitative science. Biologists traditionally needed little mathematical training beyond an introductory course in statistics to analyze their data, which were few and hard won. At a symposium on molecular genetics held by the Cold Spring Harbor Laboratory on Long Island in 2002, I felt like a fish out of water because I was the only one giving a computational talk. Speaking before me was Leroy Hood, a molecular geneticist who was on the faculty at Caltech for many years. While on sabbatical at Caltech in 1987, I was astonished to find that Hood's lab filled an entire building. Since then, he had moved to Seattle, where, in 2000, he cofounded the Institute for Systems Biology, a new field that is attempting to understand the complexity of all the molecular interactions within cells.

In his talk, Hood said that one day he asked himself why he had more computer scientists than biologists on his payroll. The reason, he concluded, was that biology had become an information science and that computer scientists knew far more about analyzing information than did biologists, who had been overwhelmed by the vast amounts of data generated by modern techniques such as gene sequencing. I could not have asked for a better way to motivate my talk, which was about understanding how information is stored at synapses between neurons in the brain.

Today systems biology is attracting many computer scientists and physicists to analyze and understand the information that is being generated by DNA sequencing and the signals in cells that are controlled by RNA and proteins. The 3 billion base pairs in the DNA of a human cell contain all the information the cell needs to survive, replicate, and specialize. Some base pairs are templates for making proteins, but other parts of the genome contain an abstract code to regulate genes that are used during development to guide the construction of the body and brain. Perhaps the most demanding construction project in the universe, the construction of brains is guided by algorithms embedded in the DNA that orchestrate the development of connections between thousands of different types of neurons in hundreds of different parts of the brain.

Playing the Long Game

The commercialization of technology developed by basic science research typically takes about fifty years. The great discoveries that were made in relativity and quantum mechanics during the first decade of the twentieth century gave rise to CD players, GPS, and computers in the second half of that century. The discovery of DNA and the genetic code in the 1950s gave rise to applications in medicine and agribusiness that are having an economic impact today. The basic discoveries that the BRAIN Initiative and other brain research programs around the world are making today will lead to applications fifty years from now that would be considered science fiction today.[13] We can expect AIs to have operating systems comparable to the one in our brain by 2050. But which companies and which countries will control this technology depends on investments and big bets being made today.

16　Consciousness

When his mother asked young Francis Crick what scientific problems he wanted to pursue in life, he told her there were only two that interested him: the mystery of life and the mystery of consciousness.[1] Crick clearly had a keen sense for what is important, but he may not have appreciated the difficulty of these problems. Little did his mother know that, decades later in 1953, her son and James Watson would discover the structure of DNA—the loose thread that would eventually unravel one of life's great mysteries. But Crick (figure 16.1) was not content with this achievement.

After moving to the Salk Institute in 1977, Crick took up his long-standing interest in consciousness. He decided to focus on the question of visual awareness since a great deal was already known about the visual parts of the brain, and understanding the neural basis of visual perception would serve as a solid foundation for exploring the neural basis of other aspects of consciousness.[2]

That the study of consciousness was out of fashion among biologists in the 1980s did not deter Crick. Visual perception was filled with illusions and mysteries that defied understanding. Seeking explanations for them in anatomical and physiological mechanisms, he developed the novel "searchlight hypothesis."[3] Ganglion cells project down the optic nerve to the thalamus, which in turn relays the spikes to the visual cortex. But why couldn't the ganglion cells project directly to the cortex? Crick pointed out that there was a feedback projection from the cortex back to the thalamus that, like a searchlight, might highlight parts of the images for further processing.

Neural Correlates of Consciousness

Crick's closest colleague on the quest to understand consciousness was neuroscientist Christof Koch, then at Caltech, with whom he published a

Figure 16.1
Francis Crick with his wife, Odile, and daughter Jacqueline punting on the Cam in Cambridge, England, around 1957. Courtesy of Maurice S. Fox.

series of papers exploring the "neural correlates of consciousness" (NCCs; the brain structures and neural activities responsible for generating states of conscious awareness).[4] In the case of visual awareness, this meant finding correlations between the firing properties of neurons in different parts of the brain and visual perception. Crick and Koch hypothesized that we are not aware of what happens in the primary visual cortex,[5] which is the first area of the cerebral cortex to receive input from the retinas; rather, we are only aware of what happens at the highest levels of the hierarchy of the visual cortex (figure 5.11). Support for this possibility comes from the study of binocular rivalry, in which two different patterns are presented to the two eyes, such as vertical stripes to one eye and horizontal stripes to the other eye: rather than seeing a blend of the two images, visual perception flips abruptly between the disparate images every few seconds. Different neurons in the primary visual cortex respond to the patterns from each eye, regardless of which is being consciously perceived at any moment. At the higher levels of the visual hierarchy, however, many neurons respond only to the perceived image. Thus it is not enough for a neuron to be firing for it to be a neural correlate of perception. Apparently, we are only aware of what is represented in a subset of the active neurons distributed over the hierarchy of visual areas working together in a coordinated way.

Grandmother Cells

In 2004, an epilepsy patient at the UCLA Medical Center whose brain was being monitored to detect the origin of the seizures was shown a series of pictures of celebrities. Electrodes implanted into the memory centers of the patient's brain reported spikes in response to the photos. In one of these patients, a single neuron responded vigorously to several pictures of Halle Berry and her name (figure 16.2), but not to pictures of Bill Clinton or Julia Roberts or the names of other famous people.[6] Neurons were found that responded to other celebrities, to specific objects, and to buildings, like the Sydney Opera House.

The neurons found by the team led by Itzhak Fried and Christof Koch at the University of California, Los Angeles, had been predicted fifty years ago when it first became possible to record from single neurons in the brains of cats and monkeys. Researchers thought that, in the hierarchy of visual areas of the cerebral cortex, the response properties of neurons became more and more specific the higher the neurons were in the hierarchy, perhaps so specific that a single neuron at the top of the hierarchy would only respond to pictures of a single person. This became known as the "grandmother cell hypothesis," after the putative neuron in your brain that "recognizes" your grandmother.

Even more dramatic were experiments in which patients looked at a blend of two images representing familiar individuals and were asked to imagine one individual at the expense of the other, competing one, while recording from neurons that preferred one or the other image. The subjects were able to increase the firing rates of the neuron that represented the face they favored in the blend, while simultaneously decreasing the rates of other neurons that preferred the competing face, even though the

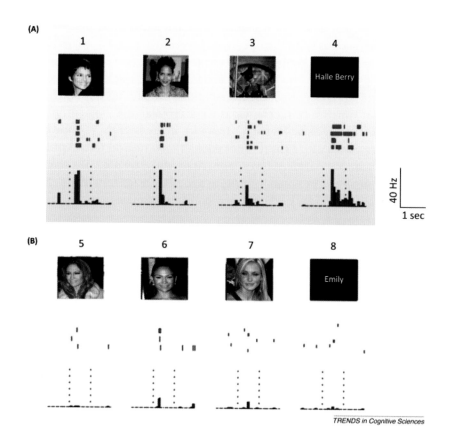

Figure 16.2
Halle Berry cell. The responses to photos of a single neuron recorded from the hippocampus of a patient. Spikes (blue tics) from six individual trials are shown below each photo, along with the average (histograms). (A) Photos of Halle Berry and her name elicited a burst of spikes, whereas (B) photos of other actresses and their names did not. Halle Barry starred in the 2004 action superhero film *Catwoman* (photo 3). From A. D. Friederici and W. Singer, "Grounding Language Processing on Basic Neurophysiological Principles," *Trends in Cognitive Sciences* 19, no. 6 (2015): 329–338, figure 1.

visual stimulus was not changing. The experimenters then closed the loop by controlling the ratio of the two images in the mixture according to the firing rates of the neurons preferring the images, so the subjects could control the input—the ratio of the two faces—by imagining one or the other image. This illustrates that the process of recognition is not simply a passive process, but depends on active engagement of memory and internal attentional control.

Despite this striking evidence, the grandmother cell hypothesis is unlikely to be the whole story of visual perception. According to the hypothesis, you perceive your grandmother when the cell is active, so it should not fire to any other stimulus. Only a few hundred pictures were tested, so we really don't know how selective the "Halle Berry cell" was. Second, the likelihood that the electrode happened to record from the only Halle Berry neuron in the brain is low; it is more likely that there are many thousands of these cells in the brain. There must also be many copies of neurons that respond to other famous faces, and many more for everyone you know and every object you can recognize. Although there are billions of neurons in the brain, there aren't enough to exclusively represent every object and name that a person knows by a large dedicated population of neurons. Finally, the response is only a correlation with the sensory stimulus and may not be causal. Equally important is the output of the neuron and its downstream impact on behavior (the projective field introduced in chapter 5). Nonetheless, the selectivity of the responses is striking. Before the recordings began, the patient was asked to identify a favorite celebrity, so Halle Barry might be overrepresented in the patient's brain.

Recordings from hundreds of cortical neurons simultaneously in mice, monkeys, and humans are leading to an alternative theory for how neurons collectively perceive and decide.[7] In recordings from monkeys, stimuli and task-dependent signals are broadly distributed over large populations of neurons, each tuned to a different combination of features of the stimuli and task detail.[8] Before long, it will be possible to record from millions of neurons and to manipulate their firing rates, as well as to distinguish different types of neurons and how they are connected with one another.[9] This could lead to theories beyond the grandmother cell and a deeper understanding of how activity in populations of neurons gives rise to thoughts, emotions, plans, and decisions. Of course, there may be more than one way for neurons to represent faces and objects. With new recording techniques coming online, however, we should soon know the answer.

We have known since the 1980s in trained neural network models with one layer of hidden units, and more recently in deep networks, that patterns of activity for each input in neural networks are highly distributed in a way that is qualitatively similar to the variety of responses that have been observed in populations of cortical neurons (figure 9.2).[10] A distributed representation can be used to recognize many versions of the same object, and the same set of neurons can recognize many different objects by differentially weighting their outputs. When individual hidden units in neural networks are tested in the same way that neurophysiologists record from neurons in the visual cortex, sometimes one simulated neuron near the top of the hierarchy is found to develop a specific preference for one of the objects. But, because the remaining neurons carry redundant signals representing the object, the performance of the neural network does not appreciably change when such a unit is cut out of it. The robust performance of neural networks despite damage is a major difference between the architecture of both these networks and the brain itself and that of digital computers.

How many cortical neurons are needed to discriminate between many similar objects such as faces? From imaging studies, we know that several areas of the human brain respond to faces, some with a high degree of selectivity. But, within these areas, the information about any single faces is broadly distributed among many neurons. Doris Tsao at Caltech has recorded from neurons in monkey cortex that respond selectively to faces and has shown that it is possible to reconstruct faces by combining the inputs from 200 face cells, a relatively small subset of all face-selective neurons.[11]

When Is the Time of a Visual Event Perceived?

Another aspect of visual awareness are the brain's efforts to register events, like flashes of light, as occurring at specific times. The time delays of neurons in the visual cortex in response to a flashed visual stimulus vary from 25 to 100 milliseconds, often within the same region of the cortex. Nonetheless, we can determine the order of two flashes that occur within 40 milliseconds of each other, and the order of two sounds with less than a 10-millisecond time difference. To make this even more paradoxical, the processing in the retinas takes a certain amount of time, which is not fixed but depends on the intensity of the flash, so that there is a delay in the arrival time of the first spike from a dim flash compared to one from a bright flash, even though the dim and bright flashes appear to occur simultaneously. This raises the question of why visual percepts seem to have a unity that is not at all apparent from the temporally and spatially distributed patterns of activity throughout the cortex.

The question of simultaneity becomes even more vexing when we make cross-modal comparisons. When you watch someone chop down a tree, assuming you're close enough, you simultaneously see and hear the axe hit the tree with each blow, even though the speed of sound is much slower than that of light. Moreover, the illusion of simultaneity is maintained as the distance from the tree increases,[12] even though the absolute delay between the visual and auditory signals as they reach your brain can vary more than 80 milliseconds before the illusion is broken, and the sound is no longer perceived as simultaneous with the axe hit (at about 100 feet away).

Researchers who study the temporal aspects of vision have uncovered another phenomenon called the "flash-lag effect." This can be observed when an airplane with a flashing taillight passes overhead and the flashes and tail don't seem to line up—the flashes seem to lag behind the tail. Another common occurrence is at soccer matches when a running player appears to be ahead of a kicked ball (the flash), which can elicit an offside call from an assistant referee who has not compensated for the illusion. This can be studied in the lab with a visual stimulus illustrated in figure 16.3. In the flash-lag effect, a flash and a moving object at the same location appear to be offset.

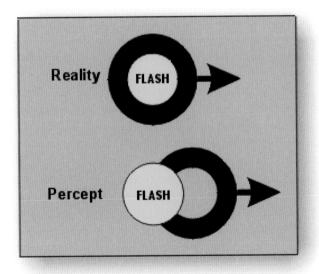

Figure 16.3

Flash-lag effect. (Top) An annulus moves from left to right (black). As it passes the center a light briefly flashes below it (yellow). (Bottom) Subjects report that the object appears to be displaced to the right at the time of the flash. Courtesy of David Eagleman.

One leading explanation—which makes intuitive sense, and for which there is some evidence from brain recordings—is that the brain predicts where the moving spot is going to be a short time later. But perceptual experiments have shown that this cannot be the explanation for the flash-lag effect because the perception attributed to the time of the flash depends on events that occur in the 80 milliseconds *after* the flash, not those which occur before the flash (which would be used to make a prediction).[13] This explanation for the flash-lag effect means that the brain is "postdictive" rather than predictive; that is, the brain is constantly revising history to make the conscious present consistent with the future. This is one example of how our brains generate plausible interpretations based on noisy and incomplete data, something that magicians have exploited for sleight-of-hand effects.[14]

Where in the Brain Is a Visual Object Perceived?

Brain imaging gives us a global picture of our brains' activity when we perceive something compared to when we don't. Using experimental evidence, researchers have developed the particularly appealing hypothesis that we only become consciously aware of something when the level of brain activity in the front of the cortex, which is important for planning and making decisions, reaches a threshold level and ignites feedback pathways.[15] Though intriguing, these observations are not compelling since they don't establish causality, but only a correlation. If a neural correlate of consciousness is responsible for—causes—a conscious state, it should be possible by changing the NCC to change that conscious state. Doris Tsao has shown that this indeed was the case in her 2017 experiment; by stimulating face areas in the visual cortex of monkeys, she was able to interfere with their discrimination of faces.[16] When a similar experiment was done in humans, subjects reported that faces looked as if they were melting.[17]

New techniques such as optogenetics[18] have recently become available to selectively manipulate the activity of neurons, which allows the causality of the NCCs to be tested. This may be difficult to do if perceptual states correspond to highly distributed patterns of activity, but, in principle, this approach could reveal how perceptions and other features of consciousness are formed.[19]

Learning Where to Look

Visual search is a task that depends on both bottom-up sensory processing and top-down attentional processing driven by expectation (figure 16.4A).

These two types of processing are intermingled in the brain and difficult to disentangle, but recently a novel search task was developed to tease them apart.[20] Participants were seated in front of a blank screen and told that their task was to explore the screen with their eyes to find a hidden target location that would sound a reward tone when their gaze fixated near it. The hidden target position varied from trial to trial and was drawn from a Gaussian distribution—a bell-shaped curve characterized by the position of its peak and width—that was not known to participants but remained constant during a session (figure 16.4D).

At the start of a session, participants had no prior knowledge to inform their search. Once a fixation was rewarded, they could use that feedback to assist on the next trial. As the session proceeded, participants improved their success rates by developing an expectation for the distribution of hidden targets and using it to guide future searches. After approximately a dozen trials, the participants' visual fixations narrowed to the region with high target probability. A characterization of this effect for all participants is shown in figure 16.4D. The search region, initially broad, narrowed as the session progressed. Surprisingly, many of the subjects were not able to articulate their search strategy, even though their first saccade after a few trials was invariably to the center of the invisible target distribution.

These experiments point toward unconscious control of actions that is guided by experience. By eliminating the visual input, the unconscious processes can be studied in isolation. The brain areas that are involved in this search task include the visual cortex and the superior colliculus, which controls the topographic map of the visual field and directs saccades to visual targets, respectively, working closely with other parts of the oculomotor system. Learning also involves the basal ganglia, an important part of the vertebrate brain that learns sequences of actions through reinforcement learning.[21] The difference between the expected and received reward is signaled by a transient increase in the firing rate of dopamine neurons in the midbrain, which regulates synaptic plasticity and influences how decisions and plans are made at an unconscious level (as discussed in chapter 10).

Passages

Near the end of his life, Francis Crick invited me to visit him at his home to discuss the claustrum, a mysterious thin layer of cells just beneath the cortex that receives projections from many cortical areas and in turn projects back. Even though Crick was terminally ill, he focused on finishing his last paper on the hypothesis that the claustrum was responsible for the unity of

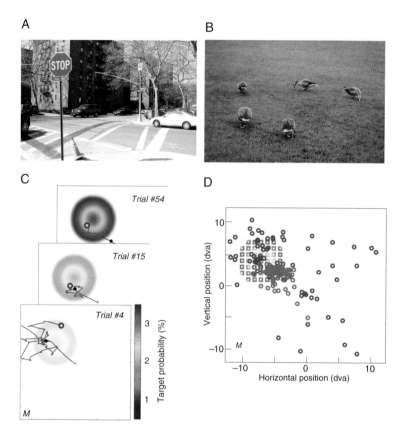

Figure 16.4

Learning where to look. (A) An experienced pedestrian has prior knowledge of where to look for signs, cars, and sidewalks in this street scene. (B) Ducks foraging in a large expanse of grass. (C) A representation of the screen is superimposed with the hidden target distribution that is learned over the session as well as sample eye traces from three trials for participant M. The first fixation of each trial is marked with a black dot. The final and rewarded fixation is marked by a shaded grayscale dot. (D) The region of the screen sampled with fixation shrinks from the entire screen on early trials (light gray circles; first five trials) to a region that approximates the size and position of the Gaussian-integer distributed target locations (squares, color proportional to the probability as given in (C) on later trials (red circles; from trials 32–39). From L. Chukoskie, J. Snider, M. C. Mozer, R. J. Krauzlis, and T. J. Sejnowski, "Learning Where to Look for a Hidden Target," figure 1.

consciousness by virtue of its central position. Only a handful of researchers had ever worked on the claustrum, and he called nearly every one of
them to ask for further information. My visit was the last time I would
ever see him. Francis died on July 28, 2004, while working to complete
the manuscript of his last paper[22] and to finish his search for the origins of
consciousness.

Fifty years after he and James Watson discovered the structure of DNA
in 1953, the human genome was sequenced. Crick told me it had never
occurred to him that it would ever be possible. How far will we be fifty
years from now on the problem of consciousness? By then, we will have
machines that interact with us in much the same way that we now interact
with one another, through speech, gestures, and facial expressions. It may
be easier to create consciousness than to fully understand it.

I suspect that we can make progress faster by first understanding unconscious processing—all the things we take for granted when we see, hear,
and move. We have already made progress on understanding motivational
systems, which strongly influence our decisions; and attentional systems,
which help guide our search for information from the world. With a deeper
understanding of the brain mechanisms that govern perception, decision
making, and planning, the problem of understanding consciousness could
disappear like the Cheshire cat, leaving only a broad grin.[23]

17 Nature Is Cleverer Than We Are

An Oxford-educated chemist who worked on the origins of life, Leslie Orgel (figure 17.1, right) was a colleague at the Salk Institute for many years and one of the smartest scientists I have ever met. Discussions with him at faculty lunch on Fridays were always fascinating. The origin of life goes back billions of years to a time when the earth was so different from today that it would not support life as we know it. Conditions were harsh, and there was little oxygen in the atmosphere. Bacteria were preceded on the earth by archaea, but what came before archaea? DNA is common to all cells today, but what came before DNA? In 1968, Leslie Orgel and Francis Crick speculated that RNA, which is derived from DNA in cells, might have been the precursor, but this would require RNA to self-replicate. Evidence for this possibility was found in the form of ribozymes, RNA-based enzymes that can catalyze RNA reactions,[1] and today most researchers in the field believe it is quite possible that all life descended from an earlier "RNA world."[2] But where did RNA come from? Unfortunately, we have little evidence from that period to go on.

Orgel's Second Rule

Time and again, universally held truths have been shattered by surprising discoveries. We looked up and saw the sun going around the earth, but we were the ones going around the sun. The theory of evolution put us humans in our place, though even today it remains difficult for many to accept. Many years from now, our descendants will look back at our era and say that our intuitions about intelligence were at best oversimplified and held back progress in artificial intelligence for fifty years. As Orgel's second rule states, evolution is cleverer than you are.

Our conscious awareness is the tip of an iceberg, most of the workings of our brain are inaccessible to introspection. We have words like "attention"

Figure 17.1
Francis Crick (left) and Leslie Orgel (right) at the Salk Institute in 1992 on the trail of the origins of consciousness and the origins of life, respectively. Courtesy of The Salk Institute.

and "intention" that we use to describe our behavior, but these are slippery concepts that hide the complexity of the brain processes underlying them. And artificial intelligence based on intuitive folk psychology has been disappointing. We see, but we know not how. We think, and therefore believe that we are, but the machinery behind thinking is a mystery. There is no survival advantage for nature to reveal to us how the brain really works. Orgel's second rule prevails.

As noted in chapter 2, we have highly evolved visual systems, but this does not make us experts on how we see.[3] Many of us are not even aware we have a fovea with sharp vision that is only 1 degree of arc across, about the size of a thumb at arm's length, and that we are legally blind beyond the fovea. When I once pointed this out to my mother, she said she didn't believe me because it was perfectly clear everywhere she looked. But we have the illusion of high resolution everywhere because we can rapidly reposition our eyes. Are you aware that when you gaze at an object, your eyes dart back and forth over the object at three times a second? Peripheral vision may have low spatial resolution but is exquisitely sensitive to changes in brightness and motion. A major stream in visual cortex, separate from the one that recognizes objects, is devoted to moving around in space.

When the pioneers of computer vision set out to engineer vision, their goal was to create a complete internal model of the world from an image, a goal that has proven difficult to achieve. But a complete and accurate model may not be necessary for most practical purposes, and it might not even be possible given the low sampling rate of current video cameras.

Based on evidence from psychophysics, physiology, and anatomy, Patricia Churchland, neuropsychologist V. S. Ramachandran, and I came to the conclusion that the brain represents only a limited part of the world, only the part needed at any moment to carry out the task at hand.[4] This also makes it easier for reinforcement learning to narrow down the number of possible sensory inputs that contribute to obtaining rewards. The apparent modularity of vision (its relative separateness from other sensory processing streams) is also an illusion. The visual system integrates information from other streams, including signals from the reward system indicating the values of objects in the scene, and the motor system actively seeks information by repositioning sensors, such as moving eyes and, in some species, ears to gather information that may lead to rewarding actions.

Brains evolved through a long process of progressive adaptation to the environment; nature could not afford to start with a clean slate but had to make do by modifying parts and pieces while keeping the current species viable. In his book *Evolving Brains*,[5] John Allman illustrates progressive evolution on an urban human scale by recounting a visit to the boiler room of an old power plant in San Diego, where he noticed an intricate array of small pneumatic tubes next to a bank of vacuum tubes, alongside several generations of computer control systems. Because the plant was needed for continuous power output, it could not be shut down and retrofitted with each new technology, so the old control systems were left in place and the new ones integrated into them. So, too, with evolving brains: nature could not afford to throw out an old brain system, but tinkered with the current developmental plan, occasionally adding a new layer of control. Gene duplication was a favorite route for introducing a copy of a gene that could mutate for a new function. Whole genome duplication also occurred, which could lead to an entirely new species.

The Case against Noam Chomsky

Psychologists who studied learning in the 1930s approached behavior as a transformation of sensory inputs into motor outputs and called themselves "behaviorists." Associative learning was the focus for behaviorism, and many laws of learning were uncovered by training animals on different reward schedules. B. F. Skinner at Harvard University was a leader in this field and wrote several popular books to explain the consequences of his discoveries for society.[6] Interest about behaviorism was high in the popular press at that time.

In 1971, the eminent linguist Noam Chomsky (figure 17.2) wrote a devastating attack on behaviorism in general, and B. F. Skinner in particular, in the *New York Review of Books* (figure 17.3).[7] Here is a sample of his argument specifically on language:

> But what does it mean to say that some sentence of English that I have never heard or produced belongs to my "repertoire," but not any sentence of Chinese (so that the former has a higher "probability")? Skinnerians, at this point in the discussion, appeal to "similarity" or "generalization," but always without characterizing precisely the ways in which a new sentence is "similar" to familiar examples or "generalized" from them. The reason for this failure is simple. So far

Figure 17.2

Noam Chomsky in 1977, after he wrote "The Case against B. F. Skinner" for the *New York Review of Books*. Chomsky's essay had a profound impact on a generation of cognitive psychologists, who would embrace symbol processing as a conceptual framework for cognition and discount the essential role of brain development and learning in cognition and intelligence. Hans Peters/Anefoto.

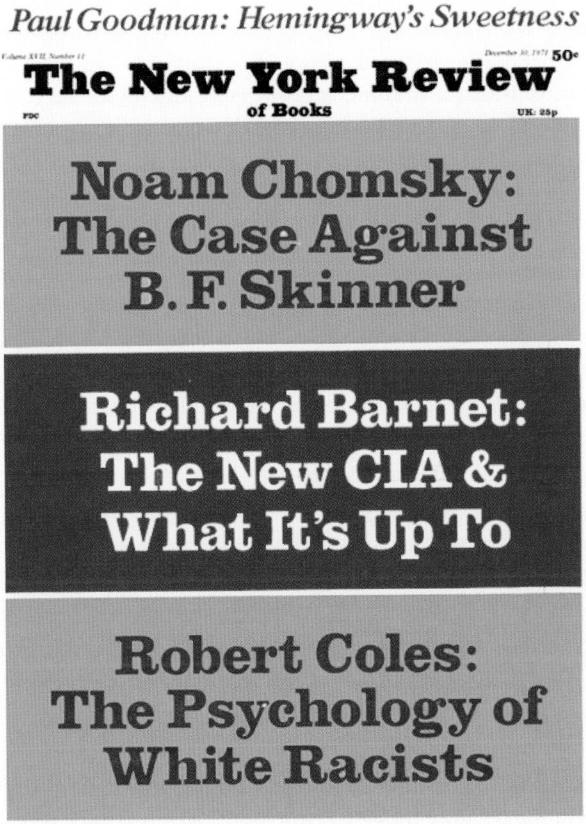

Figure 17.3
Cover headline for Noam Chomsky's 1971 takedown of B. F. Skinner in the *New York Review of Books*. Chomsky's essay would influence a generation of scientists to abandon behavioral learning and take up symbol processing as a way to explain cognition. But with the symbolic approach, artificial intelligence never achieved cognitive levels of performance. B. F. Skinner was on the right track with reinforcement learning, which Chomsky derided: today's most compelling AI applications are based on learning, not logic. Courtesy of the *New York Review of Books*.

as is known, the relevant properties can be expressed only by the use of abstract theories (for example, a grammar) describing postulated internal states of the organism, and such theories are excluded, a priori, from Skinner's "science." The immediate consequence is that the Skinnerian must lapse into mysticism (unexplained "similarities" and "generalization" of a sort that cannot be specified) as soon as the discussion touches the world of fact. While the situation is perhaps clearer in the case of language, there is no reason to suppose that other aspects of human behavior will fall within the grasp of the "science" constrained by a priori Skinnerian restrictions.[8]

From today's perspective, we can see that Chomsky understood what was at stake, but that he simply didn't know the power of learning. Deep learning has shown us that, like the neural networks of the brain itself, model neural networks are capable of "generalization" of the sort that Chomsky dismissed as "mysticism," and that they can be trained to selectively recognize speech from many languages, to translate between languages and to generate captions for images, with perfectly good syntax. The ultimate irony is that machine learning has solved the problem of automatically parsing sentences, something that Chomsky's "abstract theories" of syntax never accomplished despite strenuous efforts by computational linguists. When coupled with reinforcement learning, whose study in animals Skinner pioneered, complex problems can be solved that depend on making a sequence of choices to achieve a goal. This is the essence of problem solving and ultimately the basis of intelligence.

Dripping with disdain, Chomsky's essay went far beyond taking down B. F. Skinner: it challenged—and indeed dismissed—learning as a way to understand cognition. This had a decisive influence on cognitive psychology in the 1970s. That associative learning could ever give rise to a cognitive behavior as complex as language, the crux of Chomsky's argument ran, was simply unimaginable (at least to Chomsky). Note, however, that this argument was based on ignorance. Just because the world's leading linguist says he cannot imagine something doesn't make it impossible. But Chomsky's rhetoric, which resonated with the zeitgeist of the 1970s, was persuasive. By the 1980s, the symbol processing approach to cognition had become the only game in town and formed the basis for a new field called "cognitive science," an amalgam of cognitive psychology, linguistics, philosophy, and computer science. Neuroscience was the weak sister of cognitive science and was more or less ignored until cognitive neuroscience was launched in the 1990s.

Poverty of Imagination

Chomsky has since used the same rhetorical arguments many times, most notably in his argument for the innateness of language based on "poverty of the stimulus,"[9] which asserts that a baby does not hear enough examples of sentences to be able to learn the rules of syntax. But a baby is not a computer getting a string of disembodied symbols from the world. A baby is immersed in a world of rich sensory experiences and is learning about the nature of the world at a breathtaking pace.[10] The world is filled with meaningful experiences that are tied to sounds, which begin in the womb, a form of unsupervised learning, and it is only after this foundation is laid that language generation begins, first with babbling, then with single words, and much later with syntactically correct sequences of words. What is innate is not grammar, but the ability to learn language from experience and to absorb the higher-order statistical properties of utterances in a rich cognitive context.

What Chomsky could not imagine was that, when coupled with deep learning of the environment and a deeply learned value function honed by a lifetime of experience, a weak learning system like reinforcement learning can indeed give rise to cognitive behaviors, including language. This was not at all obvious to me in the 1980s, although I should have realized that, if a tiny network like NETtalk could handle English pronunciation, it was likely that, in their representations of words, learning networks, whether model or cortical, would have a natural affinity for language. Chomsky's position was based on a poverty of imagination, but it follows logically from Orgel's second rule: evolution is cleverer than you are, and that includes experts like Chomsky. Indeed, when an expert tells you something in nature is impossible, beware—no matter how plausible or convincing the argument.

Chomsky's emphasis on word order and syntax became the dominant approach in linguistics in the latter half of the twentieth century. But even a "bag of words" model neural network that throws away word order does remarkably well at determining the topic of an article, such as sports or politics, and its performance can then be improved by taking into account the immediate neighborhoods of words in the article. The lesson from deep learning is that, even though word order carries some information, semantics, based on the meaning of words and their relationships with other words, is more important. Words are represented in the brain by a rich internal structure. And as we learn more about how words are semantically represented in deep learning networks, we may have the beginnings of a new linguistics. Just as there is no reason why nature should burden us with knowing how we see, there is no reason why our intuition into how we use language should be any better.

Let's consider what the internal structure of words might look like in a model network trained on a natural language task. Although a network may be trained on a particular problem, the way the network represents its inputs can be used to solve other problems. A good example is a network trained to predict the next word in a sentence. The representations of words in the trained network have internal structure, in the form of patterns of activity of all the units in the network, that can be used to draw analogies between word pairs.[11] For example, when these activity patterns are projected onto a plane, vectors connecting countries to their capital cities are all the same. The network learned to automatically organize concepts and learn implicitly the relationships between them, without having any supervised information about what a capital city means (figure 17.4). This shows that the semantics of countries and capitals can be extracted from text using unsupervised learning.

I once opened a presentation at MIT by declaring, "Language is too important to be left to the linguists."[12] What I meant was that we shouldn't stop at describing language at the behavioral level. We should seek to understand the biology of language, the underlying biological mechanisms, and how language ability evolved in *Homo sapiens*. This has become possible with noninvasive brain imaging and with recordings directly from the brains of epilepsy patients. Equally important are brain studies to understand the differences that made language possible by comparing human brains with those of chimpanzees and other higher primates; the ability to use language happened in an evolutionary instant compared to the earlier and much slower acquisition of sensorimotor skills. Powerful genetic tools will allow us to dissect the development of the brain and to understand how evolution gave rise to our innate ability to learn languages by tinkering with development.

Language can be used to mislead and control by appealing to plausibility and by arguing from ignorance, which has unfortunate consequences far beyond science. History is filled with demagogues, who are eventually abandoned when the poverty of their imaginations is exposed. Fortunately, brains have been around a lot longer than language, and we will be better served if we rely on the parts of our brains that evolved long before language.[13]

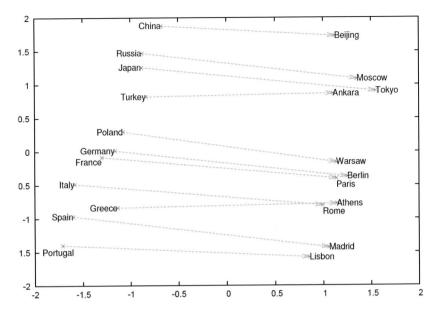

Figure 17.4
Internal representation of words in a network trained to predict the next word in a sentence. Each word is a vector of activity in the network, which can be projected down to the two-dimensional plane as shown above. The arrows connect countries to their capitals. Because all these arrows are parallel to each other and about the same length, the word pairs are represented analogously. For example, if you want to find out the capital of a different country, you can add this arrow to the vector of the country and retrieve its capital vector. From: T. Mikolov, I. Sutskever, K. Chen, G. Corrado, and J. Dean, "Distributed Representations of Words and Phrases and Their Compositionality," figure 2. Courtesy of Jeffrey Dean.

The Case against Black Boxes

In retrospect, behaviorism and cognitive science, which in the twentieth century took opposite approaches to behavior, made the same mistake by ignoring the brain. Behaviorists did not want to be misled by introspection, so they made it a point of honor not to look into the brain for guidance. They believed that it would be possible to discover behavioral laws for any contingency by carefully controlling the inputs and outputs of the black box. Functionalist cognitive scientists, for their part, rejected behaviorism, believing they could discover the internal representations of the mind, but because they also believed that the details of how the brain implemented the representations were irrelevant,[14] the internal representations they developed were based on unreliable intuition and folk psychology. Nature was cleverer than they were.

The internal states of the black box are tremendously complex; discovering internal representations and the laws of behavior is thus exceedingly difficult. If someday we do discover the laws of behavior, we may well be able to give a functional account of them, although this account will probably be as counterintuitive as quantum mechanics was to physicists. To discover the laws of behavior, we will need all the help we can get from the brain. Deep learning networks are good examples of the progress that can be made by paying attention to some general features of brain architecture and general principles of brain function. I have no doubt that the hard-line functionalists will protest, but we need to move forward, not look backward. At every step along the way, adding a new feature from brain architecture has boosted the functionality of deep learning networks: the hierarchy of cortical areas; the brain's coupling of deep with reinforcement learning; working memory in recurrent cortical networks; and long-term memory of facts and events—to name just a few. There are many more computational principles of the brain that we can learn from and make the most of.[15]

In their experiments, neuroscientists who study perception, memory, and decision making typically use trial-based tasks, in which laboratory animals are trained to give the desired response to a stimulus. After months of training, these stimulus-driven responses become reflexive, rather than reflective, which can reveal mechanisms underlying habitual behaviors but not cognitive behaviors. Thinking is not a reflex; it can occur in the absence of any sensory stimulus; but the traditional way that experiments are designed ignores ongoing spontaneous activity that is present in the absence of sensory inputs. New methods are needed to study internal activity that is neither sensory nor motor related, which includes conscious thinking and unconscious processing. This is beginning to happen now that brain imaging experiments have revealed resting states that spontaneously occur when someone is put in a scanner and asked to "rest." The mind wanders when there is nothing to do and thoughts show up as a changing pattern of brain activity that we can see but do not yet understand.

Brain imaging, and especially noninvasive functional magnetic resonance imaging (fMRI), has opened up new ways to study social interactions and decision making, spawning a new field called "neuroeconomics."[16] Because humans are not the rational actors often assumed in classical economics, we need to build a behavioral economics based on actual not idealized human judgment and motivation as these emerge from complex internal brain states.[17] As noted in chapter 10, dopamine neurons have a powerful influence on motivation by representing reward prediction error. Brain imaging of social interactions has probed human motivation in ways that purely behavioral experiments could not. The goal is to replace a theory of rational decisions based on logic with a theory of probabilistic decisions based on prior experience.

The Case against Marvin Minsky

The early history of neural networks is a case study in how a small but influential group can derail the exploration of a competing research direction. Near the end of *Perceptrons*, Marvin Minsky and Seymour Papert (figure 17.5) expressed the opinion that the perceptron learning algorithm could not be extended to multilayer perceptrons:

> The problem of extension is not merely technical. It is also strategic. The perceptron has shown itself worthy of study despite (and even because of!) its severe limitations. It has many features to attract attention: its linearity; its intriguing learning theorem; its clear paradigmatic simplicity as a kind of parallel computation. There is no reason to suppose that any of these virtues carry over to the many-layered version. Nevertheless, we consider it an important research

Figure 17.5
Marvin Minsky and Seymour Papert in 1971, shortly after they wrote *Perceptrons*. This excellent mathematical analysis of simple networks had a chilling effect on a generation of researchers pursuing approaches to artificial intelligence based on learning in multilayer networks. Cynthia Solomon/Courtesy of MIT.

problem to elucidate (or reject) our intuitive judgment that the extension is sterile. Perhaps some powerful convergence theorem will be discovered, or some profound reason for the failure to produce an interesting "learning theorem" for the multilayered machine will be found.[18]

Sterile, indeed. This ungrounded "intuition" in Minsky and Papert's otherwise excellent book had a chilling influence on the development of learning in neural networks and set back research for a generation, although I personally benefited from this delay because it made my career possible. But I had an opportunity to look behind the curtain in the twilight of Minsky's career.

I was invited to attend the 2006 Dartmouth Artificial Intelligence Conference, "AI@50," a look back at the seminal 1956 Summer Research Project on artificial intelligence held at Dartmouth and a look forward to the future of artificial intelligence.[19] Five of the original ten pioneers from the 1956 project were in attendance: John McCarthy (Stanford), Marvin Minsky (MIT), Trenchard More (IBM), Ray Solomonoff (University of London), and Oliver Selfridge (MIT). It was a fascinating meeting both scientifically and sociologically.

In his talk "Artificial Intelligence Vision: Progress and Non-Progress," Takeo Kanade (from Carnegie Mellon) noted that computer memories back in the 1960s were tiny by today's standards and could hold only one image at a time. For his doctoral dissertation in 1974, Takeo had shown that, though his program could find a tank in one image, it was too difficult for it to do so in other images where the tank was in a different position and the lighting was different. But, by the time his early students graduated, the programs they designed could recognize tanks under more general conditions because computers were more powerful. Today his students' programs can recognize tanks in any image. The difference is that today we have access to millions of images that sample a wide range of poses and lighting conditions, and computers are millions of times more powerful.

In "Intelligence and Bodies," Rodney Brooks (from MIT) spoke about his experience with building robots that crawl and meander. Intelligence evolved in brains to control movements, and bodies evolved to interact with the world through that intelligence. Brooks departed from the traditional controllers used by roboticists and used behavior rather than computation as the metaphor for designing robots. As we learn more from building robots, it will become apparent that the body is a part of the mind.

In "Why Natural Language Processing is Now Statistical Natural Language Processing," Eugene Charniak explained that a basic part of grammar is to tag parts of speech in a sentence. This is something that humans can be trained to do much better than the extant parsing programs. The field of computational linguistics initially tried to apply the generative grammar approach pioneered by Noam Chomsky in the 1980s, but the results were disappointing. What eventually worked was to hire Brown undergraduates to hand-label the parts of speech for thousands of articles from the *Wall Street Journal,* and then to apply statistical techniques to identify the most likely part of speech for a particular word in the neighborhood of other specific words. Many examples are needed because most words have multiple meanings, and there are many different contexts for each word. Automatic tagging of parts of speech in sentences is now a solved problem based on machine learning.

These success stories had a common trajectory. In the past, computers were slow and only able to explore toy models with just a few parameters. But these toy models generalized poorly to real-world data. When abundant data were available and computers were much faster, it became possible to create more complex statistical models and to extract more features and relationships between the features. Deep learning automates this process. Instead of having domain experts handcraft features for each application, deep learning can extract them from very large data sets. As computation replaces labor and continues to get cheaper, more labor-intensive cognitive tasks will be performed by computers.

In his summary talk at the end of the conference, Marvin Minsky started out by saying how disappointed he was both by the talks and by where AI was going. He explained why: "You're not working on the problem of general intelligence. You're just working on applications." The conference was supposed to be a celebration of the progress we had made, so his rebuke stung. My talk about recent progress with reinforcement learning and the remarkable results achieved by TD-Gammon in teaching networks to play champion-level backgammon had not impressed him. He dismissed this as a mere game.

What did Minsky mean by "general intelligence"? In his book *The Society of Mind,*[20] the premise is that general intelligence emerges from the interactions between simpler agents. Minsky once said that the biggest source of ideas about his theory came from trying to create a machine that used a robotic arm, a video camera, and a computer to build a structure from children's blocks (figure 2.1).[21] Which sounds suspiciously like an application. But a concrete application forces you to focus and get to the bottom of a problem in a way that abstract theorizing cannot. The successes reported by the speakers at the Dartmouth conference came with deep insights into concrete problems that paved the way for a more general theoretical understanding. Perhaps a better theory of general intelligence will someday emerge from these narrow AI successes.

Our brains don't simply sit around generating abstract thoughts. They are connected intimately with all parts of our bodies, which in turn are connected intimately with the world through our sensory inputs and motor effectors. Biological intelligence is therefore embodied. Even more important, our brains develop through a long process of maturation while interacting with the world. Learning is a process that coincides with development and continues long after we reach adulthood. Learning is therefore central to the development of general intelligence. It is interesting that one of the most difficult unsolved problems in artificial intelligence is common sense, something noticeably absent in children, and something that emerging slowly in most adults only after prolonged experience with the world. Emotions and empathy, which often are ignored in AI, are also an essential aspect of intelligence.[22] Emotions are global signals to prepare the brain for actions that cannot be decided by local brain states.

There was a banquet on the last day of AI@50. At the end of the dinner, the five returning members of the 1956 Dartmouth Summer Research Project on Artificial Intelligence made brief remarks about the conference and the future of AI. In the question and answer period, I stood up and, turning to Minsky, said: "There is a belief in the neural network community that you are the devil who was responsible for the neural network winter in the 1970s. Are you the devil?" Minsky launched into a tirade about how we didn't understand the mathematical limitations of our networks. I interrupted him—"Dr. Minsky, I asked you a yes or no question. Are you, or are you not, the devil?" He hesitated for a moment, then shouted out, "Yes, I am the devil!"

In 1958, Frank Rosenblatt built an analog computer that was designed to emulate a perceptron because digital computers were painfully slow at simulating network models, which were highly compute intensive. By the 1980s, computer power had increased greatly and we were able to explore learning algorithms through simulations of small networks. But it was not until the 2010s that sufficient computer power became available to scale up networks to sizes that could solve real-world problems.

Minsky's doctoral dissertation in mathematics from Princeton in 1954 was a theoretical and experimental study of computing with neural networks. He had even built small networks from electronic parts to see how they behaved. The story I heard when I was a graduate student at Princeton in physics was that there wasn't anyone in the Mathematics Department who was qualified to assess his dissertation,[23] so they sent it to the mathematicians at the Institute for Advanced Study in Princeton who, it was said, talked to God. The reply that came back was, "If this isn't mathematics today, someday it will be," which was good enough to earn Minsky his Ph.D. And neural networks have indeed given rise to a new class of mathematical functions that are spurring new studies and are on their way to becoming a new branch of mathematics. The youthful Minsky was ahead of his time.

Passages

Marvin Minsky died in 2016, steadfast in his belief that neural networks were a dead end on the way to achieving general artificial intelligence. In a thoughtful essay on his friendship with Minsky, Stephen Wolfram wrote: "And although I don't think anyone could have known it then, we now know that the neural networks Marvin was investigating as early as 1951 were actually on a path that would ultimately lead to just the kind of impressive AI capabilities he was hoping for. It's a pity it took so long, and Marvin barely got to see it."[24]

Shortly after Minsky's death, Alex Graves, Greg Wayne, and colleagues, researchers at DeepMind, achieved the next step toward a general artificial intelligence based on deep learning by adding a dynamic external memory.[25] Activity patterns can only be stored temporarily in a deep recurrent neural network, which makes it difficult to emulate reasoning and inference. By adding a stable memory to the network that can be written to and read back with the same flexibility as a digital computer memory, the researchers demonstrated a network trained with reinforcement learning that could answer questions that required reasoning. For example, one such network reasoned about paths in the London Underground and another answered questions about genealogical relationships in a family tree. The dynamic memory network was also able to master the Blocks World transfer task that had challenged the MIT AI Lab in the 1960s (figure 2.1). This brings us back to where we started in chapter 2.

Francis Crick died in 2004 and Leslie Orgel shortly thereafter, in 2007, marking the end of an era at the Salk Institute. Now that these scientific giants are no longer with us, a new generation is forging ahead. I have been at the Salk Institute for thirty years, half of its lifetime. Starting out as a family in 1960, with faculty and staff in the same little boat, the Salk was small enough that everyone knew one another. But even today, with a complement of 1,000, it still has a family feeling, testimony to the enduring culture of an institution.

We are one species in a great chain of being, going back to bacteria and before. It is a miracle that we have arrived at the brink of understanding brains and how they evolved, which will forever change how we think about ourselves.

18 Deep Intelligence

Francisco Crick in Paradiso

Born and educated in South Africa, Sydney Brenner participated in the early days of molecular genetics at Cambridge University (figure 18.1). He shared an office at the Laboratory of Molecular Biology (LMB) with Francis Crick. What do you do for your next project after discovering the structure of DNA and working out the genetic code? Francis decided to focus on the human brain, and Sydney inaugurated a new model organism, *Caenorhabditis elegans* (*C. elegans*), a roundworm that lives in the soil, is only 1 millimeter long, and has only 302 neurons. This nematode has served as the starting point for many breakthroughs in understanding, by following every cell in the body over time, how a creature develops from an embryo, for which Sydney shared the Nobel Prize in Physiology or Medicine in 2002 (with H. Robert Horvitz and John E. Sulston). Brenner also is famous for his wit. In his Nobel speech, he praised the worm: "The title of my lecture is 'Nature's gift to Science.' It is not a lecture about one scientific journal paying respects to another, but about how the great diversity of the living world can both inspire and serve innovation in biological research."[1] Sydney Brenner, it would seem, was present at the Creation.

The three lectures given by Brenner at the Salk Institute under the series title "Reading the Human Genome"[2] in 2009 were tour de forces, delivered without a single slide or prop. Noting that no human, but only computers, had ever read the entire human genome, base pair by base pair, Sydney took it as his goal to do just that, and when he did, he discovered all sorts of interesting similarities between stretches of DNA in different genes and across species.

Sydney is peripatetic. He has an experimental project in Singapore; he was the founding president of the Okinawa Institute of Science and Technology; and he is a senior fellow at the Janelia Research Campus at the

Figure 18.1
Sydney Brenner is a legendary figure in biology. He worked on the genetic code, the way that base pairs in DNA are transcribed into proteins, and received a Nobel Prize for his pioneering work on a new model organism. This photo was from a 2010 interview with *The Science Network*, http://thesciencenetwork.org/programs/the-science -studio/sydney-brenner-part-1.

Howard Hughes Medical Institute, near Ashburn, Virginia, and at the Crick-Jacobs Center for Theoretical and Computational Biology that I direct at the Salk Institute in La Jolla (I have abbreviated his list of affiliations). Brenner hired David Marr at the LMB to work on computing after Marr had completed his doctorate and later arranged a position for Marr at the MIT AI Lab through his friend and fellow South African Seymour Papert. The ties between molecular genetics and neurophysiology were deep, and Sydney was at the center of both fields.

At a dinner on one of his visits to La Jolla, I told Sydney a story that I had heard many years ago when I was a postdoctoral fellow at the Harvard Medical School. Francis Crick dies and goes to heaven. St. Peter is surprised to see this devout atheist, but Francis is there to ask God a question. Directed to a wooden shack amid a field strewn with all manner of wheels and cogs—failed experiments—Francis finds God at his workbench in a leather apron, tinkering with a new organism. "Francis," says God, "how delightful to see you. What can I do for you?" "All my life," says Francis, "I've wanted to know the answer to this question: Why do flies have imaginal discs?"[3] "Dear Francis," replies God, "what a surprise! No one's ever asked me that question before. I've been putting imaginal discs into flies for hundreds of millions of years and I haven't had a single complaint."

Sydney was silent and I wondered whether a story at the expense of his close friend may not have been a good idea. "Terry," he said, "I can tell you the moment when that story came to me. Francis and I were sitting together in our office and Francis was reading a book on developmental biology when he suddenly threw up his hands and said: 'God knows why flies have imaginal discs!'"

I was stunned. How often do you come across the origin of a story you've known for decades and told innumerable times? I asked Sydney to tell me the original version. He said it was entitled "Francisco Crick in Paradiso"; his story had the same basic structure as mine but the details were different[4]—just as evolution holds to the basic core of its story while changing many of the details.

I visited Sydney in Singapore in January 2017 to celebrate his ninetieth birthday. He no longer travels because of health problems and is confined to a wheelchair, but he was as lively and I have ever seen him. Theodosius Dobzhansky once said that nothing in biology makes any sense except in the light of evolution.[5] Sydney gave a riveting lecture on February 21, 2017, on bacterial evolution as part of a series, "10-on-10: The Chronicle of Evolution," at the Nanyang Technological University in Singapore.[6] My talk in this series on July 14, 2017, about the evolution of the brain began with a variation on this theme: Nothing in biology makes any sense except in the light of DNA.[7]

Evolution of Intelligence

Intelligence evolved in many species to solve the problems they faced to survive in their environmental niches. Animals that evolved in the ocean have different problems to solve than animals that evolved on land. Visual perception allows us to sense the world around us, and we have developed visual intelligence for interpreting those visual signals. Ethologists, who study the behavior of nonhuman animals in their natural settings, have uncovered abilities and skills that are foreign to humans, such as echolocation: bats actively send out auditory signals to probe their environments and analyze the returning echoes. This creates an internal representation of the outside world that is, to all appearances, as vivid as our visual experience. Bats have an auditory intelligence that sorts through signals from fluttering insects (to be hunted) and obstacles (to be avoided).

Thomas Nagel, a philosopher at New York University, wrote a paper in 1974 entitled "What Is It Like to Be a Bat?" and concluded that we cannot imagine what the bat world is like without the direct experience of echo-location.[8] But lack of such experience has not stopped us from inventing radar and sonar, technologies that allow us to actively probe the world we cannot see, nor does it stop blind people from navigating the world by becoming attuned to sound reflections. We may not know what it is like to be a bat, but we can build bat-like intelligence that helps self-driving cars navigate using radar and lidar.

We humans are nature's champion learners. We can learn faster on a broader range of topics, remember more, and accumulate more knowledge over more generations than any other species. We created a technology called "education" for enhancing how much we can learn in our lifetimes. Children and adolescents now spend their formative years sitting in class-rooms and learning about things in the world that they have never directly experienced. Relatively recent human inventions, reading and writing take many years to master. But these inventions allow more accumulated knowl-edge to be passed down to the next generation—as books to be written, printed or displayed, and read—than was possible by oral tradition. It is writing, reading, and learning, not spoken language, that have made mod-ern civilization possible.

Where Did We Come From?

What are our evolutionary origins? The La Jolla Group for Explaining the Origin of Humans, which I helped found in 1998, started out as a small group that held regular meetings to discuss the many sources of evidence that might help us answer this question, from paleontology, geophysics, anthropology, biochemistry, and genetics all the way to comparative neu-roscience. It gradually attracted an international membership, becoming the UCSD/Salk Center for Academic Research and Training in Anthropog-eny (CARTA) in 2008.[9] And just as NIPS assembled all the tribes of science and engineering to understand neural computation, so, in exploring where we humans came from and how we got here and in training a new gen-eration of thinkers to seek answers to these age-old questions, CARTA has drawn on insights from all areas of science.[10]

The lineage that eventually generated the genus *Homo* split from the lineage that led to chimpanzees about 6 million years ago (figure 18.2). Chimps are a highly intelligent species, but chimp intelligence is quite dif-ferent from ours. Attempts to teach chimpanzees the rudiments of language resulted in their learning no more than a few hundred signs, which the chimps used to express simple needs, though this is an unfair measure of

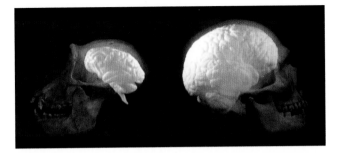

Figure 18.2
Comparison between the chimpanzee brain and the much larger human brain, which has evolved a greatly expanded cerebral cortex with many more convolutions. From Allman, *Evolving Brains*, p. 164. Courtesy of John Allman.

their intelligence. How well would we do if we had to survive in a chimp troop? Are all species as self-centered as ours?

One place to find differences between humans and chimps is in our DNA. We have known for some time that only 1.4 percent of our 3 billion DNA base pairs are different from those in chimps. When the chimpanzee genome was first sequenced, it was thought that we would be able to read the book of life and discover what makes humans different from chimps. Unfortunately, we have still not learned how to read some 90 percent of this book.[11] Our brains are remarkably similar to those of chimps; neuro-anatomists have identified the same brain areas in both species. But most of the differences between humans and chimps are at the molecular level and are subtle, compared to the dramatic differences in our behaviors. Once again, nature is cleverer than we are.

The Logic of Life

Orgel's first rule, Leslie told me, states that every essential reaction in a cell has evolved an enzyme to catalyze that reaction. The enzyme not only speeds up the reaction but also makes it possible to regulate the reaction through interactions with other molecules, so that the cell can be both more efficient and more adaptable. Nature starts out with a clever reaction pathway, then gradually refines it by adding enzymes and backup pathways, but none of it would work in the absence of certain core processes, which for cells are the maintenance and replication of DNA, the queen bee of cellular biochemicals.

Single cells have adapted to many different conditions and evolved into many niches. For example, bacteria have adapted to extreme environments that range from hydrothermal vents on the ocean floor to sheets of ice in Antarctica and to many more moderate environments, like our stomachs and intestines, which harbor thousands of species. Bacteria like *Escherichia coli* (*E. coli*; figure 18.3) have developed algorithms for swimming up gradients toward food sources. Because they are too small to sense a gradient directly (a few micrometers across), bacteria use chemotaxis, which involves periodically tumbling and setting off in a random direction.[12] This may seem counterproductive, but by adjusting their swim times to be longer at higher concentrations, bacteria can reliably climb up the gradient. Theirs is a primitive form of intelligence, but bacteria are smarter than the smartest biologists, who have yet to figure out how they manage to survive

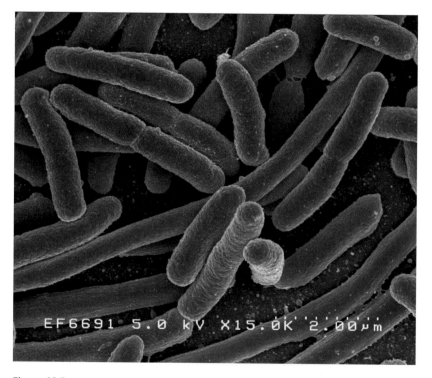

Figure 18.3

Scanning electron micrograph of *E. coli*. Bacteria are the most diverse, robust, and successful life-forms on earth. We can learn much about autonomous artificial intelligence by studying them. (NIAID, NIH)

in such a wide range of environments. More complex forms of intelligence are found in multicellular animals.

We have seen that the temporal difference learning algorithm that underlies reinforcement learning can lead to highly complex behaviors, made still more complex in humans by deep learning in the cerebral cortex. There is a spectrum of intelligent behavior in nature that artificial systems can learn from. A new field of science that straddles computer science and biology, algorithmic biology, seeks to use the language of algorithms to describe problem solving strategies used by biological systems.[13] The hope is that identifying such biological algorithms will both inspire new computing paradigms in engineering, and will provide a systems-level understanding of biological networks. This is the edge of the wedge that could eventually explain the nested levels of complexity in biological systems across spatial and temporal scales: gene networks, metabolic networks, immune networks, neural networks, and social networks—it's networks all the way down.

Deep learning depends on optimizing a cost function. What are the cost functions in nature? The inverse of cost in evolution is called fitness, but that is a concept that only has meaning in the context of a concrete set of constraints, either from the environment or from the system being optimized. In the brain, there are some innate costs that regulate behavior, such as the need for food, warmth, safety, oxygen, and procreation. In reinforcement learning, actions are taken to optimize future rewards. But beyond rewards that insure survival, a wide range of rewards can be optimized, as is apparent from the bewildering range of human behaviors. Is there some underlying universal cost function that is responsible for this diversity?

We are still looking for the core concepts that will give the game away for the highest forms of intelligence. We have identified a few key principles, but we do not have a conceptual framework that explains how brains work as elegantly as DNA does the nature of life. Learning algorithms are a good place to look for unifying concepts. Perhaps the progress we are making in understanding how deep learning networks solve practical problems will yield more clues. Perhaps we will discover the operating systems in cells and brains that make evolution possible. If we could solve these problems, unimaginable benefits might follow. Nature may be cleverer than we are individually, but I see no reason why we, as a species, cannot someday solve the puzzle of intelligence.

Acknowledgments

The Salk Institute for Biological Studies, where I work, is a special place. From the outside, it looks like a concrete fortress, but as you enter the central courtyard, a broad expanse of travertine stretches out to the Pacific, with towers rising along the sides anchoring the otherworldly space (figure 19.1).[1] My lab is in the South Building, located off the courtyard (left side of photo). You are greeted on the left with a wall-sized electron microscopic photo of the hippocampus, which looks like a cross-section of a plate of spaghetti; the entryway opens onto the tearoom, the heart of the Computational Neurobiology Laboratory.

Some of the world's most distinguished scientists, including Francis Crick, who loved to hold forth with students and colleagues, have gathered around the circular white tea table for discussions on all things scientific (figure 19.2). Indeed, the tearoom became a scene in Crick's book *The Astonishing Hypothesis*:

> Terry Sejnowski's group at the Salk Institute has an informal tea on most afternoons of the week. These teas are ideal occasions to discuss the latest experimental results, throw out new ideas, or just gossip about science, politics, or the news in general. I went over to tea one day and announced to Pat Churchland and Terry Sejnowski that the seat of the Will had been discovered! It was at or near the anterior cingulate. When I discussed the matter with Antonio Damasio, I found that he also had arrived at the same idea.[2]

I especially remember the day when Francis Crick arrived at tea with Beatrice Golomb in 1989. He told me that she wanted to work on neural networks and I should hire her.[3] Beatrice was a medical/doctoral student at UC, San Diego, and had briefly worked with Crick as a graduate student. She had wanted to work on neural networks for her doctoral dissertation but was not allowed to do so by the Biology Department. I took Crick's advice and learned as much from Beatrice as she learned from me—and

Figure 19.1
Salk Institute for Biological Studies at La Jolla, California, overlooks the Pacific Ocean. This landmark building designed by Louis Kahn is a temple of science. This is where I come to work every day. Courtesy of Kent Schnoeker, Salk Institute for Biological Studies

I've continued to learn from her ever since we were married at Caltech's Athenaeum in 1990.

The tea table traveled with me from Johns Hopkins University; it was the first item I purchased for my new lab at my first job there in the Thomas C. Jenkins Department of Biophysics in 1981. The department was like an old family, and I was the young doted-on son; they gave me the confidence to strike out in new directions, for which I am forever grateful. I had adopted the afternoon tea tradition as a postdoctoral fellow in the Department of Neurobiology at Harvard Medical School. In a large, diverse department, this was a way to keep in touch and hear about the experiments that were under way down the hall. My lab at the Salk Institute is a miniature university, with students from many different backgrounds in science, mathematics, engineering, and medicine, and teatime is when we all come together as a group.

I have been fortunate. My parents valued education and trusted me from an early age; I have lived at a time of unprecedented economic growth

Figure 19.2
Tearoom of the Computational Neurobiology Laboratory at the Salk Institute in 2010. Daily teas have been a social incubator for the development of the many learning algorithms and scientific discoveries that are described in this book. Courtesy of the Salk Institute for Biological Studies.

and opportunities, which opened my horizons; I have had mentors and collaborators who generously shared their insights and advice; and I have had the privilege of working with a generation of exceptionally talented students. I am especially grateful to Geoffrey Hinton, John Hopfield, Bruce Knight, Stephen Kuffler, Michael Stimac, and John Wheeler, as I am to my-father-in-law, Solomon Golomb, who at various turning points in my career helped me take the right turn. Beatrice Golomb is a critical thinker and I learned from her how to avoid groupthink. Just because everyone believes in an explanation does not make it true. It sometimes takes a generation for a commonly held belief to be flushed from a community.

I am grateful to many others who have helped me write this book. Discussions with Patricia Churchland, a longtime collaborator, and Roger Bingham, founder of *The Science Network* on the Internet, were a source of inspiration. John Doyle's insights from control theory illuminated my discussion of the brain's operating system. A long hike with Cary Staller in the mountains around Klosters and Davos in Switzerland clarified the universe of algorithms. Barbara Oakley taught me how to reach out to a much bigger audience than the classroom. Both Cary and Barbara helped shape the way I have told the story of deep learning. Many others helped with feedback and ideas for the book, including Yoshua Bengio, Sydney Brenner, Andrea Chiba, Gary Cottrell, Kendra Crick, Rodney Douglas, Paul Ekman, Michaela Ennis, Jerome Feldman, Adam Gazzaley, Geoffrey Hinton, Jonathan C. Howard, Irwin Jacobs, Scott Kirkpatrick, Mark and Jack Knickrehm, Te-Won Lee, David Linden, James McClelland, Saket Navlakha, Barbara Oakley, Tomaso Poggio, Charles Rosenberg, Hava Siegelmann, David Silver, James Simons, Marian Stewart-Bartlett. Richard Sutton, Paula Tallal, Gerald Tesauro, Sebastian Thrun, Ajit Varki, Massimo Vergassola, Stephen Wolfram (who also suggested the title for this book), and Steven Zucker.

The Woods Hole Workshop on Computational Neuroscience has met every summer since 1984 with a small core of regulars and new participants for in-depth discussions in the mornings and evenings, leaving the afternoons free for outdoor activities—a perfect combination. Alumni from this workshop have gone on to stellar careers. The Woods Hole Workshop has continued to this day but moved to Telluride in 1999 to coincide with the annual Neuromorphic Engineering Workshop. I am grateful to all of those who came to these workshops over the past thirty years, especially John Allman, Dana Ballard, Robert Desimone, John Doyle, Katalin Gothard, Christof Koch, John Maunsell, William Newsome, Barry Richmond, Michael Stryker, and Steven Zucker.

My colleagues at the Salk Institute for Biological Studies and the University of California, San Diego, are a remarkable community of entrepreneurial and cooperative researchers who are creating the future of the biomedical sciences. Faculty and students at the Institute for Neural Computation at UCSD have integrated neuroscience and computation in ways that I never dreamed would happen when I founded it in 1990.

The Computational Neurobiology Laboratory (CNL) at the Salk Institute has been my home for the last thirty years, and my many academic children have gone on to lead thriving careers throughout the world. A lab is like a family, and generations of enthusiastic graduate students and postdoctoral fellows have greatly enriched my life. Good ship CNL was well cared for by my lab managers, Rosemary Miller and Mary Ellen Perry. Mary Ellen has been the managing director for NIPS during the last decade of growth, and Lee Campbell has developed a computer platform that has allowed us to scale up the size of the conference by a factor of ten.

I am grateful to the MIT Press, which has been a reliable partner for forty years, publishing a book series on computational neuroscience that I edited with Tomaso Poggio; *Neural Computation*, a journal that I founded in

1989; my book *The Computational Brain* in 1992; and many other foundational books on machine learning, including Richard Sutton and Andrew Barto's *Reinforcement Learning: An Introduction*, and the leading textbook *Deep Learning* by Ian Goodfellow, Yoshua Bengio, and Aaron Courville. The Press's Robert Prior helped guide the present volume around many an unexpected bend in its long road to publication.

I thank the NIPS community, without whom I would not have written *The Deep Learning Revolution*, though, far from a comprehensive history of the field, it focuses on only a few of the topics and people who were involved in research on neural networks. The International Neural Network Society's journal *Neural Networks* has been a stalwart in expanding the reach of neural networks. In partnership with the Institute of Electrical and Electronic Engineering (IEEE), the society holds an annual International Joint Conference on Neural Networks. Machine learning also has spawned many excellent conferences including the International Conference on Machine Learning (ICML), a sister conference to NIPS. The field has benefited greatly from all of these organizations and the researchers who contributed to them.

At the opening session at NIPS 2018 in Long Beach, I marveled at the growth of NIPS: "Little did I know 30 years ago at the first NIPS conference that I would be standing here today addressing 8,000 attendees—I thought it would only take 10 years." I visited Geoff Hinton at Mountainview in April, 2016. Google Brain has an entire floor of a building. We reminisced about the old days and came to the conclusion that we had won, but it took a lot longer than we had expected. Along the way, Geoff was elected to the Royal Societies of both England and Canada and I was elected to the National Academy of Sciences, the National Academy of Medicine, the National Academy of Engineering, the National Academy of Inventors, and the American Academy of Arts and Sciences, a rare honor. I owe Geoffrey Hinton a great debt of gratitude for sharing his insights into computing with networks over many years.

As a graduate student at Princeton University, I pursued research on black holes and gravitational waves in general relativity, Albert Einstein's theory of gravity. After receiving my doctorate in physics, however, I changed fields to neurobiology, and brains have captured my interest ever since. I don't yet know what my third act might be. Solomon Golomb once told me that careers happen in retrospect, which I confirmed while writing this book. Revisiting my past revealed the events and decisions that led me to where I am today, though, of course, I did not know this at the time.

Recommended Reading

An Introduction to Neuroscience

The Deep Learning Revolution only briefly touches on neuroscience, which is itself a vast field with a rapidly advancing scientific frontier. The part of neuroscience most relevant to deep learning is called "systems neuroscience." If you want to learn more about the brain and neural networks, a good place to start is *The Computational Brain*, 2nd ed. (MIT Press, 2016) by

Patricia S. Churchland and Terrence J. Sejnowski. This book introduces the basics of neuroscience and gives applications of neural networks to a wide range of brain structures such as the visual system, the oculomotor system that guides our eye movements and the way that space is represented in the cortex.

Written for a general audience, *Liars Lovers, and Heroes: What the New Brain Science Reveals about How We Become Who We Are* (Harper-Collins, 2002) by Steven R. Quartz and Terrence J. Sejnowski explores how both our noblest and darkest traits are rooted in brain systems so ancient that we share them with insects—the same reinforcement algorithms that Deep-Mind used to train AlphaGo.

The Society for Neuroscience hosts a website (http://www.brainfacts.org/brain-basics/neural-network-function/) where you can look up information about many aspects of brain function and brain disorders.

Biological Intelligence

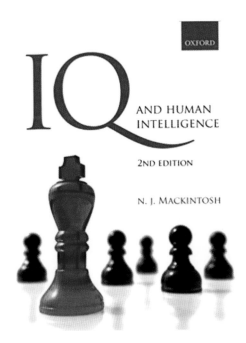

IQ *and Human Intelligence* (Oxford University Press, 2002) by Nicholas Mackintosh is a reliable and comprehensive introduction to the psychology of intelligence, including social and emotional intelligence. The biological basis of intelligence depends on the interaction of the brain with the world during brain development. Animal intelligence has also been extensively studied, and *Animal Minds: Beyond Cognition to Consciousness* (University of Chicago Press, 1992) by Donald R. Griffin is a good introduction.

Machine Learning

Neural Networks for Pattern Recognition (Oxford University Press, 1995) by Christopher M. Bishop is a good place to learn the fundamentals of neural networks. The deep connection between information theory and learning algorithms is beautifully expounded in *Information Theory, Inference, and Learning Algorithms* (Cambridge University Press, 2003) by David J. C. MacKay. Deep learning is growing rapidly: *Deep Learning: A Practitioner's Approach* (O'Reilly Media, 2017) by Josh Patterson and Adam Gibson is a good introduction, and *Deep Learning* (MIT Press, 2016) by Ian Goodfellow, Yoshua Bengio, and Aaron Courville is currently the definitive textbook, available online (http://www.deeplearningbook.org). *Machine Learning: A Probabilistic Perspective* (MIT Press, 2014) by Kevin P. Murphy is a compendium that covers the broader range of machine learning algorithms. Deep reinforcement learning is at the forefront of research, and the definitive textbook is *Reinforcement Learning: An Introduction* (MIT Press, 1998) by Richard S. Sutton and Andrew G. Barto (online draft of forthcoming second edition available at http://www.incompleteideas.net/sutton/book/the-book-2nd.html).

Glossary

adaptive signal processing Methods that improve the quality of a signal, such as an automatic grain control or an adjustable filter that automatically reduces noise.

algorithm A step-by-step recipe that you follow to achieve a goal, not unlike baking a cake.

backprop (backpropagation of errors) Learning algorithm that optimizes a neural network by gradient descent to minimize a cost function and improve performance.

Bayes's rule Formula that updates the probability of an event based on new data and prior knowledge of conditions related to the event. More generally, Bayesian probabilities are beliefs about outcomes based on current and prior data.

Boltzmann machine A neural network model consisting of interacting binary units in which the probability of a unit being in the active state depends on its integrated synaptic inputs. Named after Ludwig Boltzmann, a nineteenth-century physicist who laid the foundations for statistical mechanics.

constraints Conditions that the solution to an optimization problem must satisfy to have a positive value.

convolution Blending one function with another by computing the amount of overlap of the one as it is shifted over the other.

cost function Function that specifies the goal of a network and quantifies its performance. The goal of learning is to reduce the cost function.

digital assistant A virtual assistant that can help with tasks, like Alexa on Echo, Amazon's smart speaker.

epoch Update of weights during learning after the average gradient has been calculated from a specified number of examples.

equilibrium Thermodynamic state in which there are no net macroscopic flows of matter or of energy. In a Boltzmann machine, where the units are probabilistic, the system settles down to an equilibrium state when the inputs are kept constant.

feedback Connections that travel backward in a neural network from higher to lower layers creating a loop in the network that allows signals to circulate within it.

feedforward network Layered neural network in which connectivity between layers is one way, starting at the input layer and ending at the output layer.

gradient descent Optimization technique in which the parameters are changed on every epoch to reduce a cost function, which is a measure of how well a network model is performing.

Hopfield net A fully connected neural network model introduced by John Hopfield. It was guaranteed to converge to a fixed attractor state, which depended on the starting state, and could be used to store and retrieve information. This network launched a thousand papers.

learning algorithm Algorithm for changing the parameters of a function based on examples. Learning algorithms are said to be "supervised" when both inputs and desired outputs are given or "unsupervised" when only inputs are given. Reinforcement learning is a special case of a supervised learning algorithm when the only feedback is a reward for good performance.

logic Mathematical inference based on assumptions that can only be true or false. Mathematicians use logic to prove theorems.

machine learning Branch of computer science that gives computers the ability to learn to perform a task from data without being explicitly programmed.

millisecond One thousandth of a second (0.001 sec). The time it takes for one cycle of a 1 kilohertz tone.

MOOC (massive open online course) Course of lectures freely available over the Internet on any of a wide range of topics. The first MOOC was offered in 2006, and there are now more than 9,400 MOOCS attended by 91 million learners in January, 2018.

neuron Specialized brain cell that integrates inputs from other neurons and sends outputs to other neurons.

normalization Maintaining the amplitude of a signal within fixed limits. One way to normalize a time-varying positive signal is to divid it by its maximum value which is then bounded by 1.

optimization Process of maximizing or minimizing a function by systematically searching through input values from within an allowed set to find the optimal value of the function.

overfitting State reached by a learning algorithm when the number of adjustable parameters in a network model is much greater than the number of training data and the algorithm uses the excess capacity to memorize the examples. Although overfitting greatly reduces a network's ability to generalize to new examples, it can be reduced by **regularization**.

perceptron   A simple neural network model consisting of one unit and inputs with variable weights that can be trained to classify inputs into categories.

plasticity   Changes in a neuron that alter its function, such as changes in its connection strengths ("synaptic plasticity") or in how the neuron responds to its inputs ("intrinsic plasticity").

probability distribution   Function that specifies the probability of occurrence of all possible states of a system or outcomes in an experiment.

recurrent network   Neural network whose feedback connections allow signals to circulate within it.

regularization   Method to avoid overfitting a network model with many parameters when the training data are limited, such as weight decay, in which all the weights in the network decrease on every epoch of training, and only the weights with large positive gradients survive.

scaling   How the complexity of an algorithm scales with the size of the problem:; For example, adding up n number scales with n, but multiplying all pairs of n number scales with n^2.

skunk works   A group working on advanced or secret projects with a high degree of autonomy within an organization. Derived from the name of the moonshine factory in the comic strip Li'l Abner.

sparsity principle   A sparse representation of a signal, such as EEG and fMRI, is one that approximates the signal by the weighted sum of only a few fixed basis functions, which for **independent component analysis** are called sources. In a population of neurons, a sparse representation of an input is one where only a few neurons are highly active. This reduces interference with other patterns of activity that represent other inputs.

spine   Thorny excrescence on a dendrite of a neuron that serves as the postsynaptic site of a synapse.

synapse   Specialized junction between two neurons where a signal is passed from the presynaptic to the postsynaptic neuron.

training and test sets   Because performance on a training set is not a good estimate of how well a neural network will perform on new inputs, a test set not used during training gives a measure how well the network generalizes. When data sets are small, a single sample left out of the training set can be used to test the performance of the network trained on the remaining examples, and the process repeated for every sample to get an average test performance. This is a special case of cross-validation where $n = 1$, in which n subsamples are held out.

Turing machine   Hypothetical computer invented by Alan Turing (1937) as a simple model for mathematical calculation. A Turing machine consists of a "tape" that can be moved back and forth, a "head" that has a "state" that can change the property of the active cell beneath it, and a set of instructions for how the head should modify the active cell and move the tape. At each step, the machine may modify the property of the active cell and change the state of the head. After this, it moves the tape one unit.

Notes

Preface

1. Strictly speaking, a neural network is a biological entity, and the models that are used in machine learning are artificial neural networks—ANNies. However, in this book a "neural network" means an artificial one unless otherwise indicated.

2. Conor Dougherty, "Astro Teller, Google's 'Captain of Moonshots,' on Making Profits at Google X," *New York Times*, February 6, 2015, https://bits.blogs.nytimes.com/2015/02/16/googles-captain-of-moonshots-on-making-profits-at-google-x. Deep learning has reduced the energy costs of running data centers by 15 percent, which amounts to hundreds of millions of dollars in savings per year.

3. Although the 1943 Watson quotation has never been confirmed, it reflects the almost universal failure to imagine the future of computers at that time.

Chapter 1

1. "O brave new world that has such people in't!" Miranda, in Shakespeare's *The Tempest* (5.1.182–183 [Oxford Standard Authors Shakespeare]).

2. Bill Vlasic, "G.M. Wants to Drive the Future of Cars That Drive Themselves," *New York Times*, June 4, 2017, https://www.nytimes.com/2017/06/04/business/general-motors-self-driving-cars-mary-barra.html.

3. "Full Tilt: When 100% of Cars Are Autonomous," *New York Times Magazine*, November 8, 2017. https://www.nytimes.com/interactive/2017/11/08/magazine/tech-design-autonomous-future-cars-100-percent-augmented-reality-policing.html?hp&action=click&pgtype=Homepage&clickSource=story-heading&module=second-column-region&region=top-news&WT.nav=top-news/.

4. Christopher Ingraham, "The Astonishing Human Potential Wasted on Commutes," *Washington Post*, February 24, 2016, https://www.washingtonpost.com/news/wonk/wp/2016/02/25/how-much-of-your-life-youre-wasting-on-your-commute/?utm_term=.497dfd1b5d9c.

5. Patcharinee Tientrakool, Ya-Chi Ho, and N. F. Maxemchuk, "Highway Capacity Benefits from Using Vehicle-to-Vehicle Communication and Sensors for Collision Avoidance," IEEE Vehicular Technology Conference, San Francisco, 5–8 September 2011.

6. "Google's Waymo Passes Milestone in Driverless Car Race," *Financial Times*, December 10, 2017. https://www.ft.com/content/dc281ed2-c425-11e7-b2bb -322b2cb39656/.

7. B. A. Golomb, "Will We Recognize It When It Happens?" in Brockman, J. (ed.), *What to Think About Machines That Think* (New York: Harper Perennial, 2015), 533–535.

8. Pierre Delforge, "America's Data Centers Consuming and Wasting Growing Amounts of Energy," Natural Resources Defense Council Issue Paper, February 6, 2015. https://www.nrdc.org/resources/americas-data-centers-consuming-and -wasting-growing-amounts-energy/.

9. W. Brian Arthur, "Where Is Technology Taking the Economy?" *McKinsey Quarterly* October, 2017. https://www.mckinsey.com/business-functions/mckinsey -analytics/our-insights/Where-is-technology-taking-the-economy/.

10. Gideon Lewis-Kraus, "The Great A.I. Awakening," *New York Times Magazine*, December 14, 2016. https://www.nytimes.com/2016/12/14/magazine/the-great-ai -awakening.html.

11. Aleksandr Sergeevich Pushkin, *Eugene Onegin: A Novel in Verse*, 2nd ed., trans. Vladimir Nabokov (Princeton: Princeton University Press, 1991).

12. For an early foray along these lines, see Andrej Karpathy, "The Unreasonable Effectiveness of Recurrent Neural Networks," *Andrej Karpathy Blog*, posted May 21, 2015. http://karpathy.github.io/2015/05/21/rnn-effectiveness/.

13. G. Hinton, L. Deng, G. E. Dahl, A. Mohamed, N. Jaitly, A. Senior, et al., "Deep Neural Networks for Acoustic Modeling in Speech Recognition," *IEEE Signal Processing Magazine* 29, no. 6 (2012): 82–97.

14. W. Xiong, , J. Droppo, X. Huang, F. Seide, M. Seltzer, A. Stolcke, et al., "Achieving Human Parity in Conversational Speech Recognition," Microsoft Research Technical Report MSR-TR-2016-71, revised February 2017. https://arxiv.org/pdf/ 1610.05256.pdf.

15. A. Esteva, B. Kuprel, R. A. Novoa, J. Ko J, S. M. Swetter, H. M. Blau, and S. Thrun, "Dermatologist-Level Classification of Skin Cancer with Deep Neural Networks," *Nature* 542, no. 7639 (2017): 115–118.

16. Siddhartha Mukherjee, "A.I. versus M.D: What Happens When Diagnosis Is Automated?," *New Yorker*, April 3, 2017. http://www.newyorker.com/magazine/ 2017/04/03/ai-versus-md/.

17. Dayong Wang, Aditya Khosla, Rishab Gargeya, Humayun Irshad, Andrew H. Beck, *Deep Learning for Identifying Metastatic Breast Cancer*, arXiv:1606.05718. The measure they used is called the area under the curve from signal detection theory, which is sensitive to both false negatives and false positives. https://arxiv.org/abs/1606.05718/.

18. Anthony Rechtschaffen and Alan Kales, eds., *A Manual of Standardized Terminology, Techniques and Scoring System for Sleep Stages of Human Subjects*, National Institutes of Health publication no. 204 (Bethesda, MD: U.S. National Institute of Neurological Diseases and Blindness, Neurological Information Network, 1968).

19. See Ian Allison, "Former Nuclear Physicist Henri Waelbroeck Explains How Machine Learning Mitigates High Frequency Trading," *International Business Times*, March 23, 2016, http://www.ibtimes.co.uk/former-nuclear-physicist-henri-waelbroeck-explains-how-machine-learning-mitigates-high-frequency-1551097/; Bailey McCann, "The Artificial-Intelligent Investor: AI Funds Beckon," *Wall Street Journal*, November 5, 2017. https://www.wsj.com/articles/the-artificial-intelligent-investor-ai-funds-beckon-1509937622/.

20. Sei Chong, "Morning Agenda: Big Pay for Hedge Fund Chiefs despite a Rough Year," *New York Times*, May 16, 2017. https://www.nytimes.com/2017/05/16/business/dealbook/hedge-funds-amazon-bezos.html.

21. Excluding the National Security Agency (NSA), which employs thousands of mathematicians. Alfred W. Hales, personal communication, May 4, 2016.

22. Sarfaz Manzoor, "Quants: The Maths Geniuses Running Wall Street," *Telegraph*, July 23, 2013. http://www.telegraph.co.uk/finance/10188335/Quants-the-maths-geniuses-running-Wall-Street.html.

23. D. E. Shaw, J. C. Chao, M. P. Eastwood, J. Gagliardo, J. P. Grossman, C. Ho, et al., "Anton: A Special-Purpose Machine for Molecular Dynamics Simulation," *Communications of the ACM* 51, no. 7 (2008): 91–97.

24. D. T. Max, Jim Simons, "The Numbers King," *New Yorker*, December 18 & 25, 2017. https://www.newyorker.com/magazine/2017/12/18/jim-simons-the-numbers-king/.

25. Soon to be a major motion picture.

26. John von Neumann, as quoted in Jacob Bronowski, *The Ascent of Man*, documentary TV series, episode 13 (1973).

27. See M. Moravčík, M. Schmid, N. Burch, V. Lisý, D. Morrill, N. Bard, et al., "DeepStack: Expert-Level Artificial Intelligence in Heads-Up No-Limit Poker," *Science* 356, no. 6337 (2017): 508–513. A standard deviation is the half width of a bell-shaped curve. Only 16 percent of the samples are larger than one standard deviation from the mean. Only three in ten thousand samples are more than four standard deviations from the mean.

28. The scenario in the 1983 science fiction movie *WarGames*, comes to mind. See https://en.wikipedia.org/wiki/WarGames.

29. See D. Silver, A. Huang, C. J. Maddison, A. Guez, L. Sifre, G. v. d. Driessche, et al., "Mastering the Game of Go with Deep Neural Networks and Tree Search," *Nature* 529, no. 7587 (2016): 484–489.

30. "I don't know how to start or what to say today," Sedol told members of the press, "but I think I would have to express my apologies first. I should have shown a better result, a better outcome, and better content in terms of the game played, and I do apologize for not being able to satisfy a lot of people's expectations. I kind of felt powerless. If I look back on the three matches, the first one, even if I were to go back and redo the first match, I think that I would not have been able to win, because I at that time misjudged the capabilities of AlphaGo." As quoted in Jordan Novet, "Go Board Game Chapion Lee Sedol Apologizes for Losing to Google's AI," *VentureBeat*, March, 12, 2016. https://venturebeat.com/2016/03/12/go-board-game-champion-lee-sedol-apologizes-for-losing-to-googles-ai/.

31. Surveyor 1 landed on the lunar surface on June 2, 1966, at 6:17:36 UT (1:17:36 a.m. EST). The landing site was on a flat area inside a 100-kilometer crater north of Flamsteed Crater.

32. Ke Jie, as quoted in Selina Cheng, "The Awful Frustration of a Teenage Go Champion Playing Google's AlphaGo," *Quartz*, May 27, 2017. https://qz.com/993147/the-awful-frustration-of-a-teenage-go-champion-playing-googles-alphago/.

33. Ke Jie, as quoted in Paul Mozur, "Google's A.I. Program Rattles Chinese Go Master As It Wins Match," *New York Times*, May 25, 2017. https://www.nytimes.com/2017/05/25/business/google-alphago-defeats-go-ke-jie-again.html.

34. Paul Mozur, "Beijing Wants A.I. to Be Made in China by 2030," *New York Times*, July 20, 2017. https://www.nytimes.com/2017/07/20/business/china-artificial-intelligence.html.

35. Silver D., J. Schrittwieser, K. Simonyan, I. Antonoglou, A. Huang, A. Guez, T. Hubert, L. Baker, M. Lai, A. Bolton, Y. Chen, T. Lillicrap, F. Hui, L. Sifre, G. van den Driessche, T. Graepel, and D. Hassabis, "Mastering the Game of Go Without Human Knowledge," *Nature* 550 (2017): 354–359.

36. David Silver, Thomas Hubert, Julian Schrittwieser, Ioannis Antonoglou, Matthew Lai, Arthur Guez, Marc Lanctot, Laurent Sifre, Dharshan Kumaran, Thore Graepel, Timothy Lillicrap, Karen Simonyan, Demis Hassabis, *Mastering Chess and Shogi by Self-Play with a General Reinforcement Learning Algorithm*, arXiv:1712.01815 (2017).

37. Harold Gardner, *Frames of Mind: The Theory of Multiple Intelligences*, 3rd ed. (New York: Basic Books, 2011).

38. J. R. Flynn, "Massive IQ Gains in 14 Nations: What IQ Tests Really Measure," *Psychological Bulletin* 101, no. 2 (1987):171–191.

39. S. Quartz and T. J. Sejnowski, *Liars, Lovers, and Heroes: What the New Brain Science Reveals About How We Become Who We Are* (New York: Harper Collins, 2002).

40. Douglas C. Engelbart, *Augmented Intelligence: Smart Systems and the Future of Work and Learning*, SRI Summary Report AFOSR-3223 (Washington, DC: Doug Engelbart Institute, October 1962). http://www.dougengelbart.org/pubs/augment -3906.html.

41. M. Young, "Machine Learning Astronomy," *Sky and Telescope*, December (2017): 20–27.

42. "Are ATMs Stealing Jobs?" *The Economist*, June 15, 2011. https://www.economist .com/blogs/democracyinamerica/2011/06/technology-and-unemployment/.

43. John Taggart and Kevin Granville, "From 'Zombie Malls' to Bonobos: What America's Retail Transformation Looks Like," *New York Times*, April 15, 2017.

44. E. Brynjolfsson and T. Mitchell, "What Can Machine Learning Do? Workforce Implications." *Science* (2017): 358:1530–1534. doi: 10.1126/science.aap8062.

45. "Technology Is Transforming What Happens When a Child Goes to School: Reformers Are Using New Software to 'Personalise' Learning," *Economist*, July 22, 2017. https://www.economist.com/news/briefing/21725285-reformers-are-using -new-software-personalise-learning-technology-transforming-what-happens/.

46. The education market is estimated to be more than $1.2 trillion dollars, with three major sectors: early childhood education: $70 billion; K–12: $670 billion; and higher education: $475 billion. See Arpin Gajjar, "How Big Is the Education Market in the US: Report from the White House," *Students for the Future*, October 10, 2008. https://medium.com/students-for-the-future/how-big-is-the-education-market-in -the-us-report-from-white-house-91dc313257c5.

47. "Algorithmic Retailing: Automatic for the People," *Economist*, April 15, 2017, 56.

48. T. J. Sejnowski, "AI Will Make You Smarter," in Brockman, J. (ed.), *What to Think About Machines That Think* (New York: Harper Perennial, 2015), 118–120.

Chapter 2

1. Though not formally founded until 1970, the MIT Artificial Intelligence Laboratory began its research in 1959, merging with the MIT Laboratory of Computer Science (LCS) in 2003 to form the MIT Computer Science and Artificial Intelligence Laboratory (CSAIL). For the sake of simplicity and continuity, however, I refer to the laboratory as the "MIT AI Lab" from its earliest days to the present.

2. See Seymour A. Papert, "The Summer Vision Project," AI Memo AIM-100. July 1, 1966, DSpace@MIT. https://dspace.mit.edu/handle/1721.1/6125. According to Michaela Ennis, MIT Class of 2016: "The story about the MIT undergrad that got

assigned 'computer vision' as a summer project is actually told by Professor Patrick Winston every year in class, and he also says that this student was Gerald Sussman."

3. See, for example, Roger Peterson, Guy Mountfort, and P. A. D. Hollom, *Field Guide to the Birds of Britain and Europe*, 5th ed. (Boston: Houghton Mifflin Harcourt, 2001).

4. Bruce G. Buchanan and Edward H. Shortliffe, *Rule Based Expert Systems: The MYCIN Experiments of the Stanford Heuristic Programming Project* (Reading, MA: Addison-Wesley, 1984).

5. S. Mukherjee, "A.I. versus M.D.: What Happens When Diagnosis Is Automated?" *New Yorker*, April 3, 2017

6. Pedro Domingos, *The Master Algorithm: How the Quest for the Ultimate Learning Machine Will Remake Our World* (New York: Basic Books, 2015), 35. No one even knows how to quantify all of the commonsense knowledge that we have and take for granted.

7. Cats are lighter than humans and can rotate in the air even if they are dropped back first. J. A. Sechzera, S. E. Folsteina, E. H. Geigera, R. F. and S. M. Mervisa, "Development and Maturation of Postural Reflexes in Normal Kittens," *Experimental Neurology* 86, no. 3 (1984): 493–505.

8. B. Katz, *Nerve, Muscle, and Synapse* (New York: McGraw-Hill, 1996); A. Hodgkin, *Chance and Design: Reminiscences of Science in Peace and War* (Cambridge: Cambridge University Press, 1992).

9. M. Stefik, "Strategic Computing at DARPA: Overview and Assessment," *Communications of the ACM* 28, no.7 (1985): 690–704.

10. G. Tesauro and T. J. Sejnowski, "A Parallel Network That Learns to Play Backgammon," *Artificial Intelligence* 39 (1989): 357–390.

Chapter 3

1. At a local level, differences in cellular properties and connectivity are found between different parts of the cortex, which presumably reflect specialization for different sensory systems and different levels in the hierarchies.

2. P. C. Wason, "Self-Contradictions," in P. N. Johnson-Laird and P. C. Wason, eds., *Thinking: Readings in Cognitive Science* (Cambridge: Cambridge University Press, 1977).

3. Norbert Wiener, *Cybernetics, or Control and Communication in the Animal and the Machine* (Cambridge, MA: MIT Press, 1948).

4. O. G. Selfridge, "Pandemonium: A Paradigm for Learning," in D. V. Blake and A. M. Uttley, eds., *Proceedings of the Symposium on Mechanisation of Thought Processes* (1959): 511–529.

5. See Bernard Widrow and Samuel D. Stearns, *Adaptive Signal Processing* (Englewood Cliffs, NJ: Prentice-Hall, 1985).

6. See Frank Rosenblatt, *Principles of Neurodynamics: Perceptrons and the Theory of Brain Mechanisms* (Washington, DC: Spartan Books, 1962).

7. A shy bachelor who nonetheless liked to drive a sports car around the Cornell campus, Rosenblatt was a polymath who had wide interests. Among these was how to find planets orbiting distant stars by measuring the slight dip in the brightness of the stars as the planets transited them, a method now routinely used to detect exoplanets orbiting stars in our galaxy.

8. M. S. Gray, D. T. Lawrence, B. A. Golomb, and T. J. Sejnowski, "A Perceptron Reveals the Face of Sex," *Neural Computation* 7, no. 6 (1995): 1160–1164.

9. B. A. Golomb, D. T. Lawrence, and T. J. Sejnowski, "SEXNET: A Neural Network Identifies Sex from Human Faces," in R. Lippmann, and D. S. Touretzky, eds., *Advances in Neural Information Processing Systems* 3 (1991): 572–577.

10. Posner's pun is an allusion to *Dragnet*, a popular TV series from the 1950s showcasing crime busters from the Los Angeles Police Department.

11. M. Olazaran. "A Sociological Study of the Official History of the Perceptrons Controversy," *Social Studies of Science* 26, no. 3 (1996): 611–659.

12. Vladimir Vapnik, *The Nature of Statistical Learning Theory* (New York: Springer 1995), 138.

13. Weifeng Liu, José C. Principe, and Simon Haykin, *Kernel Adaptive Filtering: A Comprehensive Introduction* (Hoboken, NJ: Wiley, 2010).

14. Marvin Minsky and Seymour Papert, *Perceptrons* (Cambridge, MA: MIT Press, 1969). See also Marvin Lee Minsky and Seymour Papert, *Perceptrons: An Introduction to Computational Geometry*, expanded ed. (Cambridge, MA: MIT Press, 1988).

15. According to Harvey Karten, a colleague at UCSD, Rosenblatt was an experienced sailor who took out a group of students for a cruise. He was hit by a boom and fell overboard, but none of the students were able to save him (personal conversation, November 8, 2017).

Chapter 4

1. Christoph von der Malsburg, "The Correlation Theory of Brain Function," Internal Report 81–2 (Göttingen: Max-Planck Institute for Biophysical Chemistry, 1981), https://fias.uni-frankfurt.de/fileadmin/fias/malsburg/publications/vdM_correlation.pdf.

2. P. Wolfrum, C. Wolff, J. Lücke, and C. von der Malsburg. "A Recurrent Dynamic Model for Correspondence-Based Face Recognition," *Journal of Vision* 8, no. 34 (2008): 1–18.

3. K. Fukushima, "Neocognitron: A Self-Organizing Neural Network Model for a Mechanism of Pattern Recognition Unaffected by Shift in Position." *Biological Cybernetics* 36, no. 4 (1980): 93–202.

4. T. Kohonen, "Self-Organized Formation of Topologically Correct Feature Maps," *Biological Cybernetics* 43, no. 1 (1982): 59–69.

5. Judea Pearl, *Probabilistic Reasoning in Intelligent Systems: Networks of Plausible Inference* (San Mateo, CA: Morgan Kaufmann, 1988).

6. Which gave rise to their collected volume: Geoffrey E. Hinton and James A. Anderson, eds., *Parallel Models of Associative Memory* (Hillsdale, NJ: Erlbaum, 1981).

7. Terrence J. Sejnowski, "David Marr: A Pioneer in Computational Neuroscience," in Lucia M. Vaina, ed., *From the Retina to the Neocortex: Selected Papers of David Marr* (Boston: Birkhäuser, 1991), 297–301; see, for example, D. Marr, "A Theory of Cerebellar Cortex," *Journal of Physiology* 202 (1969): 437–470; D. Marr, "A Theory for Cerebral Neocortex," *Proceedings of the Royal Society of London: B Biological Sciences* 176 (1970): 161–234; D. Marr, "Simple Memory: A Theory for Archicortex," *Philosophical Transactions of the Royal Society of London: B Biological Sciences* 262 (1971): 23–81.

8. D. Marr and T. Poggio, "Cooperative Computation of Stereo Disparity," *Science* 194, no. 4262 (1976): 283–287; for a description of random-dot stereograms see also Béla Julesz, *Foundations of Cyclopean Perception* (Chicago: University of Chicago Press, 1971).

9. Magic Eye images are autostereograms that have a hidden three-dimensional structure within the pattern that can be seen by diverging your eyes. Christopher Tyler created the first black-and-white autostereograms in 1979. See http://www.magiceye.com/.

10. David Marr, *Vision: A Computational Investigation into the Human Representation and Processing of Visual Information* (New York: W. H. Freeman, 1982).

11. Terrence Joseph Sejnowski, "A Stochastic Model of Nonlinearly Interacting Neurons" (Ph.D. diss., Princeton University, 1978).

12. T. J. Sejnowski, "Vernon Mountcastle: Father of Neuroscience," *Proceedings of the National Academy of Sciences of the United States of America* 112, no. 4262 (2015): 6523–6524.

13. There are three biophysics departments at the Johns Hopkins University, at the Schools of Medicine, Public Health, and Arts and Sciences. (I was in the Thomas C. Jenkins Department of Biophysics at the School of Arts and Sciences on the Homewood campus.)

14. T. J. Sejnowski and M. I. Yodlowski, "A Freeze-Fracture Study of the Skate Electroreceptor," *Journal of Neurocytology* 11, no. 6 (1982): 897–912.

15. T. J. Sejnowski, S. C. Reingold, D. B. Kelley, and A. Gelperin, "Localization of [³H]-2-Deoxyglucose in Single Molluscan Neurones," *Nature* 287, no. 5781 (1980): 449–451.

16. This sentence was inspired by the famous quote from the geneticist and evolutionary biologist Theodosius Dobzhansky that "Nothing in biology makes any sense except in the light of evolution." This version is due to Bill Newsome and can be found in BRAIN 2025, the NIH roadmap for the BRAIN Initiative. https://www.braininitiative.nih.gov/2025/.

17. S. W. Kuffler and T. J. Sejnowski, "Peptidergic and Muscarinic Excitation at Amphibian Sympathetic Synapses," *Journal of Physiology* 341 (1983): 257–278.

18. The System Development Corporation was a nonprofit software company in Santa Monica, California, that did contract work for the U.S. military. When the company was disbanded, they liquidated their buildings and ended up with a large profit, which is not allowed for a nonprofit. The System Development Foundation, based in Palo Alto, California, was formed in 1969 to distribute proceeds from selling from buildings through a grant-making program from 1980 to 1988.

19. Made by Symbolics, Lisp machines were designed for and good at writing symbol processing AI programs, but they were not as good at number crunching, which was needed for simulating neural networks.

20. In 1984, as an NSF presidential young investigator, I was offered a steep discount from Ridge, a new computer company, for a computer with the power of the VAX 780, the workhorse of academic computing at the time.

Chapter 5

1. Founded by Francis Crick, V. S. Ramachandran, and Gordon Shaw in the 1980s, the Helmholtz Club continued for more than twenty years. For its history, see C. Aicardi, "Of the Helmholtz Club, South-Californian Seedbed for Visual and Cognitive Neuroscience, and Its Patron Francis Crick," *Studies in History and Philosophy of Biological and Biomedical Sciences* 45, no. 100 (2014): 1–11.

2. In the words of one satisfied attendee: "I've learned a lot from everybody I've run into. I'm shameless about adopting ideas from people. ... My most intense learning experience—has been this thing called the Helmholtz Club. I don't know if you've heard of it. ... There's maybe twenty people there. I never miss one. I have somebody take my class because it lands right on top of my class. I do it anyway because it's just too important to miss." Carver Mead, in James A. Anderson and Edward Rosenfeld, eds., *Talking Nets: An Oral History of Neural Networks* (Cambridge, MA: MIT Press, 2000), 138.

3. R. Desimone, T. D. Albright, C. G. Gross, and C. Bruce, "Stimulus-Selective Properties of Inferior Temporal Neurons in the Macaque," *Journal of Neuroscience* 4, no. 8

(1984): 2051–2062. Many of the researchers in Charles Gross's lab had beards, so the neurons in the visual cortex that responded to toilet brushes might have been beard cells.

4. David Hubel, *Eye, Brain, and Vision* (New York: W. H. Freeman, 1988), 191–216.

5. The critical period in cats lasts from about 3 weeks to several months of age and in humans from a few months to 7–8 years of age. The end of the critical period may not be as abrupt as previously thought, and stereo vision can be achieved in adults with corrected strabismus after intense practice. See Susan R. Barry, *Fixing My Gaze: A Scientist's Journey into Seeing in Three Dimensions* (New York: Basic Books, 2009). I knew "stereo Sue," as Barry is now called, when I was a graduate student at Princeton.

6. There are a few exceptions to this rule: granule cells in the dentate gyrus of the hippocampus and neurons in the olfactory bulb are generated throughout our lives. See Michael Specter, "Rethinking the Brain: How the Songs of Canaries Upset a Fundamental Principle of Science," *New Yorker*, July 23, 2001. http://www .michaelspecter.com/2001/07/rethinking-the-brain/.

7. Terrence Sejnowski, "How Do We Remember the Past?" in John Brockman, ed., *What We Believe but Cannot Prove: Today's Leading Thinkers on Science in the Age of Certainty* (London: Free Press, 2005), 97–99; and R. Y. Tsien, "Very Long-Term Memories May Be Stored in the Pattern of Holes in the Perineuronal Net," *Proceedings of the National Academy of Sciences of the United States of America* 110, no. 30 (2013): 12456–12461.

8. In Alzheimer's disease, the integrity of the extracellular matrix is compromised, which may contribute to the loss of long-term memories. John Allman, private communication, July, 2017.

9. For a summary of Gehry's talk, see Shelley Batts, "SFN Special Lecture: Architecture Frank Gehry and Neuro-Architecture," *ScienceBlogs*, posted October 15, 2006. http://scienceblogs.com/retrospectacle/2006/10/15/sfn-special-lecture-architect-1/.

10. B. S. Kunsberg and S.W. Zucker, "Critical Contours: An Invariant Linking Image Flow with Salient Surface Organization," May 20, 2017. https://arxiv.org/pdf/ 1705.07329.pdf.

11. The connection between the three-dimensional contours of the surface as seen on contour maps of mountains and the constant-intensity contours on images is explained by the geometry of critical points and gradient flows on surfaces, called the "Morse-Smale complex."

12. S. R. Lehky and T. J. Sejnowski, "Network Model of Shape-from-Shading: Neural Function Arises from Both Receptive and Projective Fields," *Nature* 333, no. 6172 (1988): 452–454.

13. Terrence J. Sejnowski, "What Are the Projective Fields of Cortical Neurons?" in J. Leo van Hemmen and Terrence J. Sejnowski, eds. *23 Problems in Systems Neuroscience* (New York: Oxford University Press, 2005), 394–405.

14. C. N. Woolsey, "Cortical Localization as Defined by Evoked Potential and Electrical Stimulation Methods," in G. Schaltenbrand and C. N. Woolsey (eds.), *Cerebral Localization and Organization* (Madison: University of Wisconsin Press, 1964), 17–26; J. M. Allman and J. H. Kaas, "A Representation of the Visual Field in the Caudal Third of the Middle Temporal Gyms of the Owl Monkey (*Aotus trivirgatus*)." *Brain Research* 31 (1971): 85–105.

15. L. Geddes, "Human Brain Mapped in Unprecedented Detail: Nearly 100 Previously Unidentified Brain Areas Revealed by Examination of the Cerebral Cortex," *Nature*, July 20, 2016. doi:10.1038/nature.2016.20285.

16. One such technique, diffusion tensor imaging (DTI), tracks the direction of axons that make up the white matter in the cortex.

17. Elizabeth Penisi, "Two Foundations Collaborate on Cognitive Neuroscience," *Scientist*, October 1989. http://www.the-scientist.com/?articles.view/articleNo/ 10719/title/Two-Foundations-Collaborate-On-Cognitive-Neuroscience/.

18. U. Hasson, E. Yang, I. Vallines, D. J. Heeger, and N. Rubin, "A Hierarchy of Temporal Receptive Windows in Human Cortex," *Journal of Neuroscience* 28, no. 10 (2008): 2539–2550.

Chapter 6

1. J. Herault and C. Jutten, "Space or Time Adaptive Signal Processing by Neural Network Models," in J. S. Denker, ed., *Neural Networks for Computing, AIP Conference Proceedings* 151, no. 1 (1986): 206–211.

2. A. J. Bell and T. J. Sejnowski, "An Information-Maximization Approach to Blind Separation and Blind Deconvolution," *Neural Computation* 7, no. 6 (1995): 1129–1159.

3. Ralph Linsker at IBM earlier had introduced an algorithm called "infomax" to account for how the visual system gets wired up during development. R. Linsker, "Self-Organization in a Perceptual Network," *Computer* 21, no. 3 (1988): 105–117.

4. A. J. Bell and T. J. Sejnowski, "An Information-Maximization Approach to Blind Separation and Blind Deconvolution."

5. Other important contributions to the development of ICA were made by Pierre Comon, Jean-François Cardoso, Apo Hyvarinen, Erkki Oja, Andrzej Cichocki, Shun-ichi Amari, Te-Won Lee, Michael Lewicki, and many others.

6. A. J. Bell and T. J. Sejnowski, "The 'Independent Components' of Natural Scenes Are Edge Filters," *Vision Research* 37, no. 23 (1997): 3327–3338.

7. Bruno Olshausen and David Field came to the same conclusion with another learning algorithm based on sparsity. B. A. Olshausen and D. J. Field, "Emergence of Simple-Cell Receptive Field Properties by Learning a Sparse Code for Natural Images," *Nature* 38, no. 6583 (1996): 607–609.

8. Horace Barlow, "Possible Principles Underlying the Transformation of Sensory Messages," in Walter A. Rosenblith, ed., *Sensory Communication* (Cambridge, MA: MIT Press, 1961), 217–234.

9. A. J. Bell and T. J. Sejnowski, "Learning the Higher-Order Structure of a Natural Sound," *Network: Computation in Neural Systems* 7, no. 2 (1996): 261–267.

10. A. Hyvarinen and P. Hoyer, "Emergence of Phase- and Shift-Invariant Features by Decomposition of Natural Images into Independent Feature Subspaces." *Neural Computation* 12, no. 7 (2000): 1705–1720.

11. M. J. McKeown, T.-P. Jung, S. Makeig, G. D. Brown, S. S. Kindermann, T.-W. Lee, and T. J. Sejnowski, "Spatially Independent Activity Patterns in Functional MRI Data during the Stroop Color-Naming Task," *Proceedings of the National Academy of Sciences of the United States of America* 95, no. 3 (1998): 803–810.

12. D. Mantini, M. G. Perrucci, C. Del Gratta, G. L. Romani, and M. Corbetta, "Electrophysiological Signatures of Resting State Networks in the Human Brain," *Proceedings of the National Academy of Sciences of the United States of America* 104, no. 32 (2007):13170–13175.

13. D. L. Donoho, "Compressed Sensing," *IEEE Transactions on Information Theory* 52, no. 4 (2006): 1289–1306; Sanjoy Dasgupta, Charles F. Stevens, and Saket Navlakha, "A Neural Algorithm for a Fundamental Computing Problem," *Science* 358 (2017): 793–796. doi:10.1126/science.aam9868.

14. The brain may have implemented Independent Component Analysis in the cerebellum, at the level of mossy fiber inputs converging on the dendrites of granule cells. See D. M. Eagleman, O. J.-M. D. Coenen, V. Mitsner, T. M. Bartol, A. J. Bell, and T. J. Sejnowski, "Cerebellar Glomeruli: Does Limited Extracellular Calcium Implement a Sparse Encoding Strategy?" in *Proceedings of the 8th Joint Symposium on Neural Computation* (La Jolla, CA: Salk Institute, 2001).

15. Tony Bell is studying water structure using Independent Component Analysis and near-infrared spectroscopy. He is trying to prove that water forms coherent structures that communicate via light and form a substrate for biomolecular life at scales so far invisible to instruments. The idea is that a decision occurs when "neural schemes" relax to a sufficient degree to allow the emergence of coherent information from the more distributed atomic networks within cells throughout the body.

Chapter 7

1. The fastest that most neurons can make a decision is around 10 milliseconds, and to come to a decision in 1 second allows no more than 100 time steps.

2. When it came to electromagnetism, Michael Faraday's physics was scruffy and James Clerk Maxwell's was neat.

3. Theodore Holmes Bullock and G. Adrian Horridge, *Structure and Function in the Nervous Systems of Invertebrates* (San Francisco: W. H. Freeman, 1965).

4. E. Chen, K. M. Stiefel, T. J. Sejnowski, and T. H. Bullock, "Model of Traveling Waves in a Coral Nerve Network," *Journal of Comparative Physiology* A 194, no. 2 (2008): 195–200.

5. D. S. Levine and S. Grossberg, "Visual Illusions in Neural Networks: Line Neutralization, Tilt after Effect, and Angle Expansion," *Journal of Theoretical Biology* 61, no. 2 (1976):477–504.

6. G. B. Ermentrout and J. D. Cowan, "A Mathematical Theory of Visual Hallucination Patterns," *Biological Cybernetics* 34, no. 3 (1979):137–150.

7. J. J. Hopfield, "Neural Networks and Physical Systems with Emergent Collective Computational Abilities," *Proceedings of the National Academy of Sciences of the United States of America* 79, no. 8 (1982): 2554–2558.

8. Although the neural network of the 1976 Marr-Poggio model for stereo vision (mentioned in chapter 4) was symmetric, because Marr and Poggio used synchronous updates of all the units, the network's dynamics were much more complex than those of the Hopfield net, with its asynchronous updates. D. Marr, G. Palm, and T. Poggio T, "Analysis of a Cooperative Stereo Algorithm," *Biological Cybernetics* 28, no. 4 (1978): 223–239.

9. L. L. Colgin, S. Leutgeb, K. Jezek, J. K. Leutgeb, E. I. Moser, B. L. McNaughton, and M.-B. Moser, "Attractor-Map versus Autoassociation Based Attractor Dynamics in the Hippocampal Network," *Journal of Neurophysiology* 104, no. 1 (2010): 35–50.

10. J. J. Hopfield and D. W. Tank,"'Neural' Computation of Decisions in Optimization Problems," *Biological Cybernetics* 52, no. 3 (1985):141–152. The traveling salesman problem is famous in computer science as an example of a class of problems for which the time required to solve the problem increases very rapidly as the size of the problem grows.

11. Dana H. Ballard and Christopher M. Brown, *Computer Vision* (Englewood Cliffs, NJ: Prentice Hall, 1982).

12. D. H. Ballard, G. E. Hinton, and T. J. Sejnowski, "Parallel Visual Computation," *Nature* 306, no. 5938 (1983): 21–26; R. A. Hummel and S. W. Zucker, "On the Foundations of Relaxation Labeling Processes," *IEEE Transactions on Pattern Analysis and Machine Intelligence* 5, no. 3 (1983): 267–287.

13. S. Kirkpatrick, C. D. Gelatt Jr., and M. P. Vecchi, "Optimization by Simulated Annealing," *Science* 220, no. 4598 (1983): 671–680.

14. P. K. Kienker, T. J. Sejnowski, G. E. Hinton, and L. E. Schumacher, "Separating Figure from Ground with a Parallel Network," *Perception* 15 (1986): 197–216.

15. H. Zhou, H. S. Friedman, and R. von der Heydt, "Coding of Border Ownership in Monkey Visual Cortex," *Journal of Neuroscience* 20, no. 17 (2000): 6594–6611.

16. Donald O. Hebb, *The Organization of Behavior: A Neuropsychological Theory* (New York: Wiley & Sons., 1949), 62.

17. T. J. Sejnowski, P. K. Kienker, and G. E. Hinton, "Learning Symmetry Groups with Hidden Units: Beyond the Perceptron," *Physica* 22D (1986): 260–275.

18. N. J. Cohen, I. Abrams, W. S. Harley, L. Tabor, and T. J. Sejnowski, "Skill Learning and Repetition Priming in Symmetry Detection: Parallel Studies of Human Subjects and Connectionist Models," in *Proceedings of the 8th Annual Conference of the Cognitive Science Society* (Hillsdale, NJ: Erlbaum, 1986), 23–44.

19. B. P. Yuhas, M. H. Goldstein Jr., T. J. Sejnowski, and R. E. Jenkins, "Neural Network Models of Sensory Integration for Improved Vowel Recognition," *Proceedings of the IEEE* 78, no. 10 (1990): 1658–1668.

20. G. E. Hinton, S. Osindero, and Y. Teh, "A Fast Learning Algorithm for Deep Belief Nets," *Neural Computation* 18, no. 7 (2006): 1527–1554.

21. J. Y. Lettvin, H. R. Maturana, W. S. McCulloch, and W. H. Pitts, "What the Frog's Eye Tells the Frog's Brain," *Proceedings of the Institute of Radio Engineers* 47, no. 11 (1959): 1940–1951. http://hearingbrain.org/docs/letvin_ieee_1959.pdf.

22. R. R. Salakhutdinov and G. E. Hinton, "Deep Boltzmann Machines," in *Proceedings of the 12th International Conference on Artificial Intelligence and Statistics, Journal of Machine Learning Research* 5 (2009): 448–455. Paul Smolensky introduced this special case of the Boltzmann machine, which he called a Harmonium: P. Smolensky, "Information Processing in Dynamical Systems: Foundations of Harmony Theory," in David E. Rumelhart and James L. McLelland (eds.), *Parallel Distributed Processing: Explorations in the Microstructure of Cognition, Volume 1: Foundations* (Cambridge, MA: MIT Press, 1986), 194–281.

23. B. Poole, S. Lahiri, M. Raghu, J. Sohl-Dickstein, and S. Ganguli, "Exponential Expressivity in Deep Neural Networks through Transient Chaos," in *Advances in Neural Information Processing Systems* 29 (2016): 3360–3368.

24. Jeffrey L. Elman, Elizabeth A. Bates, Mark H. Johnson, Annette Karmiloff-Smith, Domenico Parisi, and Kim Plunkett, *Rethinking Innateness: A Connectionist Perspective on Development* (Cambridge, MA: MIT Press, 1996).

25. Steven R. Quartz and Terrence J. Sejnowski, *Liars, Lovers, and Heroes: What the New Brain Science Reveals about How We Become Who We Are* (New York: Harper-Collins, 2002).

26. S. Quartz and T. J. Sejnowski, "The Neural Basis of Cognitive Development: A Constructivist Manifesto," *Behavioral and Brain Sciences* 20, no. 4 (1997): 537–596.

27. This is called "non-CG methylation." See R. Lister, E. A. Mukamel, J. R. Nery, M. Urich, C. A. Puddifoot, N. D. Johnson, J. Lucero, Y. Huang A. J. Dwork, M. D. Schultz, M. Yu, J. Tonti-Filippini, H. Heyn, S. Hu, J. C. Wu, A. Rao, M. Esteller, C. He, F. G. Haghighi, T. J. Sejnowski, M. M. Behrens, J. R. Ecker, "Global Epigenomic Reconfiguration during Mammalian Brain Development," *Science* 341, no. 6146 (2013): 629.

Chapter 8

1. The Cognitive Science Department at UCSD was founded by Don Norman, an expert on human factors and ergonomics, and had an eclectic faculty.

2. The mathematics used in the backpropagation learning algorithm had been around for some time, going back to the 1960s in the control theory literature, but it was the application to multilayer perceptrons that has had the biggest impact. See Arthur E. Bryson and Yu-Chi Ho, *Applied Optimal Control: Optimization, Estimation, and Control* (University of Michigan, Blaisdell, 1969).

3. See Michael Jordan's magisterial lecture on modern stochastic gradient descent: "On Gradient-Based Optimization: Accelerated, Distributed, Asynchronous, and Stochastic," May 2, 2017, Simons Institute for the Theory of Computing, UC, Berkeley. https://simons.berkeley.edu/talks/michael-jordan-2017-5-2/.

4. D. E. Rumelhart, G. E. Hinton, and R. J. Williams, "Learning Representations by Back-Propagating Errors," *Nature* 323, no. 6088 (1986), 533–536.

5. In a widely repeated account, Bertrand Russell once gave a public lecture on astronomy. At the end of the lecture, an elderly lady at the back of the room got up and said: "What you have told us is nonsense. The world is really the back of a giant tortoise." Russell smiled and replied, "And what is the tortoise standing on?" "You're very clever, young man, very clever," said the old lady. "But I know the answer. It's turtles all the way down!" The old lady had solved her problem with recursion, though at the expense of infinite regression. In practice, the loop must terminate.

6. C. R. Rosenberg And T. J. Sejnowski, "Parallel Networks That Learn to Pronounce English Text," *Complex Systems* 1 (1987): 145–168.

7. W. Nelson Francis and Henry Kucera, "A Standard Corpus of Present-Day Edited American English, for Use with Digital Computers," Brown University, 1964; revised and amplified, 1979, http://clu.uni.no/icame/manuals/BROWN/INDEX.HTM.

8. A recording of what the network sounds like during different stages of learning can be downloaded from http://papers.cnl.salk.edu/~terry/NETtalk/nettalk.mp3.

9. M. S. Seidenberg and J. L. McClelland, "A Distributed Developmental Model of Word Recognition and Naming," *Psychological Review* 96, no. 4 (1989), 523–568.

10. N. Qian and T. J. Sejnowski, "Predicting the Secondary Structure of Globular Proteins Using Neural Network Models," *Journal of Molecular Biology*, 202 (1988): 865–884.

11. David E. Rumelhart and James L. McClelland, "On Learning the Past Tense of English Verbs," in Rumelhart and McClelland, eds., *Parallel Distributed Processing: Explorations in the Microstructure of Cognition* (Cambridge, MA: MIT Press, 1986), 2:216–271; J. L. McClelland and K. Patterson, "Rules or Connections in Past-Tense inflections: What Does the Evidence Rule Out?" *Trends in Cognitive Sciences* 6, no. 11 (2002): 465–472; and S. Pinker and M. T. Ulman, "The Past and Future of the Past Tense," *Trends in Cognitive Sciences* 6, no. 11 (2002): 456–463.

12. M. S. Seidenberg and D. C. Plaut, "Quasiregularity and Its Discontents: The Legacy of the Past Tense Debate," *Cognitive Science* 38, no. 6 (2014): 1190–1228.

13. D. Zipser and R. A. Andersen, "A Back-Propagation Programmed Network That Simulates Response Properties of a Subset of Posterior Parietal Neurons" *Nature* 331, no. 6158 (1988):679–684. This network transformed the position of an object on the retina from retina coordinates to head-center coordinates, taking into account eye position.

14. G. E. Hinton, D. C. Plaut, and T. Shallice, "Simulating Brain Damage," *Scientific American* 269, no. 4 (1993): 76–82. "Adults with brain damage make some bizarre errors when reading words. If a network of simulated neurons is trained to read and then is damaged, it produces strikingly similar behavior" (76).

15. N. Srivastava, G. Hinton, A. Krizhevsky, I. Sutskever, and R. Salakhutdinov, "Dropout: A Simple Way to Prevent Neural Networks from Overfitting," *Journal of Machine Learning Research* 15 (2014):1929–1958.

16. "Netflix Prize," *Wikipedia*, last modified, August 23, 2017, https://en.wikipedia.org/wiki/Netflix_Prize.

17. Carlos A. Gomez-Uribe, Neil Hunt, "The Netflix Recommender System: Algorithms," *ACM Transactions on Management Information Systems* 6, no. 4 (2016) , article no. 13.

18. T. M. Bartol Jr., C. Bromer, J. Kinney, M. A. Chirillo, J. N. Bourne, K. M. Harris, and T. J. Sejnowski, "Nanoconnectomic Upper Bound on the Variability of Synaptic Plasticity," *eLife*, 4:e10778, 2015, doi:10.7554/eLife.10778.

19. This follows from the "law of large numbers" in probability theory. This is why casinos always win in the long run even though they may lose in the short run.

20. Bartol Jr. et al., "Nanoconnectomic Upper Bound on the Variability of Synaptic Plasticity."

21. J. Collins, J. Sohl-Dickstein, and D. Sussillo, "Capacity and Trainability in Recurrent Neural Networks," 2016, https://arxiv.org/pdf/1611.09913.pdf. It is dangerous to put too much weight on a coincidence: "24 hours in a day, 24 beers in a case. Is this just a coincidence? I think not." This coincidence is celebrated annually at Princeton University on Paul Newman Day, April 24.

22. A rough estimate of the dimensionality of synapses can be found by taking the square root of the product of the lower and upper bounds of the number of synapses. Lawrence Weinstein and John A. Adam, *Guesstimation: Solving the World's Problems on the Back of a Cocktail Napkin* (Princeton: Princeton University Press, 2009), 3. Taking, as upper bound, the total number of synapses in the cortex, 100 trillion, and, as lower bound, the number of synapses on a single neuron,10,000, a rough estimate of the number of synapses needed to represent a complex object is about a billion. Applying the same rule of thumb to the number of neurons needed: the upper bound is ten billion, the number of neurons in the cortex, and the lower bound is one neuron, so the number of neurons needed to represent a complex object is 100,000, about the number of neurons below a square millimeter of cortex. But these neurons could be distributed widely in different parts of the cortex. We can estimate the number of cortical areas that must be linked to represent a concept: an upper bound is 100, the total number of cortical areas, and a lower bound is 1, so the estimate is 10 cortical areas, each containing 10,000 neurons. New techniques being developed by the BRAIN Initiative will pin down these numbers experimentally.

23. Ali Rahimi and Benjamin Recht, "Random Features for Large-Scale Kernel Machines," *Advances in Neural Information Processing Systems* 20 (2007).

24. https://www.facebook.com/yann.lecun/posts/10154938130592143/.

25. Mukherjee, "A.I. versus M.D." *New Yorker*, April 3, 2017. http://www.newyorker.com/magazine/2017/04/03/ai-versus-md/.

26. Daniel Kahneman, *Thinking, Fast and Slow* (New York: Farrar, Straus & Giroux, 2011).

27. Clare Garvie and Jonathan Frankle, "Facial-Recognition Software Might Have a Racial Bias Problem," *The Atlantic*, Apr 7, 2016. https://www.theatlantic.com/technology/archive/2016/04/the-underlying-bias-of-facial-recognition-systems/476991/.

28. Kate Crawford, "Artificial Intelligence's White Guy Problem," *New York Times*, June 25, 2016 https://www.nytimes.com/2016/06/26/opinion/sunday/artificial-intelligences-white-guy-problem.html.

29. Barbara Oakley, Ariel Knafo, Guruprasad Madhavan, and David Sloan Wilson (eds.), *Pathological Altruism* (Oxford: Oxford University Press, 2011).

30. https://futureoflife.org/open-letter-autonomous-weapons/.

31. http://www.cnn.com/2017/09/01/world/putin-artificial-intelligence-will-rule-world/index.html.

32. Andrew Burtjan, "Leave A.I. Alone," *New York Times*, January 4, 2018. https://www.nytimes.com/2018/01/04/opinion/leave-artificial-intelligence.html.

Chapter 9

1. Thomas S. Kuhn, *The Structure of Scientific Revolutions*, 2nd ed. (Chicago: University of Chicago Press, 1970), 23

2. M. Riesenhuber and T. Poggio, "Hierarchical Models of Object Recognition In Cortex." Nat Neurosci. 2: 1019-1025, 1999; T. Serre, A. Oliva, and T. Poggio, "A Feedforward Architecture Accounts for Rapid Categorization." *Proceedings of the National Academy of Sciences of the United States of America* 104, no. 15 (2007): 6424–6429.

3. Pearl, *Probabilistic Reasoning in Intelligent Systems*. Morgan Kaufmann; 1988.

4. Yoshua Bengio, Pascal Lamblin, Dan Popovici, and Hugo Larochelle, "Greedy Layer-Wise Training of Deep Networks," in Bernhard Schölkopf, John Platt, and Thomas Hoffman, eds., *Advances in Neural Information Processing Systems 19: Proceedings of the 2006 Conference* (Cambridge, MA: MIT Press), 153–160.

5. Sepp Hochreiter, Yoshua Bengio, Paolo Frasconi, and Jürgen Schmidhuber, "Gradient Flow in Recurrent Nets: The Difficulty of Learning Long-Term Dependencies," In John F. Kolen and Stefan C. Kremer, eds., *A Field Guide to Dynamical Recurrent Neural Networks* (New York: IEEE Press, 2001), 237–243.

6. D. C. Ciresan, U. Meier, L. M. Gambardella, and J. Schmidhuber, "Deep Big Simple Neural Nets for Handwritten Digit Recognition," *Neural Computation* 22, no. 12 (2010): 3207–3220.

7. A. Krizhevsky, I. Sutskever, and G. E. Hinton, "ImageNet Classification with Deep Convolutional Neural Networks," *Advances in Neural Information Processing Systems* 25 (NIPS 2012). https://papers.nips.cc/paper/4824-imagenet-classification-with-deep-convolutional-neural-networks.

8. Ibid.

9. K. He, X. Zhang, S. Ren, and J. Sun, "Deep Residual Learning for Image Recognition," 2015. https://www.cv-foundation.org/openaccess/content_cvpr_2016/papers/He_Deep_Residual_Learning_CVPR_2016_paper.pdf.

10. Yann LeCun, "Modèles connexionistes de l'apprentissage" (Connectionist learning models) (Ph.D. diss., Université Pierre et Marie Curie, Paris, 1987).

11. Krizhevsky, Sutskever, and Hinton, "ImageNet Classification with Deep Convolutional Neural Networks."

12. M. D. Zeiler and R. Fergus, "Visualizing and Understanding Convolutional Networks," 2013. https://www.cs.nyu.edu/~fergus/papers/zeilerECCV2014.pdf.

13. Patricia Smith Churchland, *Neurophilosophy: Toward a Unified Science of the Mind-Brain* (Cambridge, MA: MIT Press, 1989).

14. Patricia Smith Churchland and Terrence J. Sejnowski, *The Computational Brain*, 2nd ed. (Cambridge, MA: MIT Press 2016).

15. D. L. Yamins and J. J. DiCarlo, "Using Goal-Driven Deep Learning Models to Understand Sensory Cortex," *Nature Neuroscience* 19, no. 3 (2016): 356–365.

16. S. Funahashi, C. J. Bruce, and P. S. Goldman-Rakic, "Visuospatial Coding in Primate Prefrontal Neurons Revealed by Oculomotor Paradigms," *Journal of Neurophysiology* 63, no. 4 (1990): 814–831.

17. J. L. Elman, "Finding Structure in Time," *Cognitive Science* 14 (1990): 179–211; M. I. Jordan, "Serial Order: A Parallel Distributed Processing Approach," *Advances in Psychology* 121 (1997): 471–495; G. Hinton, L. Deng, G. E. Dahl, A. Mohamed, N. Jaitly, A. Senior, et al., "Deep Neural Networks for Acoustic Modeling in Speech Recognition," *IEEE Signal Processing Magazine*, 29, no. 6 (2012): 82–97.

18. S. Hochreiter and J. Schmidhuber, "Long Short-Term Memory," *Neural Computation* 9, no. 8 (1997): 1735–1780.

19. John Markoff, "When A.I. Matures, It May Call Jürgen Schmidhuber 'Dad.'" *New York Times,* November 27, 2016, https://www.nytimes.com/2016/11/27/technology/artificial-intelligence-pioneer-jurgen-schmidhuber-overlooked.html.

20. K. Xu, J. L. Ba, K. Kiror, K. Cho, A. Courville, R. Slakhutdinov, R. Zemel, Y. Bengio, "Show, Attend and Tell: Neural Image Captions Generation with Visual Attention," 2015, rev. 2016. https://arxiv.org/pdf/1502.03044.pdf.

21. I. J. Goodfellow, J. Pouget-Abadie, M. Mirza, B. Xu, D. Warde-Farley, S. Ozair, A. Courville, Y. Bengio, "Generative Adversarial Nets," *Advances in Neural Information Processing Systems*, 2014. https://arxiv.org/pdf/1406.2661.pdf.

22. See A. Radford, L. Metz, and S. Chintala, "Unsupervised Representation Learning with Deep Convolutional Generative Adversarial Networks," 2016, https://arxiv.org/pdf/1511.06434.pdf ; Cade Metz and Keith Collins, "How an A.I. 'Cat-and-Mouse Game' Generates Believable Fake Photos," *New York Times*, January 2, 2018. https://www.nytimes.com/interactive/2018/01/02/technology/ai-generated-photos.html.

23. K. Schawinski, C. Zhang, H. Zhang, L. Fowler, and G. K. Santhanam, "Generative Adversarial Networks Recover Features in Astrophysical Images of Galaxies beyond the Deconvolution Limit," 2017. https://arxiv.org/pdf/1702.00403.pdf.

24. J. Chang and S. Scherer, "Learning Representations of Emotional Speech with Deep Convolutional Generative Adversarial Networks," 2017. https://arxiv.org/pdf/1705.02394.pdf.

25. A. Nguyen, J. Yosinski, Y. Bengio, A. Dosovitskiy, and J. Clune, "Plug & Play Generative Networks: Conditional Iterative Generation of Images in Latent Space," 2016, https://arxiv.org/pdf/1612.00005.pdf; Radford, Metz, and Chintala, "Unsupervised Representation Learning with Deep Convolutional Generative Adversarial Networks," 2016. https://arxiv.org/pdf/1511.06434.pdf.

26. Guy Trebay, "Miuccia Prada and Sylvia Fendi Grapple with the New World," *New York Times*, June 19, 2017. https://www.nytimes.com/2017/06/19/fashion/mens-style/prada-fendi-milan-mens-fashion.html.

27. T. R. Poggio, S. Rifkin, Mukherjee and P. Niyogi. "General Conditions for Predictivity in Learning Theory," *Nature* 428, no. 6981 (2004): 419–422.

28. Bengio is also an advisor to several companies including Microsoft and he cofounded Element AI, but his primary ties are to academia, and he is committed to the progress of science and the public good.

29. See preface in Churchland and Sejnowski, *The Computational Brain*, 2nd ed., ix–xv.

Chapter 10

1. Although the fate of our fabled inventor is unknown, he was very likely dispatched for his impudence once the king realized he had been bamboozled.

2. Tesauro and Sejnowski, "A Parallel Network That Learns to Play Backgammon."

3. R. Sutton, "Learning to Predict by the Methods of Temporal Differences," *Machine Learning* 3, no. 1 (1988): 9–44.

4. See Richard Bellman *Adaptive Control Processes: A Guided Tour* (Princeton: Princeton University Press. 1961), 51–59.

5. G. Tesauro, "Temporal Difference Learning and TD-Gammon." *Communications of the ACM* 38, no. 3 (1995): 58–68.

6. J. Garcia, D. J. Kimeldorf, and R. A. Koelling, "Conditioned Aversion to Saccharin Resulting from Exposure to Gamma Radiation," *Science* 122. no. 3160 (1955): 157–158.

7. P. R. Montague, P. Dayan, and T. J. Sejnowski, "A Framework for Mesencephalic Dopamine Systems Based on Predictive Hebbian Learning," *Journal of Neuroscience* 16, no. 5 (1996): 1936–1947.

8. W. Schultz, P. Dayan, and P. R. Montague, "A Neural Substrate of Prediction and Reward," *Science* 275, no. 5306 (1997): 1593–1599.

9. P. N. Tobler, J. P. O'Doherty, R. J. Dolan, and W. Schultz, "Human Neural Learning Depends on Reward Prediction Errors in the Blocking Paradigm," *Journal of Neurophysiology* 95, no. 1 (2006): 301–310.

10. M. Hammer and R. Menzel, "Learning and Memory in the Honeybee," *Journal of Neuroscience* 15, no. 3 (1995): 1617–1630.

11. L. A. Real, "Animal Choice Behavior and the Evolution of Cognitive Architecture," *Science* 253, no. 5023 (1991): 980–986.

12. P. R. Montague, P. Dayan, C. Person, and T. J. Sejnowski, "Bee Foraging in Uncertain Environments Using Predictive Hebbian Learning," *Nature* 377, no. 6551 (1995): 725–728.

13. Y. Aso and G. M. Rubin, "Dopaminergic Neurons Write And Update Memories With Cell-Type-Specific Rules," in L. Luo (ed.), *eLife.* 5 (2016): e16135. doi:10.7554/eLife.16135.

14. W. Mischel and E. B. Ebbesen, "Attention in Delay of Gratification," *Journal of Personality and Social Psychology* 16, no. 2 (1970): 329–337.

15. V. Mnih, K. Kavukcuoglu, D. Silver, A. A. Rusu, J. Veness, M. G. Bellemare, et al., "Human-Level Control through Deep Reinforcement Learning," *Nature* 518, no. 7540 (2015): 529–533.

16. Simon Haykin, *Cognitive Dynamic System: Perception-Action Cycle, Radar, and Radio* (New York: Cambridge University Press, 2012).

17. S. Haykin, J. M. Fuster, D. Findlay, and S. Feng, "Cognitive Risk Control for Physical Systems," *IEEE Access* 5 (2017): 14664–14679.

18. G. Reddy, A. Celani, T. J. Sejnowski, and M. Vergassola, "Learning to Soar in Turbulent Environments," *Proceedings of the National Academy of Sciences of the United States of America* 113, no. 33 (2016): E4877–E4884.

19. G. Reddy, J. W. Ng, A. Celani, T. J. Sejnowski, and M. Vergassola, "Soaring Like a Bird via Reinforcement Learning in the Field," submitted for publication.

20. Kenji Doya and Terrence J. Sejnowski, "A Novel Reinforcement Model of Birdsong Vocalization Learning," in Gerald Tesauro, David S. Touretzky, and Todd K. Leen, eds., *Advances in Neural Information Processing Systems 7* (Cambridge, MA: MIT Press, 1995), 101–108.

21. A. J. Doupe and P. K. Kuhl, "Birdsong and Human Speech: Common Themes and Mechanisms," *Annual Review of Neuroscience* 22 (1999): 567–631.

22. G. Turrigiano, "Too Many Cooks? Intrinsic and Synaptic Homeostatic Mechanisms in Cortical Circuit Refinement," *Annual Review of Neuroscience* 34 (2011):89–103.

23. L. Wiskott and T. J. Sejnowski, "Constrained Optimization for Neural Map Formation: A Unifying Framework for Weight Growth and Normalization," *Neural Computation* 10, no. 3 (1998): 671–716.

24. A. J. Bell, "Self-Organization in Real Neurons: Anti-Hebb in 'Channel Space'?" *Advances in Neural Information Processing Systems* 4 (1991): 59–66; M. Siegel, E. Marder, and L. F. Abbott, "Activity-Dependent Current Distributions in Model Neurons," *Proceedings of the National Academy of Sciences of the United States of America* 91, no. 24 (1994): 11308–11312.

25. *H. T. Siegelmann, "Computation Beyond the Turing Limit," Science 238 (1995): 632–637.*

Chapter 11

1. All papers presented at NIPS conferences are available online at: https://nips.cc/.

2. To get a taste of biologists' jargon, consider this sentence, taken at random from a recent review in *Science*: "Oligodendrocytes present a variety of proteins inhibitory to axon regrowth, including myelin-associated glycoprotein, the neurite-outgrowth inhibitor 'Nogo,' oligodendrocyte-myelin glycoprotein, and semaphorins." B. Laha, B. K. Stafford, and A. D. Huberman, "Regenerating Optic Pathways from the Eye to the Brain," *Science* 356, no. 6342 (2017): 1032.

3. The neuroscientist turned out to be Howard Wachtel, who was studying the nervous systems of *Aplysia* at the University of Colorado at Boulder.

4. Krizhevsky, Sutskever, and Hinton, "ImageNet Classification with Deep Convolutional Neural Networks."

5. George Orwell, *Nineteen Eighty-Four* (London: Secker & Warburg, 1949). This book has recently taken on new meaning.

6. Founded in 2006, Women in Machine Learning has been creating opportunities for women in machine learning to present and promote their research. See http://wimlworkshop.org.

Chapter 12

1. The Kaggle website has a million data scientists who vie with each other to win the prize with the best performance. Cade Metz, "Uncle Sam Wants Your Deep Neural Networks," *New York Times*, June 22, 2017, https://www.nytimes.com/2017/06/22/technology/homeland-security-artificial-intelligence-neural-network.html.

2. For a video of my lecture "Cognitive Computing: Past and Present," see https://www.youtube.com/watch?v=0BDMQuphd-Q.

3. See Jen Clark, "The Countdown to IBM's IoT, Munich," *IBM Internet of Things* (blog), posted February 8, 2017. https://www.ibm.com/blogs/internet-of-things/countdown-ibms-iot-hq-munich/.

4. The BRAIN report made recommendations and set priorities for innovative technologies to help advance our understanding of neural circuits and behavior. BRAIN Working Group, *BRAIN 2025: A Scientific Vision*, Report to the Advisory Committee to the Director, NIH (Bethesda, MD: National Institutes of Health, June 5, 2014), https://www.braininitiative.nih.gov/pdf/BRAIN2025_508C.pdf.

5. See K. S. Kosik, T. J. Sejnowski, M. E. Raichle, A. Ciechanover, and D. A. Baltimore, "A Path toward Understanding Neurodegeneration," *Science* 353, no. 6302 (2016): 872–873.

6. In the 2002 science fiction film *Minority Report*, Tom Cruise, on the run from the government, was able to avoid detection by having an illegal eye transplant.

7. See Nandan Nilekani and Viral Shah, *Rebooting India: Realizing a Billion Aspirations* (Gurgaon: Penguin Books India. 2015).

8. Nandan Nilekani, as quoted in Andrew Hill, "Nandan Nilekani, Infosys, on Rebooting India," *Financial Times*, January 22, 2017, https://www.ft.com/content/058c4b48-d43c-11e6-9341-7393bb2e1b51?mhq5j=e1.

9. See, for example, M. Gymrek, A. I. McGuire, D. Golan, E. Halperin, and Y. Erlich, "Identifying Personal Genomes by Surname Inference," *Science*. 339, no. 6117 (2013): 321–324.

10. See M. Wilson, "Six Views of Embodied Cognition," *Psychonomic Bulletin & Review* 9, no. 4 (2002): 625–636.

11. P. Ruvolo, D. Messinger, and J. Movellan, "Infants Time Their Smiles to Make Their Moms Smile," *PLoS One* 10, no. 9 (2015): e0136492.

12. Abigail Tucker, "Robot Babies," *Smithsonian Magazine*, July 2009, https://www.smithsonianmag.com/science-nature/robot-babies-30075698/; Tiffany Fox, "Machine Perception Lab Seeks to Improve Robot Teacher with Intelligent Tutoring Systems," UCSanDiego News Center, July 30, 2008, http://ucsdnews.ucsd.edu/newsrel/general/07-08RobotTeachers.asp. See also F. Tanaka, A. Cicourel, and J. R. Movellan, "Socialization between Toddlers and Robots at an Early Childhood Education Center," *Proceedings of the National Academy of Sciences of the United States of America* 104, no. 46 (2008): 17954–17958.

13. "Conserve Elephants. They Hold a Scientific Mirror Up to Humans," *Economist*, June 17, 2017, 72–74. http://www.economist.com/news/science-and-technology/21723394-biology-and-conservation-elephants-conserve-elephants-they-hold.

14. See R. A. Brooks, "Elephants Don't Play Chess," *Robotics and Autonomous Systems* 6, no. 1 (1990): 3–15.

15. In Japan, where Diego San was built by Kokoro Co., the suffix "san" is an honorific.

16. See YouTube video "Diego Installed," https://www.youtube.com/watch?v =knRyDcnUc4U. The face was built by David Hanson and Hanson Robotics.

17. See Paul Ekman, Thomas S. Huang, and Terrence J. Sejnowski, eds., *Final Report to NSF of the Planning Workshop on Facial Expression Understanding July 30–August 1, 1992*, http://papers.cnl.salk.edu/PDFs/Final%20Report%20To%20NSF%20of%20 the%20Planning%20Workshop%20on%20Facial%20Expression%20 Understanding%201992-4182.pdf.

18. See J. Gottman, R. Levenson, and E. Woodin,"Facial Expressions during Marital Conflict," *Journal of Family Communication* 1, no. 1 (2001): 37–57.

19. See F. Donato, M. Stewart Bartlett, J. C. Hager, P. Ekman, and T. J. Sejnowski, "Classifying Facial Actions," *IEEE Transactions on Pattern Analysis and Machine Intelligence* 21, no. 10 (1999): 974–989.

20. See G. Littlewort, J. Whitehill, T. Wu, I. Fasel, M. Frank, J. Movellan, and M. Bartlett, "The Computer Expression Recognition Toolbox (CERT)," 2011 IEEE International Conference on Automatic Face and Gesture Recognition, Santa Barbara, California. http://mplab.ucsd.edu/wp-content/uploads/2011-LittlewortEtAl-FG-CERT.pdf.

21. See A. N. Meltzoff, P. K. Kuhl, J. Movellan, and T. J. Sejnowski, "Foundations for a New Science of Learning," *Science* 325, no. 5938 (2009): 284–288.

22. See A. A. Benasich, N. A. Choudhury, T. Realpe-Bonilla, and C. P. Roesler, "Plasticity in Developing Brain: Active Auditory Exposure Impacts Prelinguistic Acoustic Mapping," *Journal of Neuroscience* 34, no. 40 (2014): 13349–13363.

23. See J. Whitehill, Z. Serpell, Y. Lin, A. Foster, and J. R. Movellan, "The Faces of Engagement: Automatic Recognition of Student Engagement from Facial Expressions," *IEEE Transactions on Affective Computing* 5, no. 1 (2014): 86–98. The use of machine learning to register facial expressions of students automatically was a team effort that also included Gwen Littlewort, Linda Salamanca, Aysha Foster, and Judy Reilly.

24. See R. V. Lindsey, J. D. Shroyer, H. Pashler, and M. C. Mozer, "Improving Students' Long-Term Knowledge Retention through Personalized Review," *Psychological Science* 25, no. 3 (2014): 630–647.

25. B. A. Rogowsky, B. M. Calhoun, and P. Tallal, "Matching Learning Style to Instructional Method: Effects on Comprehension," *Journal of Educational Psychology* 107, no. 1 (2015): 64–78. For a webinar on this topic, see: https://www.youtube .com/watch?v=p-WEcSFdoMw.

26. International Convention on the Science of Learning (Science of Learning: How can it make a difference? Connecting Interdisciplinary Research on Learning to Practice and Policy in Education) Shanghai, 1-6 March 2014 Summary Report. https://www.oecd.org/edu/ceri/International-Convention-on-the-Science-of-Learning-1-6-March-2014-Summary-Report.pdf.

27. See B. Bloom, "The 2 Sigma Problem: The Search for Methods of Group Instruction as Effective as One-to-One Tutoring," *Educational Researcher* 13, no. 6 (1984): 4–16.

28. John Markoff, "Virtual and Artificial, but 58,000 Want Course," *New York Times,* August 15, 2011, http://www.nytimes.com/2011/08/16/science/16stanford.html.

29. One of my favorite letters was from a fifth-grade student:

February 2, 2015

Dear Professors, I took my final exams and it was great. I am in grade five. My mom was browsing through Coursera and I pestered her to make me join in. She chose this course for me. I am thankful for that. I never knew that Professors were very witty and the entire course was fun learning. Of course, I had to refer to a dictionary for scientific terms used, but it was great learning. I have learnt to overcome the discomfort in my stomach as I enter the exam hall by using the breathing technique. It really works! Now I have learnt to face exams as a tool to understand how much I have learnt and retained. I love the Pomodoro technique. My mom did a role play in the entire course. She played the opposite. She crammed her brain with video lectures (she binge watched), she did not take rest and did not even sleep before the day I took the final test. Though she is much smarter than me, she could not do well. I was amazed that simple techniques helped me score better and of course without any pressure of exams. Thanks a ton, Professors. I wish you could come up with part II of this course.

Happy Monday,

Susan

30. Barbara Oakley and Terrence Sejnowski, *Learning How to Learn: How to Succeed in School Without Spending All Your Time Studying; A Guide for Kids and Teens* (New York: TarcherPerigee, Penguin Books, August 7, 2018).

31. "Udacity's Sebastian Thrun: 'Silicon Valley has an obligation to reach out to all of the world,'" *Financial Times,* November 15, 2017. https://www.ft.com/content/51c47f88-b278-11e7-8007-554f9eaa90ba/.

32. Barbara Oakley, *Mindshift: Break through Obstacles to Learning and Discover Your Hidden Potential* (New York: Penguin Random House, 2017).

33. See D. Bavelier and C. S. Green, "The Brain-Boosting Power of Video Games," *Scientific American* 315, no 1 (2016): 26–31.

34. G. L. West, K. Konishi, and V. D. Bohbot, "Video Games and Hippocampus-Dependent Learning," *Current Directions in Psychological Science* 26. no. 2 (2017):152–158.

35. J. A. Anguera, J. Boccanfuso, J. L. Rintoul, O. Al-Hashimi, F. Faraji, J. Janowich, et al., "Video Game Training Enhances Cognitive Control in Older Adults," *Nature* 501, no. 7465 (2013): 97–101.

36. Ibid.

37. See IES: What Works Clearinghouse, *Beginning Reading Intervention Report: Fast ForWord* (Washington, DC: U.S. Department of Education, Institute of Education Sciences, 2013). https://ies.ed.gov/ncee/wwc/Docs/InterventionReports/wwc_ffw _031913.pdf.

38. See J. Deveau, D. J. Ozer, and A. R. Seitz "Improved Vision and On-Field Performance in Baseball through Perceptual Learning," *Current Biology* 24, no. 4 (2014): R146–147.

39. See Federal Trade Commission press release "FTC Charges Marketers of 'Vision Improvement' App with Deceptive Claims," September 17, 2015, https://www .ftc.gov/news-events/press-releases/2015/09/ftc-charges-marketers-vision -improvement-app-deceptive-claims/. Seitz's scientific studies are high quality and have been published in peer-review psychology journals, but the FTC wanted him to perform a randomized control trial, similar to trials used to test the efficacy of drugs. This is an expensive undertaking, difficult for a small startup company.

40. Johana Bhuiyan, "Ex-Google Sebastian Thrun Says That the Going Rate for Self-Driving Talent Is $10 Million per Person," *Recode*, September 17, 2016. https://www .recode.net/2016/9/17/12943214/sebastian-thrun-self-driving-talent-pool.

41. Geoffrey Hinton is the chief scientific advisor of the Vector Institute. See http:// vectorinstitute.ai/.

42. Paul Mozur and John Markoff, "Is China Outsmarting America in A.I.?" *New York Times*, May 27, 2017, https://www.nytimes.com/2017/05/27/technology/china -us-ai-artificial-intelligence.html.

43. Paul Mozur, "Beijing Wants A.I. to Be Made in China by 2030," *New York Times*, July 20, 2017. https://www.nytimes.com/2017/07/20/business/china-artificial -intelligence.html.

44. See Mike Wall, "JFK's 'Moon Speech' Still Resonates 50 Years Later," *Space.com* (blog), posted September 12, 2012, https://www.space.com/17547-jfk-moon-speech -50years-anniversary.html. The "We choose to go to the moon" speech by President John F. Kennedy at Rice University in Houston on September 12, 1962, which is still stirring more than fifty years later, reminds us of his leadership. See https://www .youtube.com/watch?v=WZyRbnpGyzQ/. When astronaut Neil Armstrong stepped onto the moon on July 20, 1969, the average age of an engineer at NASA was 26; in school in 1962, these engineers were inspired by Kennedy's speech.

45. J. Haskel and S. Westlake, *Capitalism without Capital: The Rise of the Intangible Economy* (Princeton, NJ: Princeton University Press, 2017), 4.

46. W. Brian Arthur, "The second economy?" *McKinsey Quarterly* October, 2011. https://www.mckinsey.com/business-functions/strategy-and-corporate-finance/our -insights/the-second-economy/.

47. "Hello, world!" is a test message from an example program in Brian Kernighan and Dennis Ritchie's classic book *The C Programming Language* (Englewood Cliffs, NJ: Prentice Hall, 1978).

Chapter 13

1. Videos of the talks by discussants at the Grand Challenges for Science in the 21st Century conference can be found at https://www.youtube.com/results?search_query =Grand+Challenges++for+Science+in+the+21st+Century.

2. See W. Brian Arthur, *The Nature of Technology: What It Is and How It Evolves* (New York: Free Press, 2009).

3. George A. Cowan, *Manhattan Project to the Santa Fe Institute: The Memoirs of George A. Cowan* (Albuquerque: University of New Mexico Press, 2010).

4. Google's PageRank algorithm, which was invented by Google founders Larry Page and Sergey Brin, uses links to a webpage to rank the importance of pages on the Internet. It has since been elaborated with many layers of algorithms to manipulate the bias on searches.

5. A. D. I. Kramer, J. E. Guillory, and J. T. Hancock, "Experimental Evidence of Massive-Scale Emotional Contagion through Social Networks," *Proceedings of the National Academy of Sciences of the United States of America* 111, no. 24 (2014): 8788–8790.

6. Stuart Kauffman, *The Origins of Order: Self Organization and Selection in Evolution* (New York: Oxford University Press, 1993).

7. Christopher G. Langton, ed., *Artificial Life: An Overview* (Cambridge, MA: MIT Press, 1995).

8. Stephen Wolfram, *A New Kind of Science* (Champaign, IL: Wolfram Media, 2002).

9. National Research Council, *The Limits of Organic Life in Planetary Systems* (Washington, DC: National Academies Press, 2007), chap. 5, "Origin of Life," 53–68. https://www.nap.edu/read/11919/chapter/7.

10. Von Neumann, J. and A. W. Burks, *Theory of Self-Reproducing Automata* (Urbana, IL: University of Illinois Press, 1966). See also Wikipedia: "Von Neumann universal constructor."

11. W. S. McCulloch, and W. H. Pitts, "A Logical Calculus of the Ideas Immanent in Nervous Activity," *Bulletin of Mathematical Biophysics* 5 (1943): 115–133.

12. The computer was called the "JOHNNIAC," to echo another early digital computer called the "ENIAC."

13. The material he prepared for these lectures gave rise to von Neumann's *The Computer and the Brain* (New Haven: Yale University Press, 1958).

14. Stephen Jay Gould and Niles Eldredge, "Punctuated Equilibria: The Tempo And Mode Of Evolution Reconsidered." *Paleobiology* 3, no. 2 (1977): 115–151, 145; John Lyne and Henry Howe, "Punctuated Equilibria': Rhetorical Dynamics of a Scientific Controversy," *Quarterly Journal of Speech,* 72, no. 2 (1986): 132–147. doi:10.1080/00335638609383764.

15. John H. Holland, *Adaptation in Natural and Artificial Systems: An Introductory Analysis with Applications to Biology, Control, and Artificial Intelligence* (Cambridge, MA: MIT Press, 1992).

16. K. M. Stiefel and T. J. Sejnowski, "Mapping Function onto Neuronal Morphology," *Journal of Neurophysiology* 98, no. 1 (2007): 513–526.

17. See Wolfram Alpha computational knowledge engine website, https://www.wolframalpha.com/.

18. Stephen Wolfram, *A New Kind of Science* (Champaign, IL: Wolfram Media, 2002).

19. For an interesting essay on how Wolfram's thinking has evolved, see Stephen Wolfram, "A New Kind of Science: A 15-Year View," *Stephen Wolfram Blog,* posted May 16, 2017. http://blog.stephenwolfram.com/2017/05/a-new-kind-of-science-a-15-year-view/.

20. See Stephen Wolfram, "Wolfram Language Artificial Intelligence: The Image Identification Project," Stephen Wolfram Blog, posted May 13, 2015. http://blog.stephenwolfram.com/2015/05/wolfram-language-artificial-intelligence-the-image-identification-project/.

Chapter 14

1. R. Blandford, M. Roukes, L. Abbott, and T. Sejnowski, "Report on the Third Kavli Futures Symposium: Growing High Performance Computing in a Green Environment," September 9–11, 2010, Tromsø, Norway, http://cnl.salk.edu/Media/Kavli-Futures.Final-Report.11.pdf.

2. Carver A. Mead and George Lewicki, "Silicon compilers and foundries will usher in user-designed VLSI," *Electronics* August 11, 55, no. 16 (1982): 107–111. ISSN 0883-4989.

3. Carver Mead, *Analog VLSI and Neural Systems* (Boston: Addison-Wesley, 1989).

4. M. A. Mahowald and C. Mead, "The Silicon Retina," *Scientific American* 264, no. 5 (1991):76–82; Tribute from Rodney Douglas: https://www.quora.com/What -was-the-cause-of-Michelle-Misha-Mahowald-death/; Misha Mahowald, "Silicon Vision" (video), http://www.dailymotion.com/video/x28ktma_silicon-vision-misha -mahowald_tech/.

5. M. Mahowald and R. Douglas, "A Silicon Neuron," *Nature* 354, no. 6354 (1991): 515–518.

6. See Carver Mead, *Collective Electrodynamics: Quantum Foundations of Electromagnetism* (Cambridge, MA: MIT Press, 2002).

7. Tobias's father, Max Delbrück, was both a physicist and a founder of molecular biology in the 1950s who (along with Alfred Hershey and Salvador Luna) received the Nobel Prize in Physiology or Medicine in 1969 (yet another link between microelectronics and molecular biology, which will be explored in chapter 18).

8. C. Posch, T. Serrano-Gotarredona, B. Linares-Barranco, and T. Delbrück, "Retinomorphic Event-Based Vision Sensors: Bioinspired Cameras with Spiking Output," *Proceedings of the IEEE* 102, no. 10 (2014): 1470–1484; T. J. Sejnowski and T. Delbrück, "The Language of the Brain," *Scientific American* 307 (2012): 54–59. https://www.youtube.com/watch?v=FQYroCcwkS0.

9. H. Markram, J. Lübke., M. Frotscher, and B. Sakmann., "Regulation of Synaptic Efficacy by Coincidence of Postsynaptic APs and EPSPs," *Science* 275, no. 5297 (1997): 213–215.

10. See T. J. Sejnowski, "The Book of Hebb," *Neuron* 24. no. 4 (1999): 773–776.

11. Hebb, *The Organization of Behavior* (New York: Wiley & Sons), 62.

12. See R. F. Service, "The Brain Chip," *Science* 345, no. 6197 (2014): 614–616. http://science.sciencemag.org/content/345/6197/614.full.

13. D. Huh and T. J. Sejnowski, "Gradient Descent for Spiking Neural Networks," 2017. https://arxiv.org/pdf/1706.04698.pdf.

14. K. A. Boahen, "Neuromorph's Prospectus," *IEEE Xplore: Computing in Science and Engineering* 19, no. 2 (2017): 14–28.

Chapter 15

1. Jimmy Soni and Rob Goodman, *A Mind at Play: How Claude Shannon Invented the Information Age* (New York: Simon & Schuster: New York, 2017).

2. Solomon Wolf Golomb, *Shift Register Sequences: Secure and Limited-Access Code Generators, Efficiency Code Generators, Prescribed Property Generators, Mathematical Models*, 3rd rev. ed. (Singapore: World Scientific, 2017).

3. See Stephen Wolfram, "Solomon Golomb (1932–2016)," *Stephen Wolfram Blog*, posted May 25, 2016. http://blog.stephenwolfram.com/2016/05/solomon-golomb -19322016/.

4. Richard Rhodes, *Hedy's Folly: The Life and Breakthrough Inventions of Hedy Lamarr, the Most Beautiful Woman in the World* (New York: Doubleday, 2012).

5. G. H. Hardy, *A Mathematician's Apology* (Cambridge: Cambridge University Press, 1940).

6. Solomon W. Golomb, *Polyominoes* (New York: Scribner, 1965).

7. L. A. Riggs, F. Ratliff, J. C. Cornsweet, and T. N. Cornsweet. "The Disappearance of Steadily Fixated Visual Test Objects," *Journal of the Optical Society of America* 43, no. 6 (1953): 495–501.

8. Rajesh P. N. Rao and Dana H. Ballard, "Predictive Coding in the Visual Cortex: A Functional Interpretation of Some Extra-Classical Receptive-Field Effects," *Nature Neuroscience* 2, no. 1 (1999): 79–87.

9. This insight was Mead's motivation for building neuromorphic systems, which, like the brain, also run in real time. C. Mead, "Neuromorphic Electronic Systems," *Proceedings of the IEEE* 78, no. 10 (1990):1629–1636.

10. Hermann von Helmholtz, *Helmholtz's Treatise on Physiological Optics*, vol. 3: *The Perception of Vision*, trans. James P. C. Southall (Rochester, NY: Optical Society of America, 1925), 25. Originally published as *Handbuch der physiologische Optik. 3. Die Lehre von den Gesichtswahrnehmungen* (Leipzig: Leopold Voss, 1867).

11. J. L. McClelland and D. E. Rumelhart, "An Interactive Activation Model of Context Effects in Letter Perception: Part 1. An Account of Basic Findings." *Psychological Review* 88, no. 5 (1981): 401–436; "Part 2. The Contextual Enhancement Effect and Some Tests and Extensions of the Model," *Psychological Review* 89, no. 1 (1982): 60–94,

12. L. Muller, G. Piantoni, D. Koller, S. S. Cash, E. Halgren, and T. J. Sejnowski, "Rotating Waves during Human Sleep Spindles Organize Global Patterns of Activity during the Night," *eLife* 5 (2016): e17267. Supported by the Office of Naval Research.

13. In what came to be known as "Clarke's third law," Arthur C. Clarke famously said, "Any sufficiently advanced technology is indistinguishable from magic."

Chapter 16

1. This chapter was adapted from T. J. Sejnowski, "Consciousness," *Daedalus* 144, no. 1 (2015): 123–132. See also Francis H. C. Crick, *What Mad Pursuit: A Personal View of Scientific Discovery* (New York: Basic Books, 1988); Bob Hicks, "Kindra Crick's Mad Pursuit," *Oregon ArtWatch*, December 3, 2015. http://www.orartswatch.org/ kindra-cricks-mad-pursuit/.

2. Although there is no single accepted scientific definition of "consciousness," which has been used to refer to many different phenomena, the term is widely understood to include the state of being awake and aware of one's surroundings, the awareness or perception of something, and the mind's awareness of itself and the world.

3. F. Crick, "The Function of the Thalamic Reticular Complex: The Searchlight Hypothesis," *Proceedings of the National Academy of Science of the United States of America* 81, no. 14 (1984): 4586–4590.

4. F. Crick and C. Koch, "The Problem of Consciousness," *Scientific American* 267, no. 3 (1992): 10–17; F. Crick and C. Koch, "Constraints on Cortical and Thalamic Projections: The No-Strong-Loops Hypothesis," *Nature* 391, no. 6664 (1998): 245–250; F. Crick and C. Koch, "A Framework for Consciousness," *Nature Neuroscience* 6, no. 2 (2003): 119–126; and F. Crick, C. Koch, G. Kreiman, and I. Fried, "Consciousness and Neurosurgery," *Neurosurgery* 55, no. 2 (2004): 273–281.

5. F. Crick and C. Koch, "Are We Aware of Neural Activity in Primary Visual Cortex?" *Nature* 375, no. 6527 (1995): 121–123; C. Koch, M. Massimini, M. Boly, and G. Tononi, "The Neural Correlates of Consciousness: Progress and Problems," *Nature Reviews Neuroscience* 17 (2016): 307–321.

6. R. Q. Quiroga, L. Reddy, G. Kreiman, C. Koch, and I. Fried, "Invariant Visual Representation by Single Neurons in the Human Brain," *Nature* 435, no. 7045 (2005): 1102–1107.

7. K. Deisseroth and M. J. Schnitzer, "Engineering Approaches to Illuminating Brain Structure and Dynamics," *Neuron* 80, no. 3 (2013): 568–577.

8. V. Mante, D. Sussillo, K. V. Shenoy, and W. T. Newsome, "Context-Dependent Computation by Recurrent Dynamics in Prefrontal Cortex," *Nature* 503, no. 7474 (2013): 78–84.

9. BRAIN Working Group, *BRAIN 2025: A Scientiific Vision,* Report to the Advisory Committee to the Director, NIH (Bethesda, MD: National Institutes of Health, June 5, 2014), 36. https://www.braininitiative.nih.gov/pdf/BRAIN2025_508C.pdf.

10. Patricia Smith Churchland and Terrence J. Sejnowski, *The Computational Brain,* 2nd ed. (Cambridge, MA: MIT Press, 2016), 183, 221.

11. L. Chang and D. Y. Tsao. "The Code for Facial Identity in the Primate Brain," *Cell* 169, no. 6 (2017): 1013–1028.e14.

12. D. A. Bulkin and J. M. Groh, "Seeing Sounds: Visual and Auditory Interactions in the Brain," *Current Opinion in Neurobiology* 16 (2006): 415–419.

13. D. M. Eagleman and T. J. Sejnowski, "Motion Integration and Postdiction in Visual Awareness," *Science* 287, no. 5460 (2000): 2036–2038.

14. See Stephen L. Macknik, Susana Martinez-Conde, and Sandra Blakeslee, *Sleights of Mind: What the Neuroscience of Magic Reveals about Our Everyday Deceptions* (New York: Henry Holt, 2010).

15. S. Dehaene and J.-P. Changeux, "Experimental and Theoretical Approaches to Conscious Processing," *Neuron* 70, no. 2 (2011): 200–227.

16. S. Moeller, T. Crapse, L. Chang, and D. Y. Tsao, "The Effect of Face Patch Microstimulation on Perception of Faces and Objects," *Nature Neuroscience* 20, no. 6 (2017): 743–752.

17. J. Parvizi, C. Jacques, B. L. Foster, N. Withoft, V. Rangarajan, K. S. Weiner, and K. Grill-Spector, "Electrical Stimulation of Human Fusiform Face-Selective Regions Distorts Face Perception," *Journal of Neuroscience* 32, no. 43 (2012): 14915–14920.

18. BRAIN Working Group, *BRAIN 2025: A Scientific Vision*, pp. 6, 35, 48.

19. Sejnowski, "What Are the Projective Fields of Cortical Neurons?"

20. L. Chukoskie, J. Snider, M. C. Mozer, R. J. Krauzlis, and T. J. Sejnowski, "Learning Where to Look for a Hidden Target," *Proceedings of the National Academy of Sciences of the United States of America* 110, supp. 2 (2013): 10438–10445.

21. T. J. Sejnowski, H. Poizner, G. Lynch, S. Gepshtein, and R. J. Greenspan, "Prospective Optimization," *Proceedings of the IEEE* 102, no. 5 (2014): 799–811.

22. Completed posthumously by his colleague Christof Koch. F. C. Crick and C. Koch, "What Is the Function of the Claustrum?" *Philosophical Transactions of the Royal Society of London* B360, no. 1458 (2005), 1271–1279.

23. See Lewis Carroll, *Alice's Adventures in Wonderland* (London: Macmillan, 1865), chap. 6.

Chapter 17

1. T. A. Lincoln and G. F. Joyce, "Self-Sustained Replication of an RNA Enzyme," *Science* 323, no. 5918 (2009): 1229–1232.

2. T. R. Cech, "The RNA Worlds in Context," *Cold Spring Harbor Perspectives in Biology* 4, no. 7 (2012), http://cshperspectives.cshlp.org/content/4/7/a006742.full .pdf+html.

3. J. A. Feldman, "Mysteries of Visual Experience" (2016; rev. 2017), https://arxiv .org/ftp/arxiv/papers/1604/1604.08612.pdf.

4. Patricia S. Churchland, V. S. Ramachandran, and Terrence J. Sejnowski, "A Critique of Pure Vision," in Christof Koch and Joel D. Davis, eds., *Large-Scale Neuronal Theories of the Brain* (Cambridge, MA: MIT Press, 1994), 23–60.

5. John Allman, *Evolving Brains* (New York: Scientific American Library, 1999).

6. B. F. Skinner, *Beyond Freedom and Dignity* (Indianapolis: Hackett, 1971).

7. Noam Chomsky, "The Case against B. F. Skinner," *New York Review of Books*, 17, no. 11 (1971): 18–24. http://www.nybooks.com/articles/1971/12/30/the-case -against-bf-skinner/

8. Ibid., para. 27. For a more detailed comparison between rule-based and statistical analysis of language, see Peter Norvig, "On Chomsky and the Two Cultures of Statistical Learning," http://norvig.com/chomsky.html.

9. Noam Chomsky, *Rules and Representations* (Oxford: Basil Blackwell, 1980).

10. A. Gopnik, A. Meltzoff, and P. Kuhl, *The Scientist in the Crib: What Early Learning Tells Us about the Mind* (New York: William Morrow, 1999).

11. T. Mikolov, I. Sutskever, K. Chen, G. Corrado, and J. Dean, "Distributed Representations of Words and Phrases and Their Compositionality," *Advances in Neural Information Processing Systems* 26 (2013): 3111–3119.

12. This was a talk at the McGovern Institute at MIT to propose a major commitment of the institute to understanding the biological basis of language and language disorders.

13. "May the Force be with you," to quote a popular line from the Jedi master Obi-Wan Kenobi in *Star Wars*.

14. J. A. Fodor, "The Mind/Body Problem," *Scientific American* 244, no. 1 (1981): 114–123.

15. D. Hassabis, D. Kumaran, C. Summerfield, and M. Botvinick, "Neuroscience-Inspired Artificial Intelligence," *Neuron* 95, no. 2 (2017): 245–258.

16. Paul W. Glimcher and Ernst Fehr, *Neuroeconomics: Decision Making and the Brain*, 2nd ed. (Boston: Academic Press, 2013).

17. Colin Camerer, *Behavior Game Theory: Experiments in Strategic Interaction* (Princeton: Princeton University Press, 2003).

18. Minsky and Papert, *Perceptrons* (1969), 231. In the expanded edition of this book published in 1988, section 13.2 that contained this excerpt was deleted. However, a new section was added, "Epilogue: The new connectionism." This is a 40-page evaluation of early results from learning in multilayer perceptrons, which is well worth reading in the light of subsequent developments.

19. See https://www.dartmouth.edu/~ai50/homepage.html. See also https://en .wikipedia.org/wiki/AI@50/.

20. Marvin Minsky, *The Society of Mind* (New York: Simon & Schuster, 1985).

21. See "Society of Mind," *Wikipedia*, last edited August 22, 2017. https://en .wikipedia.org/wiki/Society_of_Mind.

22. Cynthia Breazeal at MIT and Javier Movellan have developed social robots that interact with humans and use facial expressions to communicate, promising first steps toward a computational theory of emotions.

23. Marvin Minsky, "Theory of Neural-Analog Reinforcement Systems and Its Application to the Brain Model Problem" (Ph.D. diss., Princeton University, 1954).

24. Stephen Wolfram, "Farewell, Marvin Minsky (1927–2016)," *Stephen Wolfram Blog*, posted January 26, 2016, http://blog.stephenwolfram.com/2016/01/farewell -marvin-minsky-19272016/.

25. A. Graves, G. Wayne, M. Reynolds, T. Harley, I. Danihelka, A. Grabska-Barwińska, et al., "Hybrid Computing Using a Neural Network with Dynamic External Memory," *Nature* 538, no. 7626 (2016): 471–476.

Chapter 18

1. Sydney Brenner, "Nature's Gift to Science," Nobel Lecture, December 8, 2002, video, https://www.nobelprize.org/mediaplayer/index.php?id=523/.

2. Sydney Brenner, "Reading the Human Genome": 1. "Much Ado about Nothing: Systems Biology and Inverse Problems," January 26, 2009; 2. "Measure for Measure: The GC Shift and the Problem of Isochores," January 29, 2009; 3. "All's Well That Ends Well: The History of the Retina," January 30, 2009, videos. http:// thesciencenetwork.org/search?program=Reading+the+Human+Genome+with +Sydney+Brenner.

3. Imaginal discs are the developmental primordia of legs and antennae in flies.

4. Sydney Brenner has published his original story in S. Brenner, "Francisco Crick in Paradiso," *Current Biology*. 6, no. 9 (1996): 1202: "I shared an office with Francis Crick for twenty years in Cambridge. At one time he was interested in embryology and spent a lot of time thinking about imaginal discs in *Drosophila*. One day, he threw the book he was reading down onto his desk with an exasperated cry. 'God knows how these imaginal discs work!' In a flash I saw the whole story of Francis arriving in heaven and Peter welcoming him with 'Oh, Dr. Crick, you must be tired after your long journey. Do sit down, have a drink and relax.' 'No,' says Francis, 'I must see this fellow, God; I have to ask him a question.' After some persuasion, the angel agrees to take Francis to God. They cross the middle part of heaven, and finally right at the back, across the railway tracks, they come to a shed, with a corrugated iron roof, surrounded by junk. And in the back part, there is a little man in overalls with a large spanner in his back pocket. 'God,' says the angel, 'this is Dr. Crick; Dr. Crick, this is God.' 'I am so pleased to meet you,' says Francis. 'I must ask you this question. How do imaginal discs work?' 'Well,' comes the reply, 'We took a little bit

of this stuff and we added some things to it and ... actually, we don't know, but I can tell you that we've been building flies up here for 200 million years and we have had no complaints.'"

5. T. Dobzhansky, "Nothing in Biology Makes Sense Except in the Light of Evolution," *American Biology Teacher* 35, no. 3 (1973): 125–129, http://biologie -lernprogramme.de/daten/programme/js/homologer/daten/lit/Dobzhansky.pdf.

6. Sydney Brenner, "Why We Need to Talk about Evolution," in "10-on-10: The Chronicle of Evolution" lecture series, Nanyang Technological University, Singapore, February 21, 2017. http://www.paralimes.ntu.edu.sg/NewsnEvents/10-on-10 %20The%20Chronicle%20of%20Evolution/Pages/Home.aspx. Video. https://www .youtube.com/watch?v=C9M5h_tVlc8.

7. Terrence Sejnowski, "Evolving Brains," in "10-on-10: The Chronicle of Evolution" lecture series, Nanyang Technological University, Singapore, July 14, 2017. https://www.youtube.com/watch?v=L9ITpz4OeOo.

8. T. Nagel, "What Is It Like to Be a Bat?" *Philosophical Review* 83, no. 4 (1974): 435–450.

9. "Anthropogeny" is the study of the origins of humankind. See Center of Academic Research and Training in Anthropology (CARTA) website, https://carta .anthropogeny.org/.

10. The La Jolla Group and CARTA were founded under the leadership of Ajit Varki, a physician-scientist at UC, San Diego, with a passion for evolution.

11. About 1 percent of the DNA is sequences coding for proteins, and 8 percent is regulatory sequences that bind proteins.

12. Howard C. Berg, *E. coli in Motion* (New York: Springer, 2004).

13. S. Navlakha and Z. Bar-Joseph, "Algorithms in Nature: The Convergence of Systems Biology and Computational Thinking," *Molecular Systems Biology* 7 (2011): 546.

Acknowledgments

1. See Sarah Williams Goldhagen, *Louis Kahn's Situated Modernism* (New Haven: Yale University Press, 2001).

2. Francis Crick, *The Astonishing Hypothesis: The Scientific Search for the Soul* (New York: Scribner's Sons, 1994), 267.

3. Crick also gets credit for introducing me to Beatrice.

Index